The Grand Prix

1906 to 1972

The Grand Prix
1906 to 1972

L J K Setright

W. W. Norton & Company, Inc. New York, New York.

Published by W. W. Norton & Company, Inc.

© Thomas Nelson and Sons Ltd 1973

First American Edition 1973

ISBN 0 393 8680 1
Printed in Great Britain

Contents

Plates

Acknowledgements

All that good money going on a mere picture, when it might have been spent on something useful . . .
from *Time Must Have A Stop*, by Aldous Huxley

All illustrations in this work, other than those listed below, are the author's.
Colour:
Daimler-Benz AG: 1956 Mercedes-Benz chassis
Geoffrey Goddard: 1960 Cooper
Monochrome (identified by caption numbers):
British Leyland Motor Corporation: 12
Michael Cooper: 157, 159–61, 164, 165
William Court: 106, 124
Daimler-Benz AG: 13–15, 22–4, 65–7, 69, 76, 78, 79, 83, 84, 87–9, 107–9
The Donington Collection: 64, 95, 163, 181
Fiat: 1, 7–10, 16, 20, 26, 30, 34, 35, 39, 40, 44, 56
Ford: 190, 228, 234, 248, 249
Lola: 169
March Engineering: 229, 230
Officine Alfieri Maserati SpA: 63, 81, 92
Engins Matra: 191, 192, 207, 208
Lynton Money: 158, 170
Montagu Motor Museum: 31, 38, 41–3, 48, 50, 52, 54, 55, 58, 62, 68, 70, 71, 73, 75, 77, 86, 90, 97–9, 100, 102, 134, 156
Owen Organization: 119, 168
David Phipps: 186
Pirelli: 121, 131, 143
Charles Pocklington: 72, 73
Cyril Posthumus: 2–6, 11, 18, 19, 21, 25, 27–9, 32, 33, 37, 45, 47, 49, 51, 53, 80
John Ross: 110, 114, 120, 122, 127, 133, 135, 140, 142, 146, 149, 150, 152–4
United Press: 126

Prolegomenon

One of the perversities of historians is that they will more aggressively dispute matters of fact than they will matters of opinion. Let those who will—as some perennially do—debate the status of earlier races, for it is commonly agreed that Grand Prix motor racing properly began in 1906. At the time of completing this book, at the end of the 1972 season, there have since then been fifty-three years of effective racing, after deducting the years of the wars and their aftermaths. During the fiftieth year it had seemed possible and even likely that the then current formula—according to which the cars were constructed for this branch of the art, science, or sport which motor racing is variously considered to be—might be abandoned in favour of a new set of regulations calculated to inspire the design of cars significantly different from those then current or superseded. Alas, it was not to be: the existing set of rules was substantially perpetuated. Nevertheless there is still evidence to suggest that it will lead to the effloration of new schools of thought, the germination of which has been evident as the 1960s have given way to the 1970s, and the intensive cultivation of which may be expected to follow shortly.

The probable harvest is difficult to predict; but whatever the outcome, it is clear that motor racing has arrived at a significant and probably critical point in its history; and this encourages us in a study of what has already been achieved, what has perhaps been overlooked, and what remains to be encompassed.

There is, as one of my favourite biblical commentators has observed, no new thing under the sun; and in motor racing the demonstration of this truth may be seen in the cyclical resurgences of design philosophy among the engineers who have produced racing cars since the earliest days of motor sport. Engineering fashion swings with much of the predictability, though perhaps not the regularity, of a pendulum. Engines with two valves per cylinder may enjoy a period of supremacy; then for some further years four valves per cylinder will be preferred before the designers revert to the two-valve school again. There have been periods when aerodynamics have been cultivated, others when they have been studiously ignored; when engines have been faster than chassis, until it has been the turn of the chassis designers to catch up on development and evolve cars that seem to be wanting in power. To and fro the pendulum goes, and no sooner do we learn a lesson and begin to apply it than current values are deflated and theories jeopardised by the revival of some once cherished but long despised principle.

This alone would be sufficiently confusing, but what has most confounded motor racing in general and Grand Prix racing in particular is the swing of an entirely different pendulum, that which measures the lapse of interest in the sport on the part of any given body of people and the transfer of concern and responsibility for it to some other body. At various times in the past,

Grand Prix racing has been an arena in which rival nations have competed for prestige, or in which the main protagonists have been major car manufacturers, and occasionally there have been times when the sport has depended precariously upon the devotion of individual sportsmen. Since 1958, however, the rule books and purse strings of Grand Prix racing have been manipulated by strictly commercial corporations; and since 1968 the fostering of sponsorship and advertising have introduced powerful agencies whose businesses are quite irrelevant to motor racing but whose advisers know a good publicity medium when they see one. As a result, this particular pendulum may be said to have stopped swinging, for its mechanism has become deranged, and probably not the most serious consequence of this may be the probable checking of that other pendulum—describing the swings of engineering fashion—that was discussed earlier.

How many times have we seen, throughout recorded history, peoples or persons prospering through the youthful display of virtue until they rose to enjoy popularity, honour and affection, only to be corrupted by that very adulation they had deserved and to sink into an irredeemable course of capriciousness, dissimulation and that deadly avarice which is rationalised as being for the sake of self-preservation but finally proves self-destructive. In time there may appear another Amos or another Gibbon to measure the decline and fall of motor racing; for it appears timely already to lament that this once worthwhile and stimulating activity is doomed to pursue the same downward path. There was a time when we learned a lot from motor racing, when it was the field for the trial and development of all sorts of new ideas in automotive engineering. There have been times in its long history when, one after another, the great and famous motor manufacturers of Europe have entered the lists to try their hand or demonstrate their prowess, to give the forward planning engineers on their staffs another kind of laboratory where they could try a new idea and reject it, or, if it worked, take it away and develop it for the benefit of customers perhaps ten years later. Go back through the years and you will find that Grand Prix entries included not only racing specialists like Ferrari, Maserati, Bugatti, or Miller, but also the well-known manufacturers, including Austin, Peugeot, Renault, Sunbeam, Alfa Romeo and Daimler-Benz.

But it is no longer like that: already it is valid to argue that only the tyre manufacturers are currently learning from racing, acquiring new skills in carcass construction, tread design, and polymer chemistry, that are rapidly being applied to the tyres for the cars we buy. As for engines and chassis, there is very little to be learned from racing practice: design has stultified since about 1963, and even components and materials that are tried and proved in racing today invariably have their origin in some other technology such as aircraft engineering. Sports car racing may have taught us something about aerodynamics in the past decade, and Grand Prix racing may have added to this knowledge in the last three years or so—but the aerodynamics of two hundred miles an hour are very different from those that apply to the quoti-diurnal motoring of the multitude.

Perhaps motor racing no longer really matters, save as a means of livelihood for the few actively concerned in it and for the growing horde of parasites who infest it. Motor racing is no longer a means whereby one nation can assert its superiority over another, though goodness knows it is a system both cheaper and less bloody than most of the others that have been tried; and it is no longer a satisfactory medium for the display of corporate prowess by great automobile manufacturers. Most of the cars on today's starting grids have originated with the racing specialists, people whose interests do not extend beyond racing itself, little firms that have grown up from backyards or tuning shops, firms that have no real contribution to make to the art or science of car design and who are only racing for what they can get out of it, not because they have anything to put into it.

It is in the interests of firms like these that racing car design should remain more or less static. With limited resources they could not hope to compete with big industrial organisations should the latter enter the fray with really advanced and expensive designs: so in every class of racing we see regulations drawn up to enforce an undeserved equality upon all contestants.

Such equality might be thought a good and democratic thing; but the great pity about equality is that the enforcement of it ensures the perpetuation of mediocrity. It is even so in motor racing: look at what has happened to regulations for Grand Prix cars. For far too long we have had to put up with a series of formulae based on engine size, a form of limitation that has been proved futile time and time again since Grand Prix racing was first introduced. There was, as I have said, some hope that by 1972 a new formula might be adopted based on fuel consumption or more accurately on thermal efficiency: each car would be issued with a quantity of chosen fuel—petrol, alcohol, diesel oil, turbine kerosene, no matter what—containing a certain specified calorific content, say five million Btu. The winner of the race would be the one that had travelled furthest two hours later. But the powers that be in motor racing, entrenched firms who are in the best position to do energetic lobbying of the CSI who draw up the rules, were not at all keen on the idea: it would involve them in doing much research and some real engineering, and it might even subject them to the risk of competition from gas turbines or differential diesels or turbocharged compound engines in highly scientific cars entered by industrial concerns that are more learned and far more rich than they could ever hope to rival.

For the present motley crowd of motor racing big-timers this would not do at all, for they would be pushed out of the limelight very quickly. So instead of a forward-looking new formula we have the mixture as before, but with mediocrity guaranteed by a new stipulation that engines must not have more than twelve cylinders. To what base uses we may return . . .! Why may not imagination trace the noble dust of Newton and find it blinding the eyes of logic? What justification can there be for such a prescription? Formula One Grands Prix are supposed to be the highest form of motor racing, in which the cream of motor engineering talent devises the most exquisite machinery for the world's best drivers to put to the test. That is how it was in the old days, but now nearly everybody uses Cosworth Ford V8 engines; and were it not for the presence of BRM, Ferrari and Matra somewhere in the field, the formula would probably restrict cars to eight cylinders just to help the conservationists prosper even more.

What earthly future can there be in this attitude? It may lead to closely fought races, which are the sort of thing the lay public is supposed to enjoy, yet it as surely sends them to watch a procession of cars that all look alike, all perform alike, sound alike and are, apart from their aerodynamic warts and pustules, more or less faithful reproductions of a 1967 Lotus—and the lay public are supposed to detest watching a load of cars that all look the same.

Actually that last supposition is rapidly losing adherents. Motor racing promoters, aided by the usual unscrupulous ill-informed newspaper columnists and television opportunists, have just about succeeded now in making the car completely subservient to the driver. The introduction of the World Drivers Championship has done incalculable harm to motor racing: winning the championship is considered the *summum bonum,* with public attention focused on the personal fortunes and foibles of a small bunch of drivers of star quality. The cars they drive will before long enjoy as little attention as a sprinter's spikes or a golfer's clubs. Racing has become a competition between individual people, and 'motor sport' has become an almost meaningless expression, for the motors are becoming mere incidentals and the sport has disappeared.

It is business now, big booming business, and motor racing will very likely continue to get worse as the business gets better. Everybody in it seems to be taking a cue from the United States, where it has always been like that, where the cars have always looked, sounded, and behaved just like each other, where all that has mattered has been the drivers' names—and those of the sponsors who pay to use their cars as mobile advertisement hoardings, and who in 1972 were threatening to take over the sponsorship and therefore the virtual control of the entire Grand Prix season. America has long been accustomed to this sort of circus act, and it may or may not be fair to see in this vulgar ignorance of the sport's finer points a reflection of the crass commercialism of the American automobile industry. At Indianapolis the crowds flocked to see whether Troy Ruttman could beat Bill Vukovitch, whether A. J. Foyt might beat Rufus Parnelli Jones; and now in Europe concern is not with the rival fortunes of Ferrari and Tyrrell but with the rivalry that exists between Ickx and Stewart, *Jacky* and *Jackie* to millions who have never met them.

Nor have the manufacturers of the cars any right to complain: for the Lotus is now a Players cigarette special, and even Matra, encouraged by the French Government to represent in the world's arenas the fervour, the brilliance, and the chauvinism that are the three parts of Gaul, have sold their pride and plastered the insignia of Goodyear and Chrysler over their cars. Admitting advertising to Grand Prix racing will surely turn out to be an even more tragic mistake than the inauguration of the World Championship of Drivers.

It is pikestaff plain that this galloping degeneracy is brought about by the greed for money. The owners, managers and promoters of the world's racing circuits are most of all to blame, for it is they who control how much starting money and prize money the drivers and entrants receive, they who decide what sort of races should be run for what sort of cars. They are not concerned with progress, with the advancement of science, or even with safety, any more than they can help; what they care about is the box office, the size of the gate and how much each member of the public will pay to see the entertainment so professionally laid on. That is what motor racing is now—show business at professional level; and you know that show business depends on the star system and upon personalities, not upon props. The racing car nowadays is just a prop, at every level from Formula 1 to so-called 'poor man's motor racing' classes such as Formula Ford, Formula France and all the other half-pint categories. There is a rash of new makes of racing cars entering the sport at all levels: not one of them has anything new to offer, any real contribution to make to the art or science of motor racing, nothing to put into the sport (if sport it be) but every one concerned to get as much out of it as possible.

The blame for this does not rest entirely with the car manufacturers. If their new cars really were new rather than being refined 1972 versions of 1963 designs, if they were original or iconoclastic or unconventional, there would be no top-ranking professional drivers prepared to take them on. Make no mistake, these fellows do not stick their necks out every week for the greater glorification of Lotus, BRM, March or whatever team they honour with their services; they are hungry for fame, avid for money, beset by a compulsive urge for each to prove himself better than the others. No wonder they are suspicious and reactionary when faced with a new and different car: why should they hazard their livelihoods by taking a chance with some funny new machine that might not work? Better the devil you know— even if the wheels persistently fall off or the camshafts break on every second outing—than the devil you don't.

Thus the succeeding years bring out the old anew, mediocrity is perpetuated as virtue, error becomes received dogma, and fashion becomes habit. This year's Cosworth engine revs a thousand higher than last year's. Ho hum. Next year they might as well try stock block Chevrolets, for it is unlikely that anybody would notice. Oh yes, the accountants would: profit margins would be a bit bigger. Of course the races would have to be shortened lest the things fall to bits or run out of fuel, but the average racegoer cannot sustain concentration for more than half an hour anyway: it won't matter. So if the cars are not fast enough we can always ease the corners to make the courses faster, after the pernicious style that has affected so many of the greatest circuits since the early 1950s.

That is when the rot really started, when the public first began to take a big interest in motor racing. Before the 1950s, when motor racing began to attract the interest of the lay public first in Britain and then in America, nobody knew much about it except the people who were actually in it, and most of them didn't know all that much. Those were days beyond recall when men, grown men in linen helmets, sat up in high-sounding high-smelling super-charged cars of architectural grace and animal ferocity, whose bursts of sounds jabbed and bounded back from town walls or timbered slopes as they traced the course of real roads at places like Berne, Bari, Albi, San Remo, Syracuse or Jersey. They carried no advertising but ran under their national colours; they were more likely to pay entrance fees than to demand starting money.

We can still see some of the cars taking part in short and un-convincing races for heterogeneous collections of vintage and historic machinery. We can still encounter people with the same spirit taking part in hill climbs. But the real thing has gone beyond recall. Motor sport is dead.

From the engineer's point of view it may be argued that this does not matter, that even though the sport has degenerated into a business there is still plenty of worthwhile engineering progress to be made in motor racing and exploited elsewhere. This is a very debatable proposition; and if it is necessary to persuade the youngest generation of spectators that they do not know what good motor racing *is,* we must now go on to ask, What good is it?

It is an assertion more hackneyed than self-evident that the racing car of today is the touring car of tomorrow. It is not difficult to find examples that might illustrate the proposition: to derive the E-type Jaguar from the D-type, the Type 43 Bugatti from the Type 35, even the Leyland gas turbine truck from the Rover-BRM. But the devil can also cite scripture to his purpose: the adaptation of Mercedes-Benz 500K front suspension to the racing W125, or the emulation in racing engines from 1954 of vertical inlet porting that had been a feature of touring engines by Bristol since 1946 and BMW since 1936, might suggest just as strongly that the racing car of today was the touring car of yesterday.

It is doubtful whether many of the people involved in motor racing today care very much either way. Once upon a time such considerations mattered; but the popularisation of motor racing in the last two decades, during which commercial pressures have caused it to decline into the level of mere entertainment, have similarly caused the decline of major technical innovation over the years, and most certainly a reduction in the incidence of technical innovations relevant to typical touring car development. In those who actually enjoy or have good reason to participate in motor racing, such trends may awaken no resentment and cause no despondency. Those who merely observe it, with more or less tolerance, may be tempted to ask what good it might do. The glib response that 'racing improves the breed' is one that deserves careful examination.

If a profit and loss account were drawn up listing the technological debits and credits of motor racing, we should find that we owe the sport less than it owes us. It was not always so, but the traffic is becoming more and more one-way. The current preoccupation with ultra-high-speed aerodynamics promises to be a typical blind alley of wings and wedges, and it is even debatable whether the half-hearted endorsement of gas turbines and four-wheel-drive by Lotus will do much to further the common weal.

Of course there are some things for which we must undoubtedly thank motor racing. It has done a lot for tyre development, giving us nylon carcasses, depressed-crown contour moulding, low profiles, and some marvellous high-grip polymers—although the compounding of these was anticipated by the footwear industry many years earlier. In our engines we can trace the perfection of fuel injection, of scientific inlet and exhaust tract design, and of worthwhile improvements in pistons and piston rings, to the promptings of competition. The stability and power of disc brakes and modern friction materials is even more certainly due to the stimulus of racing. Other benefits include spin-limiting differentials, anti-lift windscreen wipers, and a number of detailed improvements in hydraulic dampers.

This hardly seems an impressive list. The benefits the production car has derived from other sources are far more numerous, more varied, more interesting and—with the exception of those tyres and brakes—more important. We owe no thanks to motor racing for any of the current sophisticated automatic transmissions, nor even for the humble synchromesh; nor for our radial-ply tyres, high viscosity-index oils and additives, our alternators, electronics, self-levelling suspensions, plugs, plastics, ceramics, heaters, ventilators, metals, paints, or servos.

That is just a random list. Even more impressive is the list of really vital things that we have inherited from aviation. Stressed skin construction is one of the most fundamental of these, though we have still not reached the levels of achievement attained by the master airframe stressmen of 1930. A younger adjunct of such techniques is the use of structural adhesives, so far playing a very limited part in touring or racing cars, though McLaren and Ford have employed such adhesives in interesting ways. Not only constructional methods but also materials themselves have been inherited from aviation: most of the well-known light alloys provide obvious examples, but glass-reinforced plastics is a more unexpected one. Then there are vital things like pressurised cooling systems, steel-backed multi-layer plain bearings, high-octane and high-performance-number fuels, and most of the worthwhile types of valve gear. By no means ending the list are some of the contributions of that American-domiciled Novacastrian, Sam Dalziel Heron, to whose four dozen years of pioneering work with aero engines we owe such current manifestations as the bowl-in-piston combustion chamber and such old favourites as the sodium-cooled exhaust valve. He even made a major contribution to gas turbine technology by drawing correct inferences from the structure and materials of his own false teeth—and I do not doubt that we can look forward to the pleasure of gas turbines in our future motorway cruisers without feeling any sense of obligation to BRM, STP or Lotus.

Let me not be too gravely misunderstood nor too treacherously misinterpreted. I am not saying that motor racing is of no use—merely that its value is not as great as is sometimes supposed. Competition is undoubtedly of some value as a tool of development. It is not that it produces any new ideas; years of dispassionate observation have convinced me that there are no new ideas. Rather, competition provides a hot-house environment that forces development of existing ideas along at a greatly quickened pace. How effectively it does so, and how easily it may be frustrated, is well exemplified by the case of four-wheel-drive, which has hung in the offing for even more years than the forty that take us back to the type 53 Bugatti. In 1969 it came in for its turn of accelerated development with Matra, McLaren, Lotus and Cosworth all building experimental cars, after taking some time to digest the lessons offered by BRM and Ferguson some years earlier. Alas, it was not a controlled experiment, for these experimental cars were generally shunned by the leading drivers, for reasons already outlined in this chapter. Furthermore, the appearance of these four-wheel-drive cars coincided with the rapid development of supplementary airfoils which *prima facie* resolved all the problems of tyre adhesion that four-wheel-drive might have remedied. The prototype cars had the briefest of heydays, and were then abandoned. At about the same time, high wings were forbidden and everybody went back to square one and busied themselves with making money instead of making progress. Yet the banning of airfoils in turn produced a good example of accelerated development, for it became a matter of urgency that the nature and effect of airflow over and around the fuselage and tyres of a racing car be understood more fully, and this was studied from 1969 onwards.

Even so, we have not yet touched upon the most profound of all the truths relevant to our discussion. This is that racing gives us not hardware but standards. Nobody with an eye for the *chiaroscuro* of motor engineering history can state positively and incontrovertibly that, say, reticular tin-aluminium bearings are better or worse than needle rollers; but where is the man who would forswear the improvements in steering, roadholding, and braking, in speed, acceleration, and stability, that distinguish the touring cars of today from their equivalents of yesteryear? The paragons of all these virtues are always the racing cars of the day; and man, who fights and loves and prays and writes and does all sorts of irrational things because he cannot help being an idealist, cannot resist the temptation to advance his standards in car behaviour, as in all things, towards the ever-receding ultimate.

17

chapter one

1906 to 1911

There were giants in the earth in those days
Genesis 6:4

Standards were already surprisingly high in some respects when motor racing emerged from its formative years of primordial chaos and entered the Grand Prix era with a two-day event which, starting on 26 June 1906, was proclaimed as the ninth Grand Prix of the Automobile Club of France, or more commonly the ninth French Grand Prix. This apparent contradiction was not due to any wish on the part of the Automobile Club of France to introduce deliberate confusion to history, but rather due to their recognition that from a purely technical standpoint the 1906 race could be considered a natural successor to those that had preceded it. Accordingly they gave retrospective recognition to eight earlier races—the Paris–Bordeaux–Paris race of 1895, Paris–Marseilles–Paris in 1896, Paris–Amsterdam in 1898, the Tour de France in 1899, Paris–Toulouse–Paris in 1900, Paris–Berlin in 1901, Paris–Vienna in 1902, and the disastrous Paris–Madrid race which, halted prematurely at Bordeaux because of the dreadful series of accidents that clearly showed the whole business to be a much too perilous undertaking, brought the days of the great inter-city races to an end in 1903.

With the Gordon Bennett races that followed, some attempt was made to regularise motor racing by the adoption of a formula which sought to discourage the manufacture of cars as gigantic as were becoming the norm in racing. The very earliest motor races were run by cars that were the same as or at least not significantly different from, those which could be bought for touring purposes; but as the popularity of racing increased, manufacturers began to build cars specifically for competition, and with automobile engineering in its then very primitive state it was natural that they should give hardly a second thought to the assumption that the key to higher performance was to have a bigger engine. Thus between 1895, when the successful Panhard had a two-cylinder engine of 1·2 litres displacement, and 1905 when the four-cylinder Fiat mustered 16·2 litres, engine capacity had increased more than thirteen times and actual power output, due to an improved understanding of the internal combustion engine, had increased no less than thirty times, the 1905 Fiat being not only very big but also notably efficient by the standards of its time.

What makes the size of the 1905 cars all the more remarkable is that it was achieved in the face of regulations which limited the the weight of a racing car to 1,000 kg (1,007 if a magneto were employed), this rule having been introduced in 1902 in an attempt to prevent racing cars from becoming too fast. Thus for the first and certainly not the most ineffectual of many times, an attempt to limit the performance of racing cars by introducing some strictly irrelevant constraint was shown to be mere folly, and to constitute nothing more than a challenge to the engineering ability of racing car constructors. How ineffectual the rule was may be seen by comparing the 7½-litre engine of the racing Panhard of 1901,

1 The pattern of the primitive GP car was already set in 1904, when Vincenzo Lancia won the Coppa Florio with his 75 hp Fiat

which weighed 1·2 tons, with the 13·7-litre engine of the 1 ton Panhard racer of the following year. Ingenious means were adopted to secure this favourable ratio of engine size to weight: for instance, the engine of the 1902 Panhard had its separate cylinders surrounded by water jackets of copper only 1 mm thick. The rest of the structure was correspondingly almost flimsy, though not necessarily dangerously so since its speeds and internal pressures were both so moderate as to keep the loadings well within the capacity of the machinery. Thus although this engine developed 90 bhp it did so at a mere 1,260 rev/min, its big pistons then travelling at a mean velocity of only 1,400 feet per minute while subjected to a mean effective pressure of less than 70 lb/in^2. In these circumstances it was quite tolerable that the engine should only weigh about 6 cwt, the vast bulk it presented to the onlooker being no more than a series of large and parsimoniously enveloped cavities.

This then was the age of Titans, a period in which long and arduous races were fought out on rudimentary roads by cars of gigantic proportions, abysmal efficiency, little scope for development, but surprisingly good balance.

Before long the chassis would be taken for granted and all attention would be concentrated on the engine. At this stage, however, there were still some conflicting schools of thought about chassis design, in particular relating to the transmission of tractive effort from the engine and gearbox to the rear tyres. Already by 1905 Hotchkiss and Itala were challenging the accepted arrangement (of chain drive to a dead beam rear axle) with the notion of shaft drive to a live axle attached to the chassis by semi-elliptic leaf springs, which thus not only provided the necessary suspension but also the link whereby the axle propelled the car. Attempts had been made by other manufacturers to use a shaft-driven live axle, but this was usually located by a torque arm fixed to the axle and, running longitudinally parallel to the propellor shaft, pivoted adjacent to the tail of the gearbox. Although in retrospect we can see that the Hotchkiss type of drive was to become almost universal at a later stage, at the time it must have seemed sheer madness to adopt the live rear axle when its sole virtue (that of enclosing all the transmission mechanism, whereas the chains of the rival school were invariably exposed to dirt and wear) could only be enjoyed at the expense of a noticeable deterioration in ride and roadholding. The chain drive arrangements that were then popular generally consisted of a bevel box located immediately behind the gearbox and fixed to the chassis, shafts from the differential gear within it terminating in sprockets, outboard of the chassis side members, engaging heavy chains which communicated with sprockets attached to the rear wheels. These wheels could therefore be mounted on a dead axle of low weight and relatively high polar inertia (that is, they had their masses arranged rather like a dumb-bell, whereas a live axle had a substantial mass at its centre), and this low unsprung weight allowed the use of fairly soft springs, well matched to those by which the even lighter front axle, bereft as it was of brakes in these early years, was suspended.

More important than this comfortably soft ride, which later racing drivers were to be denied for half a century, was the fact that such gentle springing of light masses ensured the best possible maintenance of contact between the tyres and the road surface, especially in those cars which, emulating the pioneer Mors, were equipped with dampers to modulate the action of their springs. More important still was the fact that the chain-driven rear axle was immune from transverse torque such as tended to raise the right wheel of a live rear axle clear of the road when full power was applied in a low gear. There were then no spin-limiting differentials, nor yet were cars light enough and tyres good enough always to permit the stratagem of a solid rear axle in which no differential was present: and therefore this lifting of a rear wheel would allow it to spin, and no useful tractive effort could be developed until the offending wheel were once again brought back to *terra firma*. This pernicious behaviour of the live axle was to become more and more troublesome as time went on, as cars grew more powerful and lighter, until eventually it forced the abandonment of the live axle in any car that might be a serious contender for racing honours.

With one or two trifling exceptions, the last of which occurred

2 An unheeded prophecy of future cars, the technically advanced 1905 Renault was built for Szisz to drive in the Gordon Bennett race

in 1953, no car thus equipped has won a Grand Prix since 1934. At the stage we are presently discussing, some thirty years earlier, the problems entrained by a live axle must have been perfectly obvious to the designers of those racing cars which adopted it. Their apparent folly can only be excused by the assumption that they felt it necessary for their racing cars to reflect the design features of the cars that they sold to the public, whose concern with optimising traction and roadholding would have been far less important a factor to influence their choice of a car than such matters as silence, cleanliness and freedom from maintenance, in all of which the shaft-driven live axle was clearly superior. Such good reasons not withstanding, the fact remains that the chain-driven racing car in the first years of the century was one which possessed a good ride, good handling, accurate and predictable steering, and the ability to use as much of its power as the exiguous tyres of the day could transmit. Because of its nose-heavy weight distribution and also because of its steering geometry it tended to understeer (that is, to run wide on corners as a result of the front tyres operating at a greater slip angle than those at the rear), and this made the steering quite heavy—so heavy sometimes that drivers were on occasion unable to negotiate a corner due to their sheer inability to force the steering round as much as was necessary. It must be remembered that although the ride of these cars was good, drivers nevertheless were severely fatigued by the heavy controls, by the sheer length of the races (the driver of the winning car in the 1906 Grand Prix was at the wheel for twelve hours fourteen minutes, spread over two days), and by the gruelling work involved in changing tyres, an undertaking that had to be faced with intimidating frequency, for the tyres of these cars were quite unable to sustain the loads, speeds and abrasion to which they were subjected for anything like long enough to see through a day's racing.

These tyres were made of natural rubber of dubious and inconsistent quality, reinforced with zinc oxide which gave them their characteristic whiteness, superimposed on a cotton carcass, and anchored by beads in the edges of the wheel rim. When a tyre failed it had to be removed by main force, or more quickly by being slashed away with the large and fiercesomely sharp knife which was part of the riding mechanic's tool kit, and replaced with a fresh one at some considerable cost in muscular effort and mangled fingers. In the regulations for the 1906 Grand Prix the situation was aggravated by a new rule that tyres could only be changed by the men travelling in the car, without assistance from others; but this was countered by the introduction of detachable wheel rims which greatly eased the burden of the crews of the Fiat, Itala, Renault and Richard Brasier teams.

3 Before the 1906 GP, the new Renault had wire wheels

This feature may be picked out as the only technical improvement in the cars competing in that race, which were otherwise generally similar to those that had been seen in preceding years. All of them had four-cylinder engines and all those that mattered could claim at least 12 litres displacement, Panhard producing a new giant of no less than 18 litres. The Fiat, Gobron-Brillié (actually a 1903 car), the Mercédès and the Richard Brasier had chain drive, the others shaft and live axle. Quite the most disappointing feature of the field, at least in retrospect, was the car entered by Renault, for it constituted a lamentable retrogression from their very advanced and unorthodox 1905 Gordon Bennett

1907 Fiat

FROM THE VERY BEGINNING of
Grand Prix motor racing, there
have been very few cars that have
made history by successfully
breaking with tradition. There
have been a few more which have
in their times given full expression
to the established engineering
fashions by which motor racing
has been governed. Whether to
point a moral or to adorn a tale,
these few cars of both categories
have been selected for exemplary
treatment in this book, appearing
here and on subsequent colour
plates in chronological order.

Before the pendulum of
engineering fashion began to
swing, Grand Prix cars went
through a monstrous infancy. In
the years from 1906 to 1911, the
most effective machines had
engines ranging in displacement
from about 8 litres to more than
18, and were built with such
generosity of metal as was judged
appropriate to races that might
endure for two days over public
roads that were poor to begin with
and would deteriorate rapidly as
the mighty cars passed. Yet,
giants though they were, the cars
of this period were often so finely
proportioned as to belie their
stature; and few examples better
illustrate this good balance than
the 16·2 litre FIAT which won the
Grand Prix de l'ACF in 1907. Nor
was this balance illusory or
merely visual: many of these cars
were endowed with such stability,
cornering power, and nicety of
steering as could not be equalled
by the majority of Grand Prix cars
in the next two decades. The FIAT,
employing chains to drive wheels
set on a dead axle beam,
epitomised the best of them at a
time when the appeal of the live
axle and shaft were beginning to
seduce many designers. Once the
change was made, racing car
suspension remained in the
doldrums until 1934 – by which
time the part played by this great
Italian company in fostering
racing and thus developing the
motor car would be passing from
memory to oblivion.

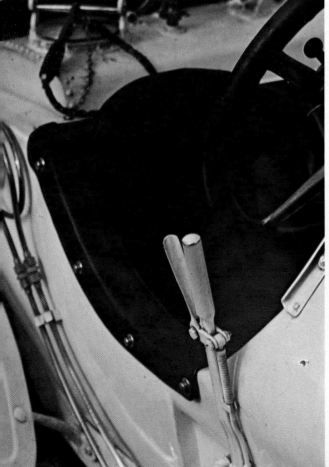

1914 Mercedes

THE CULT OF EFFICIENCY and the pursuit of lightness, ideas that had been brought to fruition by Henry and his disciples working for Peugeot in the second decade of the present century, were turned against Peugeot by Mercedes in 1914. The relatively small high-speed engine, now constrained by regulations to displace no more than 4·5 litres, gave the cars of 1914 a higher performance than anything that had previously been seen in Grand Prix racing. The engine of the Mercedes, based on aero-engine experience which conferred on it notably reliable cooling and modest weight, was also more robust (particularly within the crankcase) than those of its French rivals; and if its power was not yet as great as that of the 12·8 litre Mercedes that had won the 1908 Grand Prix, the slight deficit was more than compensated by the reduction in frontal area achieved by the new feature of a double-dropped chassis frame, lowering the entire superstructure.   (*continued over*)

1914 Mercedes Benz (continued)

The contrast with the cars of the primitive era epitomised by the 1907 FIAT was more acute in such matters as general proportions and style than in the size, construction, or efficiency of their engines. The driver's head was now less than five feet above the ground: he sat in the car, not on it, and the mechanic riding with him tucked himself away as much as was consistent with the operation of the elegant little pump with which to pressurize the fuel tank on which it was mounted. The fine execution of such details evident is but an echo of incredible devotion to detail in more important components: for example, the rear axle was constructed so as to set the driving wheels perpendicular to the surface of the cambered roads on which the 1914 race was run, and for the sake of reliability each halfshaft was made integral with its own crownwheel gear. Every feature of the course, of the opposition, and of the car itself, was subjected to exhaustive scrutiny by the Mercedes racing department: so it was as much due to strictly disciplined team control, effective signalling, and outstanding reliability as to the sheer speed of the cars that Mercedes swept to a 1-2-3 victory. There remains but one sign of human weakness: the 1914 Mercedes was the last car to win a proper Grand Prix with a front axle whose design was innocent of brakes.

4 Szisz winning the 1906 GP, his Renault now on wooden wheels

racer. There had been nothing special about its engine, but its chassis was quite extraordinary. When all about were relying on separate frames consisting either of steel channel sections or armoured wood side members, the Renault had deep pressed steel frames of light gauge, contoured to match the shape of a knife-edged wind-cheating bonnet and underslung beneath the axles so as to produce a car of uncommonly low build and consequent stability. Contemporary accounts confirm that the handling of these cars was exceptional by the standards of the time, but unfortunately they were wanting in reliability, principally due to overheating. So the design was abandoned for 1906 and we may properly lament the fact now—for the upper part of the body was riveted to the base, augmenting its strength and stiffness and constituting the first example of stressed-skin or semi-monocoque construction. Had Renault persevered with this idea into 1906 and enjoyed even reasonable success with it, there is no telling what blind alleys and red herrings might have been averted in the subsequent history of the motor car. Instead they rejected it and produced a car that was substantially orthodox. It did, in fact, have a solid rear axle—in other words, there was no differential in the final drive—since the race was on a triangular circuit which was fifty-five miles long, so that the exigencies of cornering occurred only about once every twenty minutes. Furthermore, the car boasted what were probably the first double-acting dampers to be used in racing. There was also, of course, the matter of the Michelin detachable rims, which imposed a certain weight penalty but soon proved their worth when the winning driver Szisz changed all four tyres in three minutes forty-seven seconds halfway through the first day.

The victory of the Renault is largely attributable to the driving of Szisz, which was a model of restraint, although when the cars were timed through a kilometre on the grandstand straight his

5 130 hp de Dietrich driven by Gabriel
in the 1906 GP

Renault was found to be the fastest of all competitors at a speed of
92·43 mph. His average speed for the two days of racing, covering
770 miles, was 63 mph, giving him victory by a clear margin over
the Fiat of Felice Nazzaro, who averaged 60·4 mph. The Fiat,
boasting 135 horsepower from its overhead-valve engine, was
supposed to be faster than the 105 horsepower side-valve Renault;
but in fact its time through the flying kilometre proved equivalent
to a speed of 87·2 mph. It should, however, be noted that some
authorities credit the Fiat with only 120 or even 115 horsepower.
For that matter, the Richard Brasier, less powerful still, succeeded
in turning the fastest lap of the race when the driver Baras completed his opening lap at an average of 73·3 mph. Clearly, different
cars and different drivers were at their best on different parts of the
circuit; equally clearly, both Szisz and Nazzaro were very capable
drivers, while if the Fiat were deficient in outright speed compared with the Renault, its superiority on acceleration and stability would stand it in good stead in any race run on a more sinuous
course.

6 In the 1906 Circuit des Ardennes,
this de Dietrich was handled by
Duray

7 The great Fiat year of 1907: Felice Nazzaro and his 28/40 hp Fiat plastered with dirt after winning the Targa Florio—

Just how effective was the combination of Fiat and Nazzaro was amply demonstrated in the following year. 1907 was quite busy by contemporary motor racing standards: the French organisers of the 1906 event hastened to promote it afresh in 1907, while the Germans created an event of their own, intended to attract ordinary cars rather than specialised racers and anxious no doubt to put the French firmly in their places. Furthermore the Italians were again going to run their race in Sicily for the Targa Florio, as in previous years, a race which imposed the severest demands on the roadworthiness of the cars and one in which the victor was correspondingly held in high esteem.

All three of these races were of major importance; all three were very well supported, perhaps better than ever before; and all three were won in a convincing display of superiority by Fiat. What makes this performance remarkable is that the three races were run according to different formulae, and the Torinese firm fielded entirely different cars for each event. In the case of the German race for the Kaiserpreis, the cars were limited to a maximum engine capacity of 8 litres and a minimum weight of 1,175 kg, with certain supplementary regulations dealing with dimensions designed to ensure that outright racing cars would not be admissible. In the case of the Targa Florio there was a formula based on cylinder bore, this being limited to 125 mm for cars with four cylinders, as all effective competition cars at the time had. As for the Grand Prix in France, there was only one stipulation, and this was that fuel consumption would be limited to 30 litres for 100 kilometres.

8 —*looking cleaner with the Fiat 'Taunus' on which he won the Kaiserpreis, and—*

Such a criterion had and has everything to commend it. At so early a stage in the history of the petrol-engined car, however, the manufacturers interested in competition were not generally advanced enough in their technical knowledge to be able to predict with any certainty the specific fuel consumption of a newly designed engine. In general in 1907 theory was still floundering and empiricism held sway, so it was hardly surprising that nearly all manufacturers entering cars for the French Grand Prix should rely on known devils, and field cars essentially similar and in some cases identical to those that had been seen a year earlier. Indeed Renault, having sold the 1906 team, built a set of perfect copies; and few of the other manufacturers showed much more originality. Fiat, however, responded enthusiastically to the challenges presented by all three races and did so in a manner suggesting that they were competent and confident in tailoring cars to measure, as it were—though in the next seven years, as we shall see, their confidence was somewhat dinted by the turn of events.

In 1907, however, they justifiably put their faith in low piston speeds in producing their racing engines: the Targa Florio motor was not allowed a larger bore than 125 mm, and this Fiat matched with a stroke of 130, resisting the temptation to increase engine capacity by a longer stroke and instead clinging to the already established fashion for cylinders whose stroke/bore ratio was approximately unity. For the Kaiserpreis the same stroke—

9 —radiant after treatment by a contemporary photographic artist, alongside the 130 hp Fiat with which he won the 1907 GP

indeed substantially the same engine, no doubt—was retained, but with a cylinder bore of 140 mm to produce the permitted 8 litres displacement. And for the French Grand Prix, where they could build their engine any way they liked so long as it yielded the performance likely to be necessary and displayed no greater thirst than the fuel regulations made desirable, they created an engine of 150 mm stroke and 180 mm bore. These dimensions may be converted to a displacement of $16\frac{1}{4}$ litres, and the Grand Prix Fiat may be considered as epitomising the early ideals of racing car constructors, comprising a large but very lightly stressed engine set in a reasonably compact and surprisingly light chassis and, despite the relatively short stroke, relying on piston area rather than revolutions per minute to provide the power that was communicated by chain drive. Such a car is naturally high geared, and this particular car need occasion no surprise in its ability to average better than 9·4 miles per gallon while defeating thirty-seven other starters to win the French Grand Prix in six and three-quarter hours at an average speed of 70·5 mph.

The 1907 French Grand Prix was significant in a couple of other respects. For one thing, the competing cars were required to be painted in the racing colours allotted to their respective nations— green for England, red for Italy, white for Germany, blue for France, yellow for Belgium, red and yellow for Switzerland, red and white for the United States. At least it had the effect of making

10 Lancia works on his Fiat team car (they were numbered F-1, F-2, F-3) at the pits during the 1907 GP

the Renault distinguishable from the 1906 version, which had been painted red. In 1907 it was the Renault faces that were red, for Szisz finished with over $6\frac{1}{2}$ gallons of fuel unused; and it is interesting to speculate whether, had he driven less circumspectly and allowed his motor to consume its fuel more avidly, he might have made up the deficit (less than seven minutes in six and three-quarter hours) whereby he finished second to Nazzaro in the Fiat.

The other interesting sidelight on the race is that the Mercédès team was as early as this being subjected to strict control. The crews attended lectures in which they were instructed not only in the niceties of their machines and the exigencies of the circuit but also on the features whereby they might recognise their rivals on the road (a matter of no little difficulty when peering through a dust cloud left by a preceding car), and even the weaknesses and foibles of rival drivers, with hints on how these might be exploited. It was a pity, in the light of this, that the Mercédès machinery did not work as well as the Mercédès organisation, though their driver Jenatzy was faster than the rest of the field on the fifth lap. Ten had to be covered altogether around a flat, triangular $47\frac{3}{4}$ miles circuit near Dieppe; and of these ten no less than six were covered faster by a Fiat than by any other. The record lap was put in by Duray, driving a Dietrich of 17·3 litres, who went round at 75·4 mph before retiring with a seized gearbox. We may note that the bore of the Dietrich was the same as that of the Fiat, the extra capacity coming from a stroke 10 mm longer; but the combination of longer stroke and less advanced design of cylinder head and valve gear limited it to 1,250 rev/min when the Fiat could run up to 1,500, with the result that it was the Fiat which, despite being smaller, was the more powerful.

The difference was not great, but already there was a strong undercurrent of disapproval of the tremendous size of the latest racing cars. This view was lent considerable support by a couple of races that were shortly afterwards run at a circuit in the Ardennes, one of them being for cars complying with the regulations governing the Grand Prix and the other for those conforming to the rules of the Kaiserpreis. These smaller cars proved faster than the big ones, the 8-litre race being won at 59·5 mph compared with 57·3 for the Grand Prix category, and the fastest lap in the 8-litre race being established at 67 mph compared with 66·6 in the other. The successful cars in the 8-litre category, finishing first, second, and third, and putting up fastest lap, were all Minervas from Belgium, while the cars which won the Grand Prix category and put in fastest lap were both Mercédès. Nevertheless, the Germans strongly supported the contention that the endemic elephantiasis of engines had gone too far, and they embraced as enthusiastically as anyone the regulations for the 1908 Grand Prix of the ACF which, besides stipulating a minimum weight of 1,150 kg, also provided for a maximum piston area of 117 square inches.

It is readily demonstrable that, all other things being equal, the power of an engine is proportional to its piston area. At any given stage of engineering development, the limitations being imposed

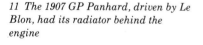
11 The 1907 GP Panhard, driven by Le Blon, had its radiator behind the engine

31

not so much by individual design or manufacturing skills, but by the metals and lubricants available (and in the first decade of the twentieth century these were of dubious quality and parlous reliability), most other variables can freely be interchanged and may be treated as mutually self-cancelling. For example, it is a somewhat inexplicable but altogether inescapable fact that throughout the history of the development of the motor car engine designers have accepted mean piston velocity as the factor limiting the performance of an engine. He is considered either brave or foolhardy who today will commit his pistons to a mean velocity in excess of 4,000 feet per minute. In 1908 the figure was more like 1,600. Given a limiting piston speed, it may be deduced that any attempt to increase engine capacity by lengthening the stroke will enforce a reduction in the permitted rate of crankshaft revolutions if the critical piston velocity is not to be exceeded. Correspondingly, if it is sought to increase the crankshaft rate, the stroke must be shortened. Thus these two factors, and therefore piston displacement itself, may be disregarded as having no bearing upon the power output of the engine: this will depend upon the piston area, upon the mean pressure that can be exerted thereupon during the combustion phase of the operating cycle, upon the mean piston velocity limit currently in fashion, and to some slight extent upon the mechanical efficiency of the engine.

It should be noted that an important variable still exists here in the mean effective pressure. It was said earlier that the power output of an engine may be considered proportional with piston area, other things being equal; but there is no reason why there should be such equality in the matter of combustion pressures, and indeed all the evidence goes to show that such was far from being the case. This was well enough known at the time, of course, but there was a general feeling that if one engineer by his skill, persistence, or good fortune, could achieve a higher mean effective pressure than another, there was no reason why he should not profit thereby. Egalitarianism was all very well, but should not be carried to stifling excess.

We may question the reasoning that permitted this freedom to exploit volumetric efficiency, which is what mean effective pressure is largely a measure of, when big engines turning slowly —and for that matter smaller engines turning faster, within the limits imposed by the bearings, lubrication and valve gear of the day—were proscribed by a kind of sumptuary law. After all, it was known at the time that, regardless of all other design factors, the ultimate power output of an engine was determined by the quantity of oxygen that could be combined with fuel to burn in the engine and thus liberate heat which could be converted into mechanical energy, and therefore that the thing which really mattered was the quantity of air that could be consumed and vitiated by the engine in a given time, since power is by definition the rate of doing work and imports time as well as force and distance. It may not have been known at the time, though ballisticians could undoubtedly have provided some clues, that the simplest and most effective way of limiting engine power was to limit the cross-sectional area of the orifice or orifices through which the engine inspired its air, since the rate of flow of air is governed to a maximum by the phenomena which intrude at the speed of sound. One has only to look at the rudimentary breathing apparatus of early engines, which invariably featured a single crude carburettor supplying all the cylinders by way of an angular and tortuous manifold, to see that the designers of the time had little or no idea of the things that affected volumetric efficiency, that encouraged good breathing—or good burning, as their combustion chambers showed.

For further confirmation one had but to examine the valve timing of these engines: developed only by cautious degrees from the sequence natural to the primitive automatic inlet valve of the very earliest engines, valve timing in the early 1900s bore little or no resemblance to modern practice. It was usual for the exhaust valve to close after the piston had reached the top of the exhaust stroke, and for the inlet valve to open even later. It was then considered futile to open the inlet valve before the piston had begun its downward stroke, creating a pressure drop within the cylinder; the notion that this pressure drop could be induced by the rapid expansion of the exhaust gases consequent upon the opening of the exhaust valve, and that the inlet valve should not only be opened before the exhaust had closed but might even be opened while the piston was still travelling upwards on the exhaust stroke, had not yet occurred to anybody. Bearing these things in mind, the mean effective pressure of 65 lb/in^2 at 1,500 rev/min in the 1907 Fiat may be considered not unreasonable, and the 93 lb/in^2 at 500 rev/min highly commendable. And indeed it was, for the Fiat boasted inclined overhead valves opposite each other in the cylinder head, at a time when all others used vertical parallel valves. Their crankshaft rates were little higher than those of the industrial engines whose valve timing they adopted, and it was therefore perfectly reasonable that at slow speeds their efficiency should have been markedly better than at higher speeds where they were simply running out of breath.

If the engineers of the time did not fully understand these things, they were extremely anxious to learn. The piston area formula gave them an excellent opportunity to do so, since it virtually imposed a moratorium on all other kinds of development and concentrated attention on the crucial business of breathing and burning.

The piston area formula that produced this result when applied to Grand Prix racing for 1908 was not then a novel idea in racing. It had been applied in a subordinate class for light cars or voiturettes in 1906, and its effect persisted for some time thereafter in this class. It was an unfortunate effect, for the contestants found it easier to satisfy themselves with the current state of the art in the matter of valve gear, ports, combustion chambers, and associated breathing apparatus, and to exploit this by the easiest means possible—which was to make an engine of very long stroke relative to the prescribed bore, accepting that it would run relatively slowly and exploiting the fact that at such speeds it would breathe fairly efficiently. The outcome was a series of grotesque engines, each more monstrously tall and narrow than the one before, until by 1908 the designers of Sizaire & Naudin (having shown earlier that when allowed to make their own decisions they favoured a stroke/bore ratio of unity) produced a racing car with a single cylinder of 100 mm bore and 250 mm stroke. Two years later the ultimate folly was achieved with a stroke/bore ratio of 4:1 when Peugeot produced a four-cylinder V engine of 3·44 litres, the bore and stroke being 65 and 260 mm respectively. Inevitably, as engine proportions passed from the extraordinary to the ludicrous, they were overtaken by the disfavour and ridicule that had long pursued them; but in the meantime they had achieved a great deal. As already mentioned, the most effective limitations on engine performance at the time were the purely mechanical ones of bearings and valve gear which together would not permit any engine to exceed 3,000 rev/min—indeed this figure was not surpassed in a four-cylinder machine until 1914, in the TT Vauxhall of that year designed by L. H. Pomeroy—and given this state of affairs it was up to designers to lengthen strokes as much as they dared and push the boundaries of limiting piston velocity as far as they could. Sizaire & Naudin in fact reached an astonishing 4,000 feet per minute in the 1908 single, and the lessons they learned about lightening reciprocating masses, about raising compression ratios (easier to do in a long-stroke engine which naturally produces a good combustion space shape when the piston is at top dead centre, compared with what can be achieved in a big-bore engine of the same compression ratio), and piston design were similar to those learned by other participants in this class of racing. The exercise was to have a profound effect upon the design of all future car engines, racing and touring alike; but in 1908, when the piston area limitation was applied to Grand Prix cars, it was too early to see what the results might be.

Those who anticipated a furious concentration upon improving volumetric efficiency were not altogether disappointed. Whereas

12 1908 GP Austin

in 1907 the Fiat had been exceptional in having its valves inclined at an included angle of 60 degrees, in 1908 the use of valves inclined in opposition at an included angle of 90 degrees was shared by Fiat with Benz, Dietrich, Clement Bayard and Weigel, these last two also having an overhead camshaft. Nor was this the only interesting new trend. Of the forty-eight cars entered, all but two had four cylinders, the exceptions being Austin and Porthos with six, whereas in the previous year the Porthos, Weigel and Dufaux had eight in line. Indeed all the cars were completely new, in detailed execution as well as in broad concept. The majority had adopted high-tension ignition, replacing the low-tension magneto that had earned little favour. Most obvious of all and most expected was the appreciable reduction in engine displacement, the largest car having less than 14 litres capacity and many combining the regulation 155-mm bore stipulated for a four-cylinder engine with a stroke of 170 mm to realise 12·83 litres displacement.

One such was the Mercédès, which bore its generally unremarkable engine in a chassis of new refinement, giving it a roadworthiness and liveliness that were exceptional even in this year when standards in these matters had generally improved considerably. Perhaps the most important change in the general disposition of the machinery was that the engine, already smaller and presumably lighter than the big fours of preceding years, was mounted further back in the frame so as greatly to improve what had hitherto been an excessively nose-heavy weight distribution. The huge flywheel, a characteristic feature of the times and one whose 550-mm diameter was really necessary in order to ensure the smooth operation of so very large and slow-running an engine, was mounted well back from the main mass of the engine, so as to be just about at mid-wheelbase; and the gearbox, bevel housing and final chain drive, all located after this flywheel beneath the floor above which the driver and his mechanic rode, were so distributed that although the weight distribution ensured a satisfactorily

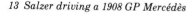
13 Salzer driving a 1908 GP Mercédès

14 Mercédès used pneumatic jacks for wheel-changes at the pits during the 1908 GP. This is Lautenschlager's winning car

large proportion on the rear wheels, it was in general concentrated amidships so as to ensure a low polar moment of inertia. In this chassis, perhaps for the first time in racing, we see a deliberate policy being applied to polar inertia—which, when minimised, gives the car very prompt steering and agile handling, these fast responses being bought at a cost of directional stability; whereas a high polar moment of inertia, where the major masses are arranged dumb-bell fashion at the front and rear extremities of the chassis, tends to make the car more ponderous in its response but better disposed to remain pointed in the desired direction.

Here was another aspect of engineering fashion which would be governed by the swing of time's pendulum: and it may be worth noticing that the next fluctuation in fashion was again dictated by Mercédès (more strictly by their successors Mercedes-Benz) when they took pains to design cars with high polar moment of inertia in the late 1930s. Together with Lancia they preached moderation in 1954, but polar moment was increased again until in 1959 the introduction of the successful rear-engined Cooper brought about a natural reduction which was made more extreme by Matra in 1969.

But we are getting ahead of ourselves. The point we made is that the chassis of the 1908 Grand Prix cars, many of them retaining chain drive, were well executed and endowed these cars with handling properties that were not to be rivalled for many years. The effect may be seen in the speeds achieved in the opening laps

15 *Benz were less advanced but well organized*

of the 1908 race, which was again held at Dieppe. The Mercédès, smaller engined but nevertheless deploying about the same power to move about the same weight with the same frontal area as the Fiat which was victorious in the previous year, set up a new lap record from a standing start, the speed being 4 per cent higher than the record established by Leon Duray on the Dietrich in the previous year. That such speeds were not subsequently maintained during the race was due to the fact that the roads were in poor condition and all the competitors suffered grievous delays while dealing with punctured tyres. The winner Lautenschlager drove with some caution and yet had to stop nine times for tyre replacements. Others stopped as many as nineteen times.

There were in the pits the means to make these stops shorter and less laborious than in the past. Quick-lift jacks were commonplace, Mercédès even having pneumatic ones. But when Napier proposed to race their Grand Prix cars with detachable wire wheels, whose removal and replacement would be considerably faster even than was possible with the now popular detachable rims on the wooden spoked wheels that were common to all other makes, they were condemned as unsound by the ACF, who showed (not for the first time, nor for the last) that they could easily allow political and patriotic issues to obscure their technical judgement.

However, it would be unfair to blame them for the fact that, after France's entries had taken such a trouncing in 1907 and 1908, the Grand Prix of the ACF was not held in 1909. In fact the

16 *The successful Fiats in the 1908 Coppa Florio did not look much different from the 1904 car in Figure 1*

principal French and German manufacturers had conspired to boycott all long-distance races, which they found increasingly burdensome, and so the proposed 1909 race came to nothing. In 1910 it was undoubtedly the Club that was to blame—or more particularly the senior French manufacturers who dominated the Club and would not foster a race which might, as seemed quite likely, be won by one of the many younger and technically more adventurous companies who had blossomed out in France. They and the French public, both avid for more and freer racing, pursued instead the honours that could be won in the voiturette class, and in particular in the series of races for the cup presented annually by the newspaper *L'Auto*. Here for the next few years was to be where the seed of future technical evolution and revolution were germinated.

This is not to say that there was no more Grand Prix racing, although the events dignified by such a title in 1911 are sometimes dismissed as being of no real character or significance. At least one important feature of 1911 was that a Grand Prix race was held in America at Savannah, where the American driver David Bruce-Brown won in the big and surpassingly ugly S74 Fiat, succeeding where Nazzaro's car had failed in 1910 with a broken chain after breaking the lap record. Big and ugly though this car looked, it was in fact of only 10 litres capacity, a genuine racing model designed in 1909 and raced in a variety of minor events as well as in the Savannah Grand Prize. It was sometimes known as the 90-horsepower model, but in fact its engine developed 120 horsepower, and this sufficed to give it victory in a race known as the Grand Prix de France, organised by the Automobile Club de la Sarthe and run at Le Mans, though not over the same roads as those used in 1906. The race was not to be confused with the French Grand Prix, which was revived the following year by the ACF, but in this 1911 event there was quite enough confusion anyway. For a start there was a contemporaneous race for the Coupe de l'Auto which was for three-litre cars of a certain minimum weight. However, what really threw the motor racing world into confusion was the appearance in the Grand Prix, running with the most sublime cheek in this unlimited category because it was *too light* to qualify as a light car within the scope of the regulations for the lesser races, of a tiny Bugatti, weighing little more than 300 kg, powered by a miniscule four-cylinder engine whose bore and stroke were 65 and 100 mm, giving a displacement of a bare 1·3 litres.

Seldom has so small a cat been set among such big pigeons, and seldom to such good purpose. This incredible little luxury car in miniature, a stripped version of the 1910 type 13 Bugatti, finished second in the Grand Prix! Admittedly its average speed was quite a bit slower than that of the winning Fiat, but the fact that it beat the rest of the Grand Prix field was quite enough to create a furore and to do a great deal to promote the reputation of the brilliant, artistic, idiosyncratic, and at this stage still young, Bugatti who had set up on his own only two years earlier. Another eleven years were to pass before Bugatti, his resources having caught up with his ambitions, presented himself again in Grand Prix racing as an entrant to be reckoned with, as an architect of change, and as the designer of Grand Prix cars embodying an ethos no less successful than his lone 1911 racer in disturbing the emotions and intellect alike.

It must not be pretended that the giant-killing performance of the little Bugatti in the 1911 Grand Prix de France had much more effect than as a temporary creator of sensation. It established no lasting precedents, sparked off no directly attributable revolution. Obviously it proved something, but it did not prove a great deal, not through any fault of its own but because the Grand Prix was so poorly supported. What it did was to underline and reinforce misgivings that were already widely felt about the course being taken by racing car design, at least as far as machines of Grand Prix status were concerned. If there were widespread dissatisfaction with the current GP cars, it was not to the pert little Bugatti that dissidents turned for inspiration, but to the cars which were racing for the Coupe de l'Auto, of which a three-litre Delage emerged victorious at 55·2 mph, compared with the 56·71 averaged by Hemery's GP Fiat. It was in fact from designs spawned in the Coupe de l'Auto series that Grand Prix racing was to draw its next inspiration.

17 Napier proposed wire wheels for the 1908 GP but the ACF prohibited them. They have been retrospectively fitted to this 1908 GP Itala, which originally had its friction dampers outboard of the dumb-irons

chapter two

1912 to 1921

The revival of Grand Prix racing in 1912, and its rise to popularity to the point where it was supported by fourteen manufacturers in 1914, was due to the fact that newly established companies calculated that the expenditure of . . . large sums would given them a really worthwhile return in the event of success. This expectation was based on selling and economic considerations far removed from those of the present day. We must picture a world in which automobile buyers were critical, knowledgeable, and few in number; indeed, in 1912 the whole output of the British industry amounted to only 23,000 vehicles. Despite this, very considerable profits could be earned and, for example, after paying for three cars in the 1913 French Grand Prix, the Sunbeam Motor Co., with a capital of only £120,000, made a net profit of £94,909 2s 3d, the equivalent of, say, £300,000 in modern money. The possibility of making racing pay can be seen from the fact that the Sunbeam profit was trebled between 1910 and 1912 and increased by nearly five times between 1910 and 1913, the very years in which they were most prominently engaged in motor sport.

L. E. W. Pomeroy

'Progress', wrote Herbert Spencer in his *Social Statics,* 'is not an accident, but a necessity . . . it is a part of nature.' Nothing could be more apposite to the situation of contestants preparing themselves for the 1912 French Grand Prix, which the ACF revived as a two-day event on the same Dieppe circuit that had been used in 1907 and 1908. The regulations governing the construction of the cars permitted virtually anything, subject only to a curious restriction of maximum width to 1·75 metres; but there was to be a concurrent race for a class of cars with engines of under three litres displacement, having at least four cylinders with a stroke/bore ratio not less than unity nor greater than 2:1. They also had to comply with a minimum weight requirement of 800 kg, and once again they would be competing for a Coupe de l'Auto. However, for those manufacturers concerned with the Grand Prix proper, it was a necessity that they prepare entirely new designs; and it was natural that, with enthusiasm for racing having passed from the older generation of car manufacturers to the younger, such designs should be based on the experience that they had garnered in the subordinate classes of racing that they had so staunchly supported in preceding years.

In fact, the division of interest was such that of the fifty-six entries received for the race, no less than forty-two were engaged in the struggle for the Coupe de l'Auto. Of the remaining French, Belgian, and Italian firms entering the Grand Prix proper, only Fiat and Lorraine Dietrich had previous Grand Prix experience; and this experience taught them to enter cars with engines much larger than any other competitors, the Lorraine having 15 litres and the Fiat over 14, although the latter had advanced somewhat

in the matter of valve gear in that its engine now mustered four vertical valves to each cylinder, all of them being operated by an overhead camshaft. It was also perhaps a sign of the times that even Fiat, whose experience and engineering logic had hitherto led them to prefer a stroke/bore ratio of about unity, should have espoused the new fashion in combining a cylinder bore of 150 mm with a stroke of no less 200. As it happened, the same length of stroke figured in the engine of the new GP Peugeot, but it was a measure of the almost startling confidence reposed in the new concepts about which it was designed that the bore of its cylinders was but 110 mm, producing a displacement of only 7·6 litres.

Progress, however, is not an accident. . . . These dimensions were arrived at by virtue of regulations for a mooted race, which never materialised, originally intended to be run concurrently with the 1911 Grand Prix. Peugeot had begun the preparation of a machine for that event, and it was natural that they should base their 1912 car on what they already had. The necessity of forswearing established fashions and striking out anew, a necessity which was recognised by their leading drivers Boillot and Zuccarelli as well as by the management of the firm, prompted the engagement of a young Swiss engineer called Ernest Henry to collaborate with these two drivers in designing an entirely new and altogether more effective racing machine. Henry was also required to produce a car for the Coupe de l'Auto; and it is a mark of his brilliance that, despite the obvious impossibility of doing a thorough job on both cars in the time available, he was so successful in both that commentators have ever since argued about the relative importance of the two designs.

There is no cause why this argument should ever be resolved. Both employed the same features to such good purpose that his designs dictated fashion until 1921, with certain features remaining current ever afterwards, even to the present day.

Although work done by Henry on the chassis must not be dismissed, it was for his engines that he will always be remembered. That of the 1912 GP Peugeot had a great deal in common with the earlier voiturette, and up to the level of the cylinder head it looked very similar—very tall and very slim, the sort of engine that might have been designed upon a wall and manufactured by offset lithography. It was in the cylinder head and its superstructure that Henry's engine was to be distinguished—not because it was replete with new features, but because Henry had combined a number of already proven ideas in an entirely original manner. Earlier engines of various makes had severally featured four valves per cylinder, an approximately hemispherical combustion chamber, inclined valves and crossflow porting, overhead camshaft operation of the valves, and even the use of two camshafts in the cylinder head. Henry combined all these features, adding as his own contribution a form of direct valve actuation that eliminated all the reciprocating or oscillating weight with which the valve springs of earlier engines had been burdened. He did this by devising a form of stirrup-shaped tappet encircling each cam inside the camshaft tunnel (which was a separate aluminium housing bolted on to the cylinder head). The stirrup was so shaped that the cam, as it rotated, in turn depressed it, whereupon it engaged axially with the valve stem in the cylinder head below, and then raised it again, this action being assisted by a light return spring which served to take up clearances between the cam and the inner surface of the stirrup. This arrangement made it possible for the valve stems and their concentric helical springs to be exposed to the air in the gap between the cylinder head and the camshaft tunnel, greatly assisting their cooling.

Prima facie, Henry was concerned with reducing reciprocating weight in the valve gear to minimum, as though his principal object were to produce an engine capable of very high rotational rates. In fact, this 7·6-litre engine gave its maximum power at 2,200 rev/min, admittedly a higher figure than anything in earlier Grand Prix practice (if one excepts the little Bugatti that ran in the 1911 race) but matched by some of the cars which competed in the Kaiserpreis and other 8-litre races of 1907, such as the Minerva. It also appears that he sought to achieve the maximum possible valve area within the narrow confines of a 110 mm bore, for the four small valves that can be placed within the circle thus circumscribed must as a geometric inevitability have a greater total area than the two largest valves that can be located therein. Undoubtedly this consideration did influence him, for we know that his valve timing had been widened to the extent that there was some overlap between the opening of the inlet valves and the closing of the exhaust, and years of voiturette racing with very long-stroke engines had demonstrated the importance of securing deep and free breathing if combustion pressures were to be maintained high enough to compensate for the small piston area.

19 *The winning 7·6 litre Peugeot, driven by Boillot, in the 1912 French GP*

By the standards of Grand Prix machinery, the Peugeot represented a great advance in this respect, for at 2,200 rev/min the brake mean effective pressure was at least 102 lb/in^2, and if the Peugeot factory's own claims were to be believed it would have been as high as 137. In fact the performance of the car never justified the claim made for 175 bhp, nor even other figures that were published at the time which ranged as low as 148. Such a figure might be reduced to 145 by conversion from the metric to the full Watt horsepower, and if measured in ideal conditions on a dynamometer might well be reduced further to perhaps 130 bhp when installed in the car and suffering the depredations of such auxiliaries as a full-length exhaust system and its own water pump, etc. In fact the late L. E. W. Pomeroy deduced this figure of 130 bhp from the observed performance of the car, and even allowing for the possibility that the losses in the transmission were higher in the Peugeot than was generally the case (for which there would seem to be no real reason), we are left wondering whether all Henry's work was justified at the time, however much the future development of Grand Prix engines may have justified it retrospectively. Despite a slight reduction in frontal area and in weight compared with its predecessors in the Grand Prix series, the 1912 Peugeot did not realise a performance that was significantly better than theirs. It was outstripped in the race by the Fiat, which itself showed no worthwhile improvement over the cars of earlier years, and it was only due to the random incidence of misfortune in both the Fiat and Peugeot teams, which suffered alike an infuriating succession of troubles with fractured petrol pipes, that the Peugeot of Boillot eventually won at a not very convincing speed. As luck would have it, it was the fastest car of the Peugeot

20 The Fiat S74 very nearly won the 1912 French GP (Bruce-Brown here fought a great duel with Boillot), and subsequent events might have been duller had it succeeded.

team that was the only example to survive until the end of the second day's racing, whereas the only Fiat to survive was Wagner's, certainly not the fastest member of the Fiat team, and he finished second. All the other unlimited cars defected, enabling the 3-litre Sunbeams to move up into third, fourth and fifth places in the Grand Prix as well as finishing first, second and third in the Coupe de l'Auto, albeit at an appreciably lower speed. In fact, the best Sunbeam performance, that of Rigal, was a final average speed of 65·29 mph, compared with 68·45 for the winning Peugeot and the 72·2 maintained throughout the first day by the Fiat of Bruce-Brown. These figures make an interesting comparison with the maximum speeds recorded by the best examples of these three makes during the race, which were, respectively, 101·67 for the Fiat, 99·86 for the Peugeot and 84·73 for the Sunbeam. The Coupe de l'Auto, be it noted, was never in contention, while the successful Sunbeams (and for that matter the 3-litre Vauxhall, which held fourth place overall for some time during the first day's racing) had side-valve engines. This being so, it becomes an interesting matter for speculation that, if Boillot's petrol pipe had also broken, or if Bruce-Brown's had not, the old-fashioned Fiat design would have emerged victorious in the Grand Prix as the elemental side-valvers did in the concurrent 3-litre race, the expectations of Peugeot and Henry might have been entirely confounded, and the lessons inferred from the event for application to future automobile design might have been entirely different. Perhaps, Herbert Spencer notwithstanding, progress is after all an accident.

What then can Henry's efforts have achieved? At 2,200 rev/min his 7·6-litre engine, in developing its 130 horsepower, displaced precisely the same total volume per minute as did the 16·2-litre Fiat of 1907 when that ran at 1,600 rev/min to produce the same power. The Peugeot enjoyed a slight superiority in horsepower per unit of frontal area; but its measured maximum speed, a fraction below 100 mph, was scarcely more than the 98 of which the Fiat was capable five years earlier. Furthermore, despite the fact that the Fiat had to be driven with some circumspection because of the fuel consumption restriction to which it was subjected, its average speed on the open road circuit was somewhat higher than that of the Peugeot, which ought to have profited from better handling and possibly better tyres but whose driver would have, if he were to achieve the full performance of which the car was capable, to have frequent recourse to a gearbox whose ratios were spaced very close together (the internal ratios were 1:1, 1·15:1, 1·52:1 and 2·05:1, making the car capable of 50 mph in bottom gear but doubtless creating some considerable difficulty in moving away from standstill) because of the relatively narrow range of crankshaft rates within which the engine would develop useful power—whereas in the first decade of the century it was the usual practice, having once ascended into top gear, to stay there. This intractability in the Peugeot could be attributed to the wider timing of the valves which Henry's operating mechanism made possible, and which would have contributed to the fact that the engine achieved a new high level for bmep among Grand Prix cars, and likewise for mean piston speed which, at 2,880 feet per minute, was nearly twice as great as that of the cars of the previous decade. These figures corresponded to a factor of 2·43 horsepower per square inch of piston area in the Peugeot, compared with about 0·82 in the Fiat; or, for what the figure is worth—which is not much—17 horsepower per litre compared with 8.

Thus in almost every respect the Peugeot is seen to have had to work much harder in order to do no better than its predecessors. The higher ratings and loadings that its engine had to accept—in particular the high piston speed and the high ratio of power output to piston area—imply mechanical hazards new to Grand Prix racing. This being so, the enquiry as to what Henry really achieved with this car can only with some temerity be met with the answer: reliability. On the evidence of the GP de l'ACF of 1912, this may appear to strain credulity, but the dominance of the GP Peugeot in the Grand Prix de France run later in the same year by the Sarthe Club helped somewhat to restore faith in the Henry concept. The point to be made is that the reliability it promised, and indeed the higher specific performance that it also promised, were to be enjoyed and cultivated by the many later cars in which Henry's principles were more effectively applied than in this his first attempt.

Mechanical, metallurgical and tribological problems were what held back the development of the petrol engine in the first fifteen years of the century more than anything else, although the general ignorance about fuel quality must have created further inhibitions. There were general difficulties in making crankshafts, bearings, and ancillaries capable of rotating at the desired speeds, difficulties that Henry was no more able (indeed, perhaps less able) to overcome than his contemporaries. However, the stoutest shackles by which engine designers were bound were imposed by the metallurgical shortcomings of materials used for valves and valve springs, and the problems ever present in this area were exacerbated by the deficiencies of contemporary fuels and lubricants. Here Henry's design showed clear and incontestable superiority. We have already seen that his use of four valves contributed to good engine breathing by allowing a greater total valve area than could be achieved with two valves; but it was a further and perhaps greater benefit that these valves, being appreciably smaller in dimension, would be very much smaller in mass, since the latter is proportional to the cube of the former. Therefore the ratio of surface area to mass would be greater, since the latter increases as the square of the former, and so Henry's small valves would be much better able to dissipate the heat that they acquired during the combustion and exhaust phases of the operating cycle. Moreover, as we have seen, the exposure of the valve stem and spring to the open air further assisted the dissipation of heat, although such exposure was not uncommon in the engines of the previous decade. At least as important was the reduction in the reciprocating weight of the valve train made possible not only by a multiplicity of smaller valves, but also by Henry's ingenious new overhead camshaft mechanism: the valve springs now had to control only the mass of the valve itself and the necessary collars and cotters by which it was retained. No longer were there any pushrods, tappets or rockers to be returned to their stations at the same time as the valves, and so the springs could be made lighter because they had less work to do, entraining a valuable reduction in valve seat loading when the valve was closed. Further possibilities were that the small valves could be raised through a greater lift, or subjected to greater acceleration, or operated at a greater cyclical rate, or some combination of all three; and it is most obviously and most immediately by such means that the power of an engine may be increased or its stamina improved. If only Henry had been capable of producing an engine whose bottom half would allow such rates of crankshaft rotation as its top half encouraged, then the prediction of L. H. Pomeroy—who told the Institution of Automobile Engineers in 1910 'There is no doubt that before the end of the next twelve months the engine which cannot develop its maximum horsepower and keep going at 3000 rpm will be a back number'—might have been judged reasonable rather than precocious. In fact, no Grand Prix engine complied with Pomeroy's stipulations until 1920 (the 1914 GP Peugeot did develop its maximum power at 3,000 rev/min, but it did not keep going quite long enough), and it was to be left to Fiat to abjure the teachings of Henry and create a new fashion in 1921 and 1922 with engines that at last achieved what Henry had set out to do, in such good measure that Fiat antedated the dictum of Sir Harry Ricardo, who in 1923 wrote: 'If a continuous mean speed of over 4000 rpm is to be maintained, some form of crankpin bearing other than a plain white metal lining will have to be employed.'

Ten years earlier, Henry was already experimenting with alternative forms of bearings, including a coated steel annulus that was free to revolve within the big-end eye of the connecting rod instead of being anchored thereto. The idea was a good one in theory, but in general it was Henry's weakness that he did not fully appreciate or could not properly cater for the lubrication requirements of his engines, especially in the crankcase regions, and the oil feeds to his crankshaft journal bearings were implausibly primitive. Still, he had to do something about all this, for the 1913 Grand Prix of the ACF was again to be run to a fuel-consumption formula considerably more rigorous than before, the permitted rate of consumption being one third lower than in 1907. We know that the 1912 car could not have complied with this requirement, for in 1913 it earned the distinction of being the first European car to win the Memorial Day Sweepstakes race at Indianapolis, covering the five hundred miles at an average speed of 75 mph and doing little more than 8 mpg in the process.

Accordingly Henry set himself to producing a new Grand Prix engine in which everything possible was done to minimise fric-

tional losses, and among the new features that he introduced were
ball and roller bearings for the crankshaft main journals. In fact
it was a two-piece crankshaft, the two halves being joined together
within the central roller bearing while ball bearings were used at
the outer extremities and the whole assembly was then inserted
axially into a new barrel-shaped crankcase which was considerably stiffer than the earlier open-bottom casting. For the rest, the
engine was but a refined and reduced version of the earlier one,
the ratio of stroke to bore being maintained as before, the dimensions reduced to give a displacement of 5·6 litres for the four
cylinders. Thus amended, the new Peugeot was claimed to be
capable of doing 15 mpg when travelling at its maximum speed
fully laden, and to have realised a specific consumption of 0·6 lb
per horsepower hour on the dynamometer, a figure which is fairly
creditable among the racing engines of any era.

When the race eventually took place on a new and unusually
short circuit at Amiens, where twenty-nine laps had to be covered
in one day to amass the total distance of 569 miles, the only serious
competition offered to Peugeot was by Delage, whose engine
was of proportions broadly similar to those of the Peugeot but
was furnished with four horizontal valves per cylinder. Shortly
after the halfway stage in the race the fastest Delage had to forego
its lead in the aftermath of a tyre stop, at which the mechanic had
jumped out too soon and was run over. This left Boillot's Peugeot
to win comfortably, with his team mate Goux supporting him in
second place.

Although there was much less to remark in its design and construction, the Delage was by no means to be despised; and when a
Delage won the poorly supported Grand Prix of France held later
in 1913, it did so at speeds which constituted new records for road
racing and demonstrated that this car at least was faster than the
1912 Peugeot, which was perhaps more than the 1913 Peugeot
could claim to be. The race was otherwise notable only for being
the last Grand Prix in which chain-driven cars were to appear,
this form of transmission being employed by all the three different
types of Mercédès that took part. The opportunity to see these

49

compared with the Peugeot had been denied by the ACF's refusal to accept the entry of Mercédès cars for their race earlier in the year, for reasons that might be arrived at without much conjecture.

Because of the absence of the Mercédès the Grand Prix of the ACF was the one in which the entire entry of twenty cars of eight different makes from France, Germany, Belgium, Italy and Great Britain had live rear axles and detachable wheels. Peugeot went farther by introducing eared locking rings for their Rudge Whitworth hubs, facilitating their rapid removal aided by a hammer rather than by a special spanner; they also confirmed the trend they had begun the previous year by dispensing with torque tubes or arms for the rear axle and relying on Hotchkiss drive through the rear springs, refinining the system by fitting double universal joints to the propellor shaft. Despite the susceptibility to transverse torque of an axle thus mounted, the system seemed to pay dividends, for the elimination of the torque arm or tube freed the axle from a geometrical constraint that had introduced spurious steering effects from the rear wheels whenever the car was in a condition of lateral roll, either when cornering or when one wheel rode over a bump or into a hollow. The importance should not be exaggerated, because the flexure of the half-elliptic springs in similar conditions could also deflect the axle from its proper position at right angles to the car's longitudinal axis, and thus produce spurious steering effects of the same nature.

Emboldened by their success the previous year, Peugeot again entered for the Indianapolis 500-mile race of 1914; and so did Delage who, despite the greater speed of the 5·6-litre Peugeot demonstrated in practice, succeeded in winning the race. Second to the Delage, ahead of the best of the Peugeot Grand Prix cars, was a privately entered 3-litre Coupe de l'Auto Peugeot, a car which had already created something of a sensation in Europe. It was essentially similar to the Grand Prix car, but while its engine was necessarily smaller the car as a whole was painstakingly made very light, and with 90 bhp available at 2,800 rev/min it was therefore able to challenge Grand Prix cars of double engine capacity and in some cases to beat them. Compared with other cars in the 3-litre class, the Peugeot was quite exceptional, demonstrating this by performances at Boulogne and at Brooklands, which showed it to be virtually in a class of its own. Its splendid performance at Indianapolis had no little effect upon the subsequent course of racing car design in America, for the 3-litre Monroe of 1920 which gave 98 horsepower at 3,200 rev/min was clearly inspired by it.

In 1914 the entire motor racing world, it seemed, was inspired by Henry—and, to be fair, by Boillot and Zuccarelli, who had been largely responsible for the original ideas upon which Henry based his subsequent designs. Not only did his refinements of chassis design enjoy widespread emulation, but his domination of design thinking among those responsible for creating new engines was almost complete, so that of the entrants for the 1914 Grand Prix of the ACF nearly all had four overhead valves per cylinder operated by an overhead camshaft, and five of the thirteen makes had adopted double overhead camshafts. The stroke/bore ratio of the various engines was generally about 1·6:1 which, if it did not exactly match Henry's precepts, approximated to them reasonably closely. Henry himself stuck to his favourite ratio of 1·8:1 almost exactly, creating an engine of 92 mm bore and 169 mm stroke for the race which was to be for cars of not more than $4\frac{1}{2}$ litres engine displacement.

This formula had been chosen, it has been said, because the 3-litre cars of the voiturette classes had demonstrated such qualities that all interested parties were now content to accept the idea of engines considerably smaller than had previously been thought appropriate to racing of Grand Prix status. Not since 1907 had races of such major importance been run to a capacity formula, the example in that year being the Kaiserpreis for 8-litre cars. Now with the size whittled down to the point where it was just sufficiently bigger than the Coupe de l'Auto cars to ensure some semblance of respectability, everybody in racing was reproducing replicas or near-replicas of Henry's Peugeot.

The only real dissidents were Delage and Mercédès, of whom the former were the less revolutionary. They continued their practice of setting the banks of valves at a wider included angle than other manufacturers, 90 degrees instead of the usual 60 degrees, and in the valve-operating mechanism they trumped Henry's card by virtually doing away with valve springs altogether. As in the Peugeot, the camshafts were located in separate cast aluminium tunnels bolted on pedestals above the cylinder head and with stirrup-type tappets completely encircling the cams; but there the resemblance ended. There was but one such tappet to each pair of valves, cross bars at the foot of the tappet engaging with the two parallel valve stems. The stirrup itself was wide, for it contained two tracks for two cams, one to depress the tappet and open the valve by a direct push on their stems, the other shaped to provide equally positive closure by pulling the tappet up again and pulling the valve stems with it, short compression springs on the valves providing a final seating pressure. It was not the first attempt to provide some alternative to the hated spring-loaded poppet valve which was such a handicap to early development of the petrol engine: Itala had, for example, had some success with rotary valves a few years earlier. It was, however, the first reasonably successful example of desmodromic operation of poppet valves, and the last to be seen in a Grand Prix engine until Daimler-Benz achieved the same ends by somewhat different means in 1954.

Desmodromic operation of the valves can improve reliability, provided it be properly arranged, simply by eliminating the treacherous valve spring. By forcing the valve positively to close instead of leaving it to the spring to effect closure as best it might, the valve timing can be made wider, the valve lift higher, and the volumetric efficiency of the engine thereby greater. Furthermore,

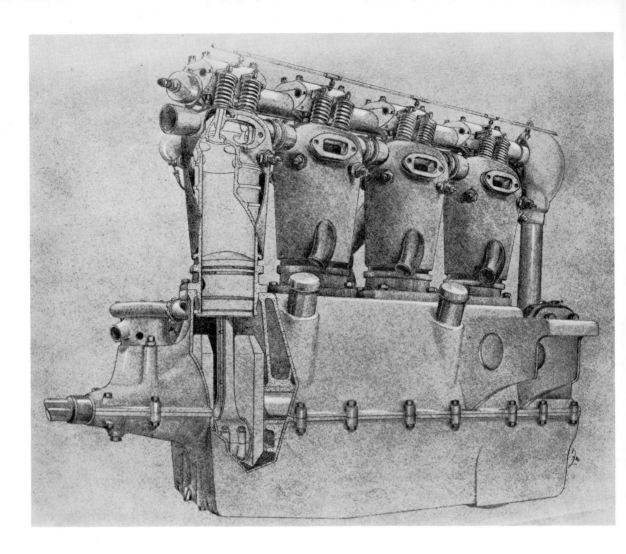

22 *The built-up cylinder construction of the 1914 GP Mercédès engine established a tradition that the German firm followed until 1955*

by eliminating the possibility of valve float due to spring inadequacy, it may enable an engine to be run at higher crankshaft rates than might otherwise be possible. In the Delage example of 1914, none of these objects was achieved, although we had the evidence of the car's third place at quarter-distance in the race to prove that it was adequately fast and at least as reliable as some of its rivals.

The departure of Mercédès from the general pattern of Henry's designs was much greater. The Daimler Company had considerable aero engine experience already, and they had recourse to this in designing the engine for their 1914 Grand Prix car which defied fashion by operating its four inclined valves with one single overhead camshaft communicating with them by rockers, and by a method of construction which was based on steel cylinders and ports all fabricated by welding and then enclosed by a thin steel water jacket that was then welded over the whole assembly. The crankcase and reciprocating parts were essentially conventional, but the Mercédès technique (copying an early idea of Panhard)

23 Mercédès in the 1914 French GP

for building up the superior portions of the engine made it fairly light in weight, allowed it to be made of more reliable materials, and permitted assured control of cooling.

The Mercédès also displayed some ingenuity in chassis design, the use of double dropped side rails and underslung rear springs allowing the car to be reduced somewhat in overall height, with commensurate reduction in frontal area that more than compensated for the reduction in power suffered by the cars of that year compared with their predecessors. The Mercédès engine actually developed 115 horsepower, and there is no doubt that this was a greater output than any of its rivals could maintain, allowing it to attain a maximum speed of no less than 116 mph, far in excess of anything previously known in racing.

However, comparable improvements in the ratio of power to frontal area were exploited by Peugeot, whose new car was virtually as powerful and as fast as the Mercédès, and it boasted of a chassis improvement which the German car did not enjoy. This was the luxury of brakes on all four wheels, a feature shared by Peugeot with Delage, Fiat and Piccard Pictet. The braking of front wheels had been introduced to touring cars five years earlier and in one or two cars raced by Isotta Fraschini in America in 1913 and 1914. At Lyon in 1914, where the Grand Prix of the ACF was held on 5 July, only the Peugeot was sufficiently powerful and therefore sufficiently fast to validate a comparison between two-

53

wheel and four-wheel brakes: eye-witness reports left no doubt but that the Peugeot gained considerably on the Mercédès in corners, due to its better braking performance as they were approached. Almost throughout the race this stood Boillot in good stead as he fought to keep the five Mercédès at bay; but team tactics, developed in the course of seven years by Mercédès until they reached a degree of sophistication unmatched until 1934, when the Germans resumed Grand Prix racing, were worth as much as one man's set of brakes, and the merciless pounding of the Peugeot eventually bore fruit in a 1, 2, 3 victory for the Mercédès team, a fourth place for the Goux Peugeot, and a broken valve for Boillot.

The war that followed within a month of this dramatic and historically important race introduced a moratorium that effectively continued until 1921, when Grand Prix racing was resumed. It was scarcely surprising that the actual years of the war saw virtually nothing in the way of chassis development for the motor car; on the other hand, we may accuse the motor manufacturers of unpardonable narrowness of outlook, evinced by their failure to

24 Fastest so far: the 115 hp of the 1914 Mercédès drove it at 115 mph

profit from the tremendous strides in engine design and manufacture, especially in the field of high-performance engines, when the emergence of the aeroplane as a weapon of first importance spurred the combatant nations to feats of technological development that might otherwise have taken a decade. The four years of World War I constituted a forcing period during which tremendous and quite fruitful research was undertaken in all aspects of engine design, not only in such matters as cooling, proportions, component design, materials, fuels and carburation, all of which were important to automobile manufacturers, but also with such concepts as turbocharging and supercharging which could and should have been recognised as of value to those interested in racing cars. A few of the more enlightened automobile designers — such as W. O. Bentley, who was definitely interested in racing, M. Birkigt, whose interest could have been revived, and F. H. Royce, who was implacably opposed to the whole idea — profited from the lessons learned in aero engine manufacture during the war, but in general the motor racing élite affected a disdainful ignorance of high-performance aero engine technology.

To this generality we must admit one important exception. Bugatti, forced by the German advance to leave his factory in Alsace early in the war, spent the years pending his return in the development and manufacture of some aero engines of marked originality. As aero engines they were not very successful, and before they could be put into production in America many of their detail shortcomings had to be eradicated there by King. Conceptually, however, they were very interesting, and automobile engine designers on both sides of the Atlantic were sufficiently

26 *Built for the 1914 French GP, the Fiat S57 was still racing after World War I, as here at Fanöe in 1919 when it was driven by Minoia. Note the front brakes*

impressed by the basic straight-eight layout (which Bugatti used in multiples to produce engines of sixteen or even thirty-two cylinders, the two or four straight-eight crankshafts being geared together) to copy the idea for their post-war racing car engines. These were by no means the first in-line eights, for Bugatti himself had produced one back in 1911 by the simple expedient of building two of his little type 13 engines together end to end; and, as we have seen, there were straight-eight engines taking part in the Grand Prix of 1907. During the war, however, Henry in France and Duesenberg in America had both been concerned in different ways with the Bugatti aero engine, and both promptly committed themselves to the production of straight-eight racing cars immediately after the war. The two had further in common an interest in the Indianapolis 500-mile race, Henry having been hurriedly commissioned by the French firm Ballot to produce a competitive car in the fearfully short time between Christmas 1918 and 26 April 1919.

The means he employed remind the author of one of the late Dorothy Parker's more barbed witticisms, *videlicet* 'If all the girls on the Yale prom were laid end to end, I shouldn't be a bit surprised'. Compared with this it must be reasonably innocent to suggest that there is nothing surprising in Henry's device of making a straight-eight Ballot by laying two of his four-cylinder Peugeot engines end to end. This, *mutatis mutandis,* is what he did, to such good purpose that the cars were the sensation of the American track, being easily the fastest there, although tyre troubles robbed them of victory, which went ironically to a pre-war 4½-litre Peugeot. Despite this setback, the 4·9-litre straight-eight Ballot engine seemed well enough vindicated by its performance, despite the handicap of being still unable (like all Henry's designs) safely to exceed 3,000 rev/min. Accordingly, when it was announced that the 1920 Indianapolis race would be run under the international regulations stipulating a 3-litre engine limit, Ballot were sufficiently encouraged to have Henry design a new

1922 Fiat   1923 Fiat

ONLY SIX MANUFACTURERS succeeded in the space of 66 years in overthrowing accepted motor racing dogma by the successful introduction of a design that could truly be called iconoclastic. Of these six, only Fiat have the distinction of doing so twice in successive years; and the magnitude of their achievement is disguised by the superficial similarity of the Fiat 804, which cast aside the habits of a decade in 1922, and the Fiat 805, which in 1923 set the world upon a new course which was to be followed faithfully for nearly three decades.

Beneath these bodies, each so carefully streamlined in plan and minimised in frontal area in a manner that was itself distinctly new, lay two engines to which many cars on the road today are yet indebted. The engine of the 804 dismissed the quadruple valves, pent-roof combustion chambers, plain bearings, and most other traditions of the current school of design, substituting the hemispherical heads with two opposed inclined valves of large size, the one-piece crankshaft with split roller bearings about the main journals and crankpins, and other constructional features which had been proved in the very fast but unfortunate 3-litre GP Fiat of 1921. The chassis was just as uncompromising; but it was the engine that counted for most. It brought about the downfall of all previous types in GP racing, and was the object of adulation and slavish copying as soon as it had proved itself successful, in its first appearance at Strasbourg in 1922.

A year later, the Fiat 805 introduced supercharging to the Grand Prix scene. Its straight-eight engine was structurally similar to that of the six cylinder 804, but the addition of forced induction gave the car such technical superiority as to assure it, after some early vicissitudes at Tours, a simply paralysing victory at Monza later in 1923. This was the car to beat, to copy, to develop under any and every guise, for the next decade; and its engine was the progenitor of nearly every successful GP engine from 1924 to 1951. No other racing car in history has exerted such a long-enduring influence.

1924-31 Bugatti

ETTORE BUGATTI has been variously represented as intuitive engineering genius, temperamental artist, freethinker, and patron of the arts of good living and good driving. It is doubtful if any of these several reputations is not exaggerated; but it would be more unjust to suggest that Bugatti be dismissed as the first quantity producer of over-the-counter racing cars. Admittedly the design of the Type 35 was strongly influenced by marketing considerations; and admittedly the large number of racing successes attributed to the machine were gained in minor events by amateurs whose custom had been attracted by Bugatti's elegant artifices. The fact remains that the Type 35 was primarily a beautiful artefact.

Unsurpassed as a vehicle for sensual gratification (whether visual, tactile, or aural), the Type 35 was not without the simple functional virtues that make a good racing car. The unusual chassis frame had its material so disposed as to provide beam stiffness and strength in the right places and to economise on weight and space in the right places. The unusual suspension combined with this structural stiffness to impart roadholding qualities that were superior to most contemporaries . The unusual wheels (originally with split rims held together by 24 set screws, later with one-piece wellbase rims) were cast integral with the brake drums, so that a tyre change in the pits during a long race could conveniently be made the occasion for a change of brake shoes as well. The engine, for all its failings, was replete with torque even though the unusual arrangement of valves denied it the high power output that it was in any case structurally incapable of supporting. When Bugatti introduced a twin-overhead-camshaft 16-valve engine to replace the 24-valve straight-eight of the type 35, to make the type 51 of 1931, the performance was markedly improved – without,

somehow, rendering the car any less unusual. For those unfortunate enough to be unable to see the Bugatti as something outstandingly beautiful, there remains the fact that it was distinctly uncommon. It set no engineering fashions, inspired no copyists (though Alfa Romeo were later to adopt the unusual rear suspension), and established no norms or standards. The Bugatti earns its place in these plates simply because it remained in contention for so long, and because Grand Prix racing would never have been the same without it.

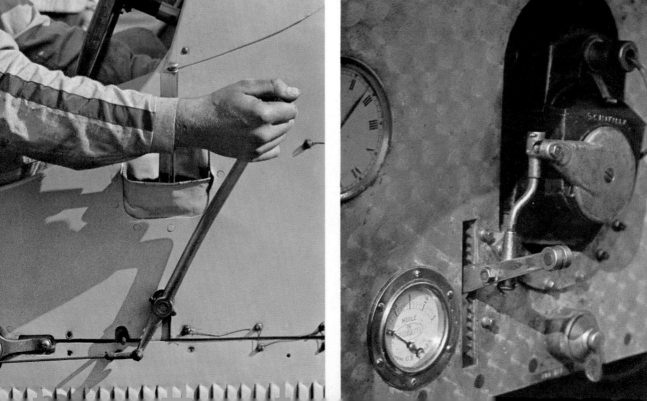

car for the occasion. This was virtually the 1919 unit scaled down and perhaps refined in some details; and it becomes germane to the story of Grand Prix racing because, when this was resumed in 1921, the 3-litre Ballot was obviously eligible and likely to be highly competitive. Once again it had been a Ballot that had been fastest at Indianapolis in 1920, leading until it caught fire only thirty-five miles from the end. At this race, incidentally, Peugeot fielded a new design of their own in which they had sought to go one better than their erstwhile designer Henry by somehow having five valves per cylinder instead of four, two sparking plugs instead of one, and three camshafts instead of two. All this evidently left insufficient room for an adequate flow of cooling water, and Peugeot quit the racing scene, never to return to it in any worthwhile strength.

Henry's 3-litre straight-eight Ballot is worthy of some examination, since it was the last competitive car that he produced. As already suggested, it was substantially similar in proportions if not in absolute dimensions to his pre-war Peugeot designs; and this similarity extends to certain chassis features such as the use of a sub-frame to carry the engine and gearbox within the chassis. In one important respect it differed, this being in the incorporation of a friction-driven servo apparatus (used under licence from Hispano Suiza) to amplify the driver's efforts at the brake pedal.

This mechanism became a popular feature of racing cars during the 1920s, only disappearing when brakes themselves and lining materials especially enjoyed some improvement some years later. We may also note that the transmission brake that had been in general use on racing cars until this time now disappeared—and likewise the fact that in many cars, the Ballot included, application of the brakes caused their torque reaction to distort the springs of the suspension and cause axle wind-up that was troublesome at the rear and positively dangerous at the front. Furthermore we must consider that the adoption of brakes on the front axle increased the unsprung mass at a time when the sprung mass of the car was being reduced, just as the abandonment of chain drive and the substitution of the live shaft-driven rear axle had produced the same effect at the rear. The inevitable consequence of all these things was that it was no longer possible to control a racing car at high speeds on the rough roads of the time if it were allowed such softness and amplitude of springing as had been the rule in the formative years of motor racing: spring rates were increased considerably, axle travel reduced correspondingly, and spring damping—almost always by simple Hartford type friction dampers—tightened up considerably. Torque-induced propensities to rear axle tramp were held in check by the same means, and for the next fifteen years the racing driver's life was a very hard one. It was not enough that the drivers should, as an English judge once instructed a barrister who complained of the hardness of the seats at the bar, 'Develop ischial callosities like baboons': they also had to adopt tight body belts in order to protect their abdominal organs from discomfort and possible injury.

27 The straight-eight Ballot in which Chassagne led the 1921 GP at Le Mans until the fuel tank was ruptured

As in the chassis, so in the engine, the 3-litre Ballot differed from the antecedent Peugeot in detail rather than in concept. For example, Henry had abandoned the stirrup type of tappet before the war, substituting in his last 3-litre car long slender cam followers of the finger type, pivoted at one end and interposed at the other between the cam and the tappet proper, which was now no more than a short length of rod butting against the tip of the valve stem. This arrangement ensured a lower total reciprocating mass in the valve gear (though the finger was still spring-loaded against the cam, as the stirrup had been in his first design) and recognised that valve springs were by now capable of returning a suitably light tappet without assistance from the cam—at least at the operational speed for which it was in Henry's competence to provide. Now in the 3-litre Ballot he abandoned the finger follower as well, and instead provided a piston type of tappet fitted over the valve springs and bearings against the cam on its upper surface. The necessary lateral support for this piston was provided by a suitably smooth cylindrical bore in which it reciprocated, and the piston tappet thus relieved the valve stem and guide of all lateral loads. On the other hand, it required complete enclosure of the valve springs, which could no longer be cooled by simple fresh air ventilation as in earlier engines.

We may also note the use of aluminium alloy pistons, as was now common, whereas they were extremely rare before the war. Bentley, Royce and Aquila-Italiana had used them in cars prior to 1914, the Italian firm (whose designer Cappa moved to Fiat in 1914) doing so as early as 1912, following the pioneer work of the Italian aviation engineer S. M. Viale, who had made an aluminium air-cooled cylinder in France in 1911 and tried aluminium pistons in it later that same year. Like the valve gear, these lightweight pistons encouraged high rates of crankshaft rotation; and in this engine, at long last, Henry's crankshaft was free to rotate faster than 3,000 rev/min. In fact the engine yielded its maximum power at 3,800, when the 107 horsepower liberated corresponded to a bmep of 122 lb/in^2, and the bore and stroke of 65 and 112 mm respectively completed the equation to give 2·61 horsepower per square inch of piston area.

Thus we see that the simple mathematical principles which encourage the adoption of a large number of small cylinders in any engine intended to produce the utmost power from a given total piston displacement are vindicated: increasing the number of cylinders offers a reduction in stresses with greater reliability at the same speed, or alternatively the possibility of raising the crankshaft rate without increasing the maximum mean piston velocity. In the 3-litre Ballot the piston speed reached 2,800 feet per minute, which is equal to that of the 200-mm stroke Peugeot of 1912; yet despite a 22 per cent increase in mean effective cylinder pressure, the piston loading in horsepower per square inch is not significantly higher. Unfortunately the inevitable Achilles heel of Henry—his incompetence with bearings and lubrication—made it inadvisable to run this engine to such speeds for a sustained time. He still employed his floating bush for the big-end bearings which continued to enjoy the justification of reducing the pv (pressure times velocity) factor, which has only in recent years been shown to be an erroneous method of rating a fixed bearing. So in practice the engine was limited to only 3,500 rev/min, and despite the engine enjoying a piston area 37 per cent greater than that of the 1913 Coupe de l'Auto Peugeot from the hand of the same designer, its continuous output was only about 11 per cent

28 In the Indianapolis Museum stands this representation of the 1921 GP Duesenberg, its engine built up from spares

greater. In short, to quote L. E. W. Pomeroy, 'Henry sowed but did not reap so far as the eight-cylinder in-line engine was concerned. The principle was used to better advantage by others, notably Duesenberg and Fiat. Both of these power units followed the long-stroke theme, but they ran reliably at high rpm and piston speeds, largely as a result of detailed refinements in mechanical construction and lubrication.'

At the 1921 French Grand Prix, the new Fiat was absent due to being in a state of advanced unreadiness. The Ballot put up a great fight, but was convincingly beaten by the Duesenberg, which was as reliable as the Ballot was not. Duesenberg's engine bore a remarkable similarity to Bugatti's straight-eight aero engine, even to the extent of having a single overhead camshaft operating three valves per cylinder, though it differed in having a detachable cylinder head in accordance with general American practice at that time. Any limitations inherent in the availability of only three forward speeds in the gearbox (whereas all its competitors in Europe offered four) were overcome firstly by the flexibility of the Duesenberg engine and, in terms of lap time on a sinuous road circuit, secondly and more importantly by the outstandingly effective hydraulic brakes which the Duesenberg brought to Grand Prix racing for the very first time at this event. They were literally hydraulic, the working fluid being water, and some very nice machining and fitting was necessary to confine this fluid within its proper circuit. Nevertheless the brakes continued to work well and the engine to drive the car fast and faultlessly throughout the four hours spent on the outrageously bad road surface of the Le Mans circuit.

Be it French or American, the 8-cylinder racing car was in the ascendant. But there was one more to come, from Italy, and it was ready in time for the newly inaugurated Brescia Grand Prix held less than two months later. This was the new Fiat 801, a 3-litre straight eight which finally completed the breakaway from the

29 The road surface at Le Mans for the 1921 French GP was bad even by contemporary standards. This is Guyot's Duesenberg at Arnage

Henry tradition and, in its necessarily limited career (in the following year Grands Prix were to be for cars of not more than two litres engine displacement), it performed sufficiently well to encourage Fiat to proceed along the avenues that they had explored with this car. The fashions created by Henry were to endure for several years in sportscars, but in Grand Prix racing it was the turn of Fiat to set the style. This they did by designing an engine with two valves per cylinder instead of four, with ten roller main bearings and even with roller big-end bearings, with a built-up form of construction similar to that used in the 1914 Mercédès and employed extensively by Fiat in their aero engines, and with an ability to operate reliably at 4,400 rev/min, higher even than the 4,250 of the Duesenberg, which it also exceeded slightly in piston area and by virtually the same proportion in power. As so often happens with a new example of fresh design thinking, the Fiat was not entirely successful on its first appearance, suffering a number of stops for minor attention which forced the fastest survivor of the team down to third place behind two Ballots. However, the fastest lap was put up by Bordino in a Fiat with which he kept at the head of the field until a puncture checked him on the twelfth lap, an oil pump failure finally causing his retirement shortly afterwards.

Thus ended in 1921 an era which, beginning in 1912, will always be associated with the work of Henry who, whatever his failings, produced a series of cars that were in many respects brilliant and by any reasonable standards eminently successful. It was an era in which the character of Grand Prix racing changed profoundly, this change being more the result than the cause of the change in the nature of the cars themselves. This period saw the beginnings of chassis development, the birth of the modern, small high-efficiency engine, and indeed the completion of the first real evolutionary phase in the history of the racing car.

30 First of a new line, the Fiat 801 (Bordino driving) was fastest but a non-finisher in the 1921 Italian GP at Brescia

chapter three

1922 to 1933

Say not thou, What is the cause that the former days were better than these?
Ecclesiastes 7:10

Let us now praise famous men
Men of little showing
For their work continueth
And their work continueth
Broad and deep continueth
Greater than their knowing!

When Kipling wrote this school song in imitation of Ecclesiasticus, it was not in any spirit of mockery but with the simple recognition (such as might be expected of any such good craftsman) that there are occasions when the best thing one can do is to take the work of a recognised master as a model. The full duality of this theme of praise by imitation was given expression in Grand Prix racing when the regulations by which such competition was governed were revised for 1922 to permit a maximum engine displacement of 2 litres and a minimum vehicle weight of 650 kg. For a brief interval there were some who clung blindly to the tenets of Henry's faith—either mediately, like Aston Martin who bought one of Henry's disciples to design them a new cylinder block and head, or immediately, like the Sunbeam–Talbot–Darracq combine which bought Henry himself to produce a new machine. There were some who went their own bizarre ways, either perishing in the attempt like Rolland Pilain, whose complex and finely executed straight eight could claim neither success nor durability save in a weakly contested 1923 San Sebastian Grand Prix, or surviving through sheer strength of character, like Bugatti. However, those who had an eye to the promising demonstration of the 3-litre straight eight Fiat in 1921 ought to have recognised this new planet swum into their ken, and to have expected further development of the new theme under the new formula.

This, as it proved, was no wild surmise; and before the year was out there was a complete swing of confidence towards the philosophy newly given expression in Turin, and a wholesale slavish adoption of Fiat's design principles by practically every other racing car constructor, excepting only the irrepressible Bugatti among those who had come to stay in motor racing.

These were the men of Fiat who became famous men—men renowned for their power, giving counsel by their understanding, and declaring prophecies: the leaders of the people by their counsels . . . men furnished with ability . . . all these were honoured in their generations, and were the glory of their times. In charge of Fiat's technical department at policy level was Fornaca and he had under him six engineers—Cavalli as leader, Bazzi, Becchia, Bertarione, Cappa and Zerbi—whose brilliance was mirrored by Jano, who was in charge of vehicle preparation. These are the men who created a new kind of racing car, whose technical inspiration was broadcast as a seed to germinate in all the leading coun-

31 *Start of the 1922 French GP: car 6
is a Rolland Pilain, 5 is a Bugatti,
7 a Ballot*

BAR

tries of the motor manufacturing world, who created a new
dynasty and set new fashions which were to endure unbroken for
a dozen years and to be revived periodically and successfully at
intervals thereafter. At their prompting dawned a new age of
classic racing cars, a golden age perhaps, during which virtually
all subsequent fashions in engine design waxed and waned,
during which supercharging began as a novelty and ended as a
sine qua non, and during which engineering intuition and artistry
enjoyed a heyday that was in no way clouded by the new burgeon-
ing of science and technology.

Let us examine the opposition that Fiat sought to defeat when
the field assembled for the Grand Prix of the ACF on 15 July 1922,
on a roughly triangular road circuit near Strasbourg. It was,
considering that this was the first race under a new set of regulations that were to remain valid for four years, an excellent entry,
amounting to twenty-two cars of which only four defected before
the race. Of the eighteen that started, three Sunbeams, three
Ballots and two Aston Martins were uncompromisingly representative of the Henry school of design. The Ballots had been designed
by him in 1920, and one of them had in fact finished third in the
1921 French Grand Prix despite giving away a litre to the other
cars and being conceived really as a sportscar rather than as an
outright Grand Prix racer. This last fact to some extent helped to
explain Henry's choice of a four-cylinder engine at a time when he
had become known as a devotee of the straight eight. He was,
however, subject to other constraints that may have even been
more effective, for a straight eight designed according to his
traditions would have had cylinders of only about 51 mm bore,
which would enforce the use of very small valves. There is no need
to accept the suggestion put forward by L. E. W. Pomeroy in

65

Volume 2 of his exceptionally fine work *The Grand Prix Car* (London, 1964), where he postulated that the stems of such valves could not be reduced in diameter to less than 5 mm (about one quarter of the probable head diameter), but Pomeroy had already shown convincingly enough that the coefficient of flow through Henry's valve gear was seldom impressive, and there is no doubt but that a reduction of valve size of this order would have impaired the engine's breathing even further. Moreover an engine with this multiplicity of such small cylinders would have to offer high crankshaft rates if it were to tempt any top-class driver with its power, and we have seen that high rates of revolution were by no means Henry's cup of tea. In fact, he was at his best when producing engines that by the standards of the 1920s would be considered of generous size, even though in 1912 his 7·6-litre iconoclast was considered small. Thus we may observe that throughout the 1920s large sports cars, of which the 3-, $4\frac{1}{2}$-, $6\frac{1}{2}$- and 8-litre Bentleys may be considered typical, continued to be very effective with engines that, if they had been modified to some extent in the light of the example given by the 1914 Grand Prix Mercédès, with which the early Bentleys had much in common, were nevertheless fundamentally aligned with Henry's theories. On the other hand, for cars that were necessarily limited by regulations to small engine capacities of which they had to make the best possible use, Henry's theories were at some variance with what could be achieved in practice.

These facts altogether eluded Louis Coatalen who directed the STD combine, the racing fortunes of which had lately declined; and he engaged Henry to design a new engine for a racing car that would bear the name of Sunbeam once more into the lists. Henry, with the experience of the 2-litre Ballot behind him, once again chose to produce a four-cylinder engine, the dimensions and proportions of which faithfully echoed his established practice.

For reasons that cannot be reliably ascertained, Henry created an engine whose piston area was somewhat less than that of the 2-litre Ballot, which was capable of developing 70 bhp at 3,800 rev/min, corresponding to a bmep of 120 lb/in^2 and 2·94 bhp per square inch of piston area. The Sunbeam exceeded expectations by developing no less than 83 at 4,250 rev/min, corresponding to 127 lb/in^2 and a piston loading of 3·7 horsepower per square inch. Henry was, in fact, squeezing his engine as hard as he could, doing everything possible to improve the volumetric efficiency and to raise the levels of piston speed and crankshaft as high as he dared. This could never be satisfactorily high because, as we have seen, Henry was not a bottom-end man. Once again I must take issue with Pomeroy who said that 'Henry was wedded to running crankshafts on roller main bearings with plain big ends *and the latter could therefore only be lubricated by jets, or to put it more crudely, by splash.'* The italics are mine, but not the opinion, for hindsight shows—and did in Pomeroy's time—examples of engines with entirely separate pressure feeds to mains and, via an end

32 Lee Guinness and Divo in the 2-litre GP Sunbeam of 1922

feed to a through-drilled crankshaft, to the big ends. Be that as it may, the Sunbeam did extraordinarily well, but not well enough, and with it Henry departed from the scene. If we evaluate it in purely quantitative terms such as piston loading or brake mean effective pressure it was the best engine he ever did; but if we relate the means he employed to the ends that he was instructed to achieve, it must be judged one of his worst.

He could at least be absolved of responsibility for the somewhat pathetic performance of the two Aston Martins. These were mere 1½-litre cars, based on existing four-cylinder engines whose nether portions were retained beneath new superstructures designed by one Gremillon, one of the Peugeot drawing office staff, whose services were obtained (quite cheaply, by some accounts) at the behest of Count Louis Zborowski. This man produced a cylinder head and all its associated apparatus bearing a resemblance to the detail design of the 8-cylinder Ballot that could better be described in the circumstances as slavish rather than as amazing.

Altogether more adventurous was the design of the three Rolland-Pilain designed by the engineer Grillot, who was more impressed by the idea of a straight eight than by the idea of a long stroke, and proportioned this intriguing machine accordingly. He specified a monobloc aluminium cylinder casting—something that had been proven to make for an admirably stiff and yet light engine when Hispano Suiza pioneered it in their famous V8 wartime aero engine—with wet iron cylinder liners inserted and carrying a detachable cast iron head. In this were machined hemispherical combustion chambers, and each accommodated but two valves: and these were spaced extraordinarily widely at an included angle of 160 degrees, Grillot having clearly recognised, as Fiat did in their 1921 3-litre car, that the greatest valve area and most efficient flow coefficients are to be achieved in an hemispherical head when its two valves are set wide apart—but Fiat contented themselves with an included angle of 96 degrees.

Presumably Grillot's valves were relatively even bigger, but he had no fears of their overloading the valve springs because he proposed to dispense with such treacherous components, adopting instead positive closure by a desmodromic mechanism. This was one respect in which he was trying a little too hard to be clever perhaps, for the mechanism proved as unsatisfactory as did most such attempts to ensure positive valve closure, and the Rolland-Pilain had returned to conventional valve operation by the time that the race was due. Nevertheless the engine was superb in its detail. The crankshaft was built up from thirteen parts, though it had only five main bearings of the roller type, and the pistons were of magnesium alloy, this being an exceptionally rare application of this material.

The feature of the crab-tracked chassis was the use of hydraulic front brakes made under licence from Duesenberg; and Duesenberg's influence was evident also in the design of the body, which was graced by a lengthy cigar-shaped tail. Tails of this nature had been employed as early as 1914 by the Grand Prix Peugeot, as a first stage in the development of some reasonable aerodynamic efficiency for cars that had hitherto been constructed with little or no thought for streamlining—a somewhat surprising omission, for the subject was already topical and the Germans in particular had done a good deal of fairly advanced aerodynamic research in order to perfect their Zeppelin series of airships.

33 Beneath the streamlined Strasbourg body, the 1922 Bugatti chassis was largely that of the medium-length Brescia, whose track and wheelbase dimensions were preserved in all GP Bugattis until 1932

Awareness of the need for minimising aerodynamic drag was displayed by several of the entrants at Strasbourg, making this 1922 Grand Prix historically important for yet another reason. The Ballot, for example, wore a fuselage of circular cross-section which gave it a most ungainly appearance and a rather large frontal area, but its hemispherical nose (with a circular hole at its centre for cooling air to enter) may have been reasonably efficient at the speeds involved. Curious though it may appear in a race of this nature, the apparently unnecessarily large diameter of the Ballot body was determined by the diameter of the spare wheel which the designer had chosen to carry within the nose—yet the 1922 GP was historic again in the sense that it was being run on a shorter circuit than had previously been fashionable, the cars making a mass start instead of being despatched in pairs at intervals, and the practice of carrying spare wheels and tyres had been abandoned.

Generically similar to the Ballot bodies but much less gross were the ovoid shells which concealed most of the interesting and unconventional features of the new Bugattis. These bodies had been built by a local panel beater immediately before the race at the insistence of the team's second-string driver de Vizcaya, Bugatti having intended to run the cars with tailless bolster-tank bodies similar to that of his early type 13 car. A feature of the streamlined body was an aperture at the tip of the cone formed by the tail, though which exhaust gases were discharged, the pipe that carried them there inconveniently heating the interior of the body to the discomfiture of the drivers and mechanics.

The Bugatti body was, however, by no means the most unusual of this new car's features. Known as the racing type 30 (it has been suggested that the correct designation was type 29), it had a straight-eight engine whose cylinders of 60 x 80 mm gave it a lower stroke:bore ratio than that of any other competitor. This suggested that Bugatti was espousing the twin causes of ample piston area and high crankshaft revolution; but he squandered the piston area by employing an arrangement for his valves which, while it may have served satisfactorily in his wartime aero engines which had so much in common with the car engine, were hardly adequate for racing purposes. There were three valves set vertically in the cylinder head and operated by a single overhead camshaft, and of these three the large singleton controlled the exhaust port while excessively small valves regulated the inlet. Bugatti was a great believer in the importance of providing clear and unobstructive exits for the waste products of combustion, and it was clear that the flow coefficient of the single large exhaust valve was substantially better than that of the little inlet valves. In fact, of course, he would have done better to reverse the arrangement, as Duesenberg had done before him, employing a large single inlet valve for the sake of good cylinder filling, and exploiting the high ratio of surface area to mass and consequent cooling of the small valves on the exhaust side.

In one respect at least Bugatti emulated Duesenberg, this being his adoption of hydraulic operation for the front brakes. Because the chassis of this otherwise new car was substantially that of the type 22 Brescia tourer, Bugatti found it convenient to retain the mechanical operation of the rear brakes, a system which proved more reliable than his hydraulics.

Much the most important defiance of convention among the cars assembled at Strasbourg in 1922 was that of Fiat, who in their

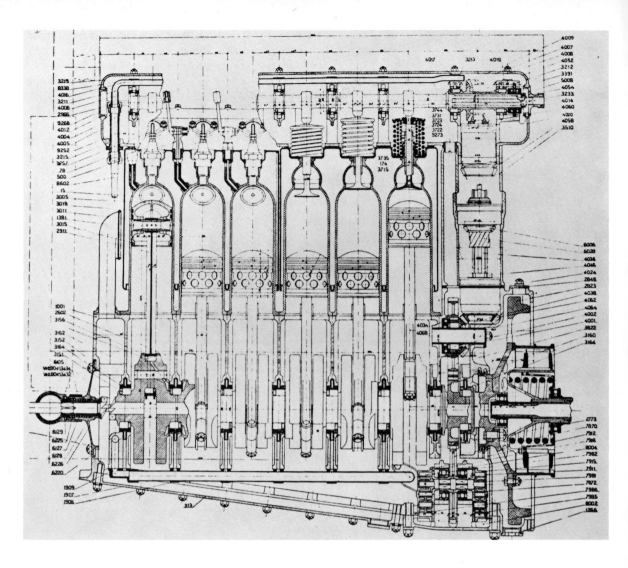

34 *The engine (type 404) of the Fiat car (type 804) which set a new fashion in 1922. The design is of great elegance: note the individual forged cylinders (with priming valves), triple valve springs, and oilways and slingers for the split roller bearings of main, big-end and camshaft journals*

new engine preferred to rely on their own initiative and on the experience that they had already amassed during three years testing and some brief racing of their eight-cylinder 3-litre and four-cylinder 1½-litre engines. These had served well enough for it to be a matter of obvious commonsense that the new 2-litre engine should be created by adapting six of the eight cylinders of the type 801 3-litre car, reducing the stroke to 100 mm and leaving the 65-mm bore unchanged. These dimensions endowed the engine of the 2-litre Fiat with 30·8 square inches of piston area, a good deal less than was mustered by the Bugatti; but because of the excellent breathing through the two large valve ports in the hemispherical cylinder head, and because of the exquisite design and consequent high mechanical efficiency of the whole construction (which was essentially that of the straight-eight 3-litre) the engine was able to sustain high speeds and loadings with safety and thus to exceed the power of all its rivals.

At 4,500 rev/min it yielded 92 bhp, equivalent to a fraction over

3 per square inch of piston area and to a bmep of no less 133 lb/in ^{2}. Thus we see that the Fiat engineers contrived to combine volumetric and combustive efficiencies comparable with the best that Henry could attain after his many years devoted work, together with the high speeds that denied him the full realisation of his design's potential.

The outcome was not for long in doubt. After a brief initial *jeu d'ésprit* on the part of Friderich, who brought his Bugatti round in the lead on the third lap, the race was completely dominated by the team of Fiats. Then on the 52nd of 60 laps the rear axle of one of them fractured and the car left the road, killing its driver Biagio Nazzaro. Then Bordino's Fiat retired with the same complaint, leaving Felice Nazzaro in the surviving Fiat (whose axle was found afterwards to have cracked), ignorant of his nephew's death, to win at an average speed of 79·2 mph. It is a measure of the Fiat's superiority that after Nazzaro's drive was completed in six hours seventeen minutes, officials had to wait nearly an hour for completion of the same distance by the first of the three Bugattis which were the only other cars to finish.

So discouraged were all the other competitors by this performance, two-thirds of the starters having failed before the race was half run, that only Bugatti turned up to challenge the Fiats in the other Grand Prix of the year, which was staged on the newly constructed Monza circuit. This artificial track promised very high speeds, suggesting that there would be a greater premium than ever on aerodynamic efficiency. In this respect it seemed likely that the Fiat would at least rival the Bugatti, for the bodywork devised for it, and seen at Strasbourg to initiate yet another fashion that was to endure for a long time, was very carefully

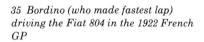
35 Bordino (who made fastest lap) driving the Fiat 804 in the 1922 French GP

shaped so as to correspond in plain with the contemporary notions of an ideal streamlined shape—notions which remain valid to this day for speeds such as were involved. In order to ensure the efficacy of this body form, Fiat had been to great pains to give it as clean and uncluttered an exterior as possible, and the chassis was shaped so that its side members were flush with the body contours from behind the front springs right through to the extreme rear. Even the outside exhaust pipe, maintained at a constant height so as to project the minimum frontal area, was carefully faired in.

Despite all this, and despite the superiority that the cars had already displayed at the French GP, Fiat were not content to present their cars at the Italian GP without further development. This had the effect of raising the peak-power bmep by 10 per cent, the corresponding crankshaft rate by 12 per cent, and the resultant power output by no less than 22 per cent—the actual figures being 145 lb/in^2, 5,000 rev/min, and 112 bhp, every one of them being of exceptional merit. In fact, the crankshaft was safe up to 5,500 rev/min, corresponding to a mean piston velocity of 3,420 feet per minute—and if the Bugatti with its shorter stroke should have been capable of equalling the Fiat's rate of revolutions, its stubbornly rudimentary system of crankshaft and big-end lubrication made it an undertaking fraught with peril.

There have been numerous occasions in the long and chequered history of Grand Prix racing when one type of car, one make, one model even, has been clearly superior to all the others. Seldom, if ever, can such superiority have been so overwhelming that three-quarters of its rivals preferred taunts of cowardice to proof of ineptitude. Yet this is what happened on the occasion of the 1922 Italian GP: Ballot, Bianchi, Delage, Rolland-Pilain, STD, and (it is said) Benz and Mercédès, all forfeited their entry fees in the conviction that the Fiats would enjoy a runaway victory. Diatto was persuaded that valour was more honourable than discretion—an attitude that has always characterised their designers who later became famous as the brothers Maserati—but their cars retired at quarter distance, the sole Bugatti at the start trailing to the finish at a speed that might have been respectable but for the ease with which the Fiats cruised around some 6 per cent faster to win at what must have been a canter, since Bordino's fastest lap was in turn 6 per cent faster still.

What could any would-be opponent of Fiat do? Louis Coatalen did what he had done in the past: he hired a demonstrably successful designer away from the home of his success to produce like results for STD. Henry, whom he had bought a year earlier, was now dismissed, his 'race of glory run, and race of shame' (though, unlike Samson Agonistes, his passing caused scarcely a ripple) and was replaced by Bertarione, whom Coatalen had induced to leave Fiat.

The Italian set about designing a car that would be called a Sunbeam by those who did not refer to it disparagingly as 'a Fiat in green paint'. Its engine was virtually identical to that of the

1922 Fiat, the only improvements made by Bertarione being a 2-mm increase in bore (supported by a 6-mm reduction in stroke), while he also made the exhaust valve larger than the inlet—which probably qualified as alteration rather than improvement. Although the chassis of the Sunbeam was basically that of the car which bore the name in 1922, the whole thing was made as much as possible in the image of the Fiat.

Coatalen was at least consistent. When previously he had seduced a rival manufacturer's designer he had left it too late. This time he had done it again: for he was not to know that the senior Fiat engineer Cavalli was treating the 1922 six-cylinder car as a mere stop-gap, while preparing for the following year an entirely new engine of even more advanced design and exploiting revolutionary principles so exotic to Grand Prix racing that the future course of technical development therein was to be wholly diverted along a new path that would be followed for another thirty years.

If Coatalen did not know, did Bertarione? Almost as fascinating a speculation is whether or not Cavalli or Fornaca connived at Bertarione's change of address, whether Bertarione knew about the gestating Fiat or not. What Fornaca in his turn could not have known was that in another year many of his outstanding team of engineers would have departed from the service of Fiat towards fresh woods and pastures new, disseminating the knowledge and experience of a generation in which Fiat had consistently been one of the most successful and often the most advanced practitioners of the motor racing sciences. Within the space of a few years Fiat would have completely withdrawn from Grand Prix racing, their glorious pre-eminence would become a rapidly fading legend, and their mantle would be assumed by newcomers who would be loath to admit the source of their inheritance.

All this was lost in the imponderable future when 1923 opened with the promise of two major Grands Prix during the summer season. The first of these was the French at Tours in July. Two months earlier the Americans had had their annual 500-mile event at Indianapolis, notable not only for the speed and quality of the Miller design which won but also for the redoubtable performance of the new supercharged Mercédès. Supercharging was even then not new, having been developed extensively during the war for aero engines, especially by the Germans, and having been used in motoring competition as early as 1908 by an American, Lee Chadwick—that being incidentally the same year in which Büchi in Switzerland invented the turbocharger, conceiving it as an adjunct of the diesel engine. By the time World War I was over, Mercédès had made more progress with supercharging than any other firm—but however liberal the other erstwhile enemies of the German nation might be, the French could not stomach the idea of German companies entering the French Grand Prix; and if the ACF had felt justified in refusing a Mercédès entry for their race in 1913, then in 1923 their cause for resentment of the Boche could hardly be said to have diminished. Accordingly there was no Mercédès at Tours; and accordingly the distinction of being

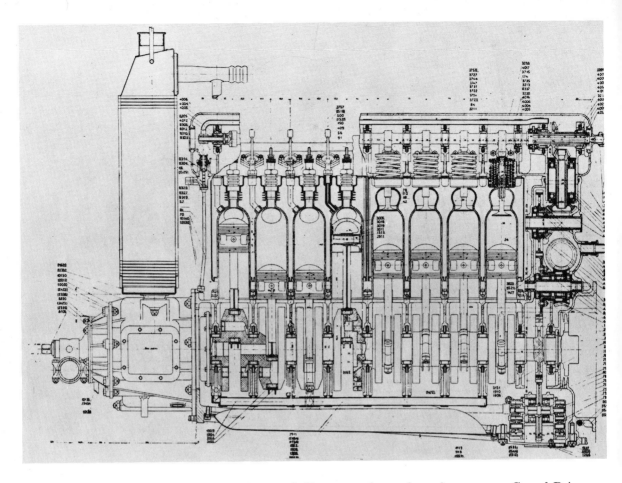

36 The type 405 engine of Fiat's 1923 type 805 car was the most influential in the history of motor racing.

the first to field a supercharged car in a proper Grand Prix race fell to Fiat, whose new type 805, while resembling the 1922 car in virtually all external aspects, in its chassis and running gear, and in the general style of construction of its engine, had become once again a straight eight in the tradition of the 1921 3-litre. The necessary reduction of cylinder dimensions gave it a lower stroke/bore ratio than even the 1922 car, and it was equipped with a Wittig vane-type supercharger blowing air into the carburettor, as indeed did the Mercédès supercharger. It was not an efficient supercharger layout, but it was better than none; and the forced induction combined with an increase in piston area and in permitted revolutions to produce a power output of 130 bhp. In view of the unchanged frontal area and the not significantly greater mass of the car (although the inevitably greater length of the engine, with its supercharger driven from the nose of the crankshaft, required a chassis of slightly longer wheelbase), it was scarcely surprising that the 1923 2-litre Fiat was appreciably faster than the 1922 car; and the completion of a record lap by Bordino proved fairly conclusively that it was also faster than any of its rivals.

Its performance in the race did not go unchallenged, however, for the Fiat suffered from some mechanical disorders which allowed the Sunbeam to challenge it from time to time. The air intake to the Fiat's blower was unscreened and unguarded, and the stones that flew from the cars' tyres on what used to pass in those days for road racing circuits entered the supercharger mechanism and there wrought such havoc as forced all the team to retire. The historian Peter Hull has implied in one of his works that it was this oversight that caused an argument to flare up after the race between chief Fornaca and his underling Bazzi, a member of the design staff; and this dissension led to Bazzi's departure from Fiat, and to his obtaining a post (at the suggestion of Enzo Ferrari) in the Alfa Romeo racing department—with what consequences we shall later see. The immediate result at Tours, however, was that the red Fiats failed and the green Fiat won, the Sunbeam of Segrave completing the distance at an average speed of 75·3 miles an hour, which may instructively be compared with the lap record (87·75 mph) of Bordino's Fiat.

There were other contestants at Tours who merited more success than the Sunbeam or deserve more attention here. The fastest of them to finish was a Bugatti, perhaps the strangest of all the strange devices that Bugatti has put on the road: described by *The Motor* as 'nightmarish monsters', the Bugattis in fact had an extraordinarily short wheelbase of only 79 inches, an extremely low chassis frame being underslung beneath the axles to carry last year's straight-eight engine—modified by the addition of roller-bearing big-ends, and in an alteration of the engine bearers to suit the novel installation which required the legs and feet of the driver and mechanic to extend on either side of the crankcase. The gearbox had been dismissed from its customary position and was now a mere three-speed affair built into the rear axle, which must have been the only place where there was room; and the whole unbelievable confection was hidden beneath a full width body of strictly rectangular cross-section and approximately lenticular longitudinal section. The streamlining idea was obviously getting a grip on Bugatti: this most original piece of designing, which appeared at the time merely grotesque to many but might attract less scorn today, was intended to displace the air vertically in the smooth manner of an airfoil, rather than to part it horizontally as had been the aim of the Fiat designers a year earlier. Eye-witness accounts have often been quoted as saying that the cars raised less dust than the others in the race, and they were certainly capable of quite high speeds, one being later timed over a kilometre at 117 mph. We may therefore accept that the body shape was successful in reducing aerodynamic drag; but it would also have suffered a forward movement of its aerodynamic centre of pressure at high speeds and must have generated appreciable lift over certain body sections, these two by-products of its contours almost certainly being responsible for the instability and indifferent roadholding which was then attributed to the chassis dimensions.

It would be interesting to know whether the wedge-shaped body of the Voisin imparted any stabilising effect to the chassis of the car, which unfortunately was so wanting in power (due to Voisin's

37 The 2-litre Voisin which ran in the 1923 French GP demands comparison with its compatriot Matra of 1971

38 1923 GP Rolland Pilain: 8 cylinders, 4 carburettors, 2 overhead camshafts, 1 minor victory

persistent use of the Knight type of sleeve valve in his engine) that it never went fast enough to permit any valid comparison to be made.

Dismissing the Rolland-Pilain which, alone of the cars present, had been constructed the previous year, we are left to consider the new Delage, the solitary example of which put up a tremendous fight before being forced to retire with a punctured fuel tank. It really was rather a surprise that it had done so well, despite its impressive specification, for it had been built in less than four months. If this time had not permitted any great care to be devoted to the chassis, which was entirely orthodox, incredible care had been lavished upon the engine, which was one of those nicely detailed and very complicated machines which can only work effectively if they are superbly wrought, as this one was. Delage's designer Plancton had, with all the remorseless logic traditionally attributed to the French, recognised that an engine-capacity formula put a premium on piston area and high rates of crankshaft revolution, which can be combined by a multiplicity of small-capacity cylinders without the ratio of stroke:bore being different from what is fashionable among other engines of like capacity but with fewer cylinders. The measure of his success is that he produced an engine whose stroke:bore ratio was 1·55:1, virtually the same as that of the 1922 Fiat, whose piston area was 30·7 square inches, which was 10 per cent greater than even the 1923 Fiat's, and which was certainly capable of running at a crankshaft rate higher than that of any other current 2-litre car. All this was achieved by the construction of a 12-cylinder engine, the two banks of six cylinders being set as a 60-degree V on a crankcase which carried a crankshaft in seven roller bearings, while the big ends and even the camshafts also ran in rollers and all other rotating members were supported in ball bearings. Broadly speaking, the principles applied by Plancton could be said to be those of Fiat, especially in respect of the free use of rolling-element bearings and in the design of the combustion chamber, valve gear, and reciprocating parts. Beyond that, the ideas were reasonably spontaneous although, of course, not new, the cast iron cylinder blocks echoing what had once been common practice, while a V12 engine had figured in racing at least as early as the Indianapolis race of 1919. In any case, no amount of virtuosity in the construction can compensate for a punctured fuel tank — and it is only fair to record that Divo's Fiat, though its blower was in an unhealthy state, was still running in the lead when forced to retire through loss of fuel out in the country.

Fiat saw to it that no such mistakes should be repeated at the Italian Grand Prix, held at Monza three months later and dignified with the title of First European Grand Prix. They did away with the troublesome and inefficient vane-type supercharger and substituted a blower of the positive displacement Roots type. This, despite offering no precompression of the air such as a vane supercharger performs, was nevertheless more efficient and very much more reliable. It was still arranged to deliver pressurised air through the carburettors, but the greater adiabatic efficiency of the Roots blower led to a reduction in the temperature of this compressed air, the advantages of a cool high-density charge being already appreciated by Fiat as of such importance that they took the further trouble to interpolate a cooler between the blower and the carburettor, with the effect that at peak power and

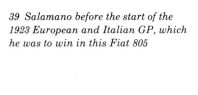

39 Salamano before the start of the 1923 European and Italian GP, which he was to win in this Fiat 805

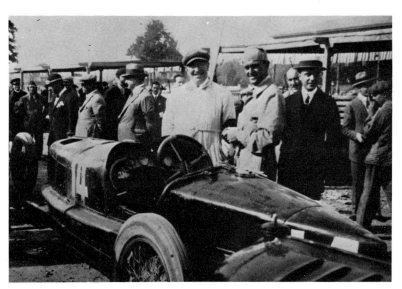

$8\frac{1}{2}$ lb/in² boost the charge temperature at the inlet ports was only 54°C instead of the 80° or thereabouts which must have been mainly responsible for the engine's poor output of a mere 130 bhp at Tours.

The effect of these innovations was to raise the power output for Monza to 146 bhp, equivalent to an improvement in the bmep from 154 to 169 lb/in² and incidentally raising the piston loading beyond four horsepower per square inch for the first time. Despite this uprating the engine wanted nothing in reliability, and the only fallibilities affecting the Fiat team in race were human: for Bordino crashed in practice, killing his mechanic and injuring an arm so that he had to drive with it bandaged in the race, steering with one hand while a mechanic operated the gear lever for him. Eventually he was constrained by sheer physical exhaustion to retire, but not before raising the Monza track lap record to 99·8 mph, 9 per cent higher than that set by the unblown six-cylinder car a year earlier. The other two members of the team, Salamano and Nazzaro, swept on to secure an untroubled victory, Salamano's winning speed being nearly 7 per cent higher than that of the previous year.

With events thus ratifying the proposals first expressed in the 3-litre type 801 a mere two years earlier, Fiat had effected a complete metamorphosis in the racing car, put an end to the many long years of doubt, neglect and prevarication on the part of the pioneers, and left almost the entire racing world anxious to endorse Fiat's engineering policies. Not only had the principles of engine design been radically revised, but also those of body shaping and even to some extent chassis design: for when Fiat resumed the use of torque-tube axle location in their 1921 car, all the others were quick to follow—whereas the similar example set by the 1914

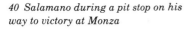

40 Salamano during a pit stop on his way to victory at Monza

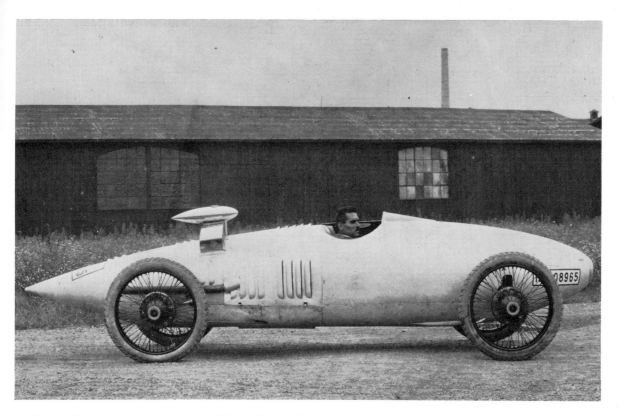

*41 The teardrop: 1923/4 Benz
Tropfenwagen 2-litre GP car*

Mercédès had been generally ignored. In all significant respects, Fiat had fixed the type of the racing car for the next ten years; and not the least important of their contribution was the use of the supercharger. This first European Grand Prix was the first international race to be won by a supercharged car; and thereafter supercharged cars were exclusively successful in Grands Prix of major standing (by which expression are excluded the Grands Prix of Pau and of Cork in 1938, which were won by an unsupercharged Delahaye) until 1947.

But for the occurrence in other quarters of human fallibility such as had afflicted Bordino in practice for the race at Monza, Fiat might not have had the distinction of achieving so much. A team of Alfa Romeo cars had been entered for the race, supercharged six-cylinder machines designed by Merosi and known as the P1. Alas, an accident in practice caused the death of one of their drivers, Sivocci, and the cars were withdrawn, never again to be run in public. Even had they enjoyed better fortune, it would still have to be admitted that in everything but their superchargers they bore a close resemblance to the 1922 six-cylinder Fiat.

So far as engines were concerned, the same applied to the new Benz machines which finished fourth and fifth at Monza. There the resemblance to the Fiat or indeed to anything else stopped: known as the Tropfwagen, the Benz had a body of circular cross-section and academically streamlined profile, its lines interrupted only by the cockpit opening and by the excrescence behind it of a

42 Engine, radiator, independent rear suspension, inboard rear brakes and underslung chassis of the Tropfenwagen

cowled radiator. Within the shell lurked the promise of a revolution which was to be long in coming: in a configuration expounded by the aeronautical engineer Doctor Rumpler, the engine was located behind the driver, communicating through a three-speed gearbox to a bevel housing that was fixed to the chassis and flanked by brakes outboard of which were pivoted swinging half axles, giving the car the first independent rear suspension of any racing car. And if this isolated experiment was crowned with less success than its proponents had perhaps hoped, at least the cars did better than the Rolland-Pilain, which appeared for the last time under their own name: they were now powered by engines incorporating the cuff valve (a kind of abbreviated and inefficient sleeve valve) developed by the Swiss Doctor Albert Schmid and, of all people, the lamented Ernest Henry. Next year the car would run (albeit unconvincingly) under the name of Schmid. Of the teardrop Benz we may be permitted to write, after Virgil, *sunt lacrimae rerum*—but it is the decline of Henry that prompts us to complete the line, *et mentem mortalia tangunt*.

So far we have said nothing about the car which finished in third place behind the fleet Fiat. It is one which, so far as its influence on European practice is concerned, is of no historical importance; but it was of the utmost technical importance. It was the Miller, a car similar to that which had won the 500 miles at Indianapolis earlier in the season. Pomeroy dismissed the Millers in a single sentence as 'Indianapolis type cars, unsupercharged, and gravely handicapped by inadequate transmission and braking systems.' True, they were not adapted to Grand Prix road racing; but the Monza track bore little or no resemblance to road racing anyway, and these American cars showed themselves here as satisfyingly fast. They were indeed the most powerful unsupercharged cars present, their finely executed straight-eight engines developing 120 bhp at between 4,500 and 5,000 rev/min. With

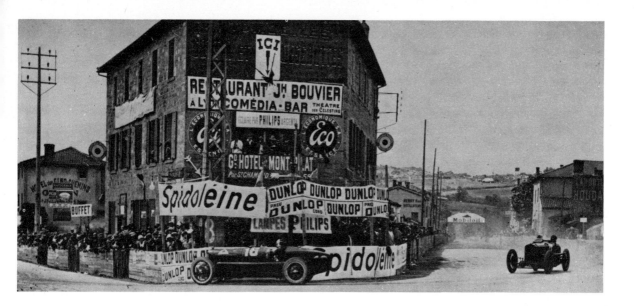

43 Wagner's new P2 Alfa Romeo leads Resta's even faster Sunbeam round the 7 Chemins hairpin during the 1924 French GP at Lyon

two valves operated by overhead camshafts and seated in hemispherical combustion chambers, these straight eights bore a certain data-sheet resemblance to the Fiat; but in fact their constructor Harry Miller, originally a carburettor manufacturer, drew his inspiration from several sources, including the Bugatti aero engine and the 1913 Peugeot, added a good deal of his own artistry, and produced from this mélange a design which deserves to be called original. What most distinguishes it from everything in Europe, and what makes it of great importance, is the fact that it was furnished with four twin-choke barrel-throttled Miller carburettors arranged to provide a completely separate induction tract for each cylinder. Nothing is more vital than this feature to the realisation of an otherwise well-designed unsupercharged engine's potential; and if the length of the tracts be determined (whether by theory, by experiment, or by chance) so as to put the column of air within it into sympathetic resonance with the engine's operating cycle at the critical speed where the most effective breathing is required, the filling of the cylinders would be improved enormously. This was achieved by Miller, with the aid of ram pipe extensions that were screwed to the downward-facing intakes of the updraught carburettors. The correct length for the tubes was ascertained empirically by the simple expedient of attending a high-speed circuit equipped with a car, an assortment of ram tubes of various lengths, and stop watch.

After Monza the Miller too acquired a supercharger. Perhaps more to our point, Alfa Romeo started afresh on the design of yet another supercharged 2-litre straight eight. Based on development work done with one of the ill-fated six-cylinder P1 machines, the new one was designated P2 and was ready by the spring of 1924. Its design, construction, and development were supervised by yet another member of the brain drain from Fiat: this was Vittorio Jano, whose acquisition by Alfa Romeo had earnestly been counselled by Bazzi, who, if we remember, had gone to them after the 1923 French Grand Prix. The car made its debut in a minor race in Italy, where it won easily and was timed along the ten-kilometre straight forming part of the circuit of Cremona at 123 mph. This was achieved with a power output of 134 bhp at 5,200 rev/min, so at this stage the car was not yet equal to the formidable type 805 Fiat that had been Jano's last concern in Turin before he moved to Milan. Nevertheless the car seemed to have sufficient promise to justify entering it for the Grand Prix of the ACF at Lyon, where it was scheduled to do battle with a new Bugatti, a new Sunbeam, a modified Delage, and of course the Fiat, as well as make-weights by Miller and Schmid.

Perhaps the biggest surprise of the event was the dismal showing of the Fiat, which suffered from a number of problems, of which far the most notable was malfunctioning of the brake system which had been extensively modified. Almost as great a surprise was the fact that the Sunbeam proved the fastest car there—and once again it was an expatriot from Fiat who could take the credit, for Bertarione had remained with STD, and during the intervening winter had rebuilt the six-cylinder engine and added a supercharger which, unlike all other European examples, drew mixture

44 Promise unfulfilled: the 1924 GP Fiat, Felice Nazzaro at the wheel

626

from the carburettor and then delivered it under pressure to the engine. This was a far better system than the older established one, principally because the latent heat of evaporation of the fuel helped to cool the charge in its passage to the blower and manifolding. Fortunately, the effect of the change has been recorded: when tried experimentally with the blower delivering air at 6 lb/in^2 above ambient to the carburettor, the bmep ranged from 140 lb/in^2 at 1,000 rev/min to 150 at 3,500, sinking again slightly to 146 at 5,200 when the engine gave its maximum power of 115 bhp. Transposing the carburettor to the suction side of the blower made no difference to the bmep at 1,000 rev/min, but beyond that speed the efficiency was increased quite remarkably, the bmep reaching 178 at 4,500 rev/min and declining only to 170 at 5,500, when the engine gave 138 bhp. No more convincing proof need be sought of the importance of the fuel being introduced upstream from the supercharger: timing during the racing at Lyon showed that when it was running properly the Sunbeam could outpace the Alfa Romeo by a clear margin, their speeds being 130 and 124 mph respectively. Alas, the Sunbeam seldom ran properly during the race, suffering misfiring from a new and untried Bosch magneto. Thus the Alfa Romeo was allowed to win its first Grand Prix; and it never looked back, going on to be the most successful racing car in Europe for a good six years.

There were three main reasons for this success. The first was that Fiat withdrew from racing, to be seen again only on one more isolated and characteristically successful occasion in 1927. The second was that Jano doubled the number of carburettors on the P2 and by this stratagem raised its power output to 145 bhp at 5,500 rev/min (virtually identical to that of the type 805 Fiat), so that the car was eventually able to reach speeds as high as 140

45 1924 type-35 Bugatti at Lyon, driven by de Vizcaya

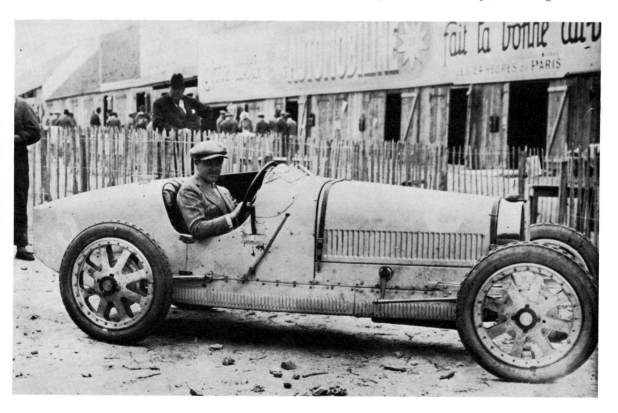

mph. Third was the fact that the utterly beautiful new type 35 Bugatti, which came as a revelation to Lyon, was condemned by its manufacturer to remain unsupercharged until as late as 1926. Bugatti publicly denounced superchargers, stoutly maintaining

46 *The type-35 Bugatti later acquired one-piece wheels, without the detachable 24-screw rim of the original cars*

that they were contrary to the piston displacement regulations by which racing was governed.

A further factor that may have inhibited the success of the type 35 to some extent was that Bugatti was aiming to do something that none of his rivals would then contemplate: to produce a racing car which had a reasonable chance of being competitive but which was so constructed that he could sell it in reasonably large numbers and at a reasonable price (which must nevertheless earn him a profit) to amateur drivers. This was why—accepting that Bugatti could show frequent flashes of genius—so many detailed features of the car were models of efficient simplicity (as in the case of his brake compensating mechanism), for the private entrant had to keep an eye on the cost and practicality of servicing. This was also why the type 35 was produced with a body which, while second to none in beauty nor possibly in efficiency, was essentially orthodox by the standards of its time, rather than curiously contrived in the manner of, say, the 1923 Tours tank.

Although it succumbed to tyre troubles at its first appearance at Lyon, the Bugatti was to prove inordinately successful, probably the most successful design in the history of motor racing. Devoted calculators have established that the type 35 won a total of more than 1,800 events, most of them admittedly minor, and this figure must be related to the surprising total of at least 400 specimens built. Nevertheless the type 35, together with the type 51 which was eventually derived from it and which it resembled very closely in everything except the cylinder head, won at least thirty-three road races of major importance in the space of seven years.

Whatever the number and quality of its victories, the most enduring and important achievement of the T. 35 Bugatti was that it elevated the racing car to a level of aesthetic sublimity which has seldom been equalled and perhaps never surpassed. Not only did Bugatti make every part of the car beautifully, he also combined these parts into a whole in which they were all concordant and contributory to an overall cultivated beauty. It is admittedly hard to give the lie to those detractors who suggest that if the type 35 engine had been designed with less concern for eye appeal and more for the laws of thermodynamics, the car might not have been somewhat lacking in power; but it must be equally difficult for them to deny the proposition that, accepting that the type 35 was never as powerful as the opposition it encountered in major events, it must have been endowed with superior qualities of roadworthiness and reliability for it to have been as competitive as it nearly always was.

An examination of the engine, essentially similar to that of the 1923 car, reveals what truth there was in the first half of this proposition. The verification of the second part must be sought by examining the chassis, which remained a convincing (and surprisingly little emulated) example of how a chassis, confined broadly within the conventions that obtained before the advent of fully independent suspension, might best be built. Everything about it—the cast aluminium alloy wheels with integral brake drums, the longitudinal frame members so deep at mid-length and so slender at their extremities, the manner in which these are united by the engine as well as by a number of tubular cross-members, the elegant proportions of the steering linkage, the care with which the axles are located, the pains taken to ensure a geometrically and kinetically precise operation of the brakes— reveals Bugatti's awareness of the importance of structural stiffness rather than mere mechanical strength, his intuitive understanding of stress distribution, and his deep-rooted concern over the consequences of laxity in the designer, his artificers, the

47 Divo driving a 1925 2-litre V12 Delage in the 1926 Targo Florio

machinery itself, and the mechanics who will maintain it.

This was all very well; but in the latter part of 1924 and certainly 1925 it was no effective substitute for a supercharger. Bugatti doggedly persisted in running his cars without this new and vital aid, whereas in 1925 the V12 Delage acquired the supercharging that it clearly needed and could, perhaps better than any other machine of the time, profit most from having. In its unsupercharged form it had most certainly been hampered by the somewhat constricted inlet manifolding whereby two carburettors served the two banks of cylinders; and it is interesting to speculate on the possibilities latent in the unsupercharged engine had it been furnished with an induction system offering a separate tract for each cylinder as had been so successfully exploited by Miller. Be that as it may, as an unblown car in 1924 it generally proved inferior not only to the Fiat and Sunbeam but even to the new and not yet shaken-down Bugatti. The acquisition of forced induction at a manifold pressure of 1·5 atmospheres completely transformed the car, which campaigned throughout 1925 with 190 bhp at its disposal, at crankshaft rates involving as much as 7,000 rev/min, and at a piston loading of no less than 4·9 horsepower per square inch. Moreover, such was the efficacy of the forced induction in improving the flow of charge through the inlet ports that the horsepower of this engine related to the total inlet valve area worked out at 15·8 per square inch, a remarkably high figure by

the standards of the time and no less than 43 per cent higher than the corresponding figure for the 1924 Fiat. In effect, the blown V12 Delage reigned supreme in 1925, only the P2 Alfa Romeo being capable of challenging it.

In 1926, however, things took an unexpected turn. It was not, of course, unknown that a new set of regulations would govern the construction of Grand Prix cars, for they had been prompted by alarm on the part of the governing body at the increasing speeds of the cars made under the existing formula—an alarm such as had been expressed on several occasions in the past and was to be voiced again with futile regularity many times in the future. As has often been the case, the reaction was almost automatic: the cars should have smaller engines. One would have thought that by 1925 the lesson that had been hammered home since 1907 might have been learned; but with their usual touching belief that nobody could possibly make things more efficient than they were already, the governors of the sport decreed that the next generation of Grand Prix cars should have engines of not more than $1\frac{1}{2}$ litres, and should weigh at least 700 kg. By thus supposedly reducing the power that would be developed and by increasing the weight that it must propel, they were confident that they would check the ever-mounting speeds of the racers; and having already banned the carriage of a mechanic in the racing car (as a result of some unfortunate accidents), they sought to forestall any unreasonable reduction in frontal area by insisting that the cars carried two-seater bodies with a certain minimum cockpit width to ensure that they should not develop into such freaks as they considered the track cars of Brooklands or Indianapolis to be.

Inevitably there were certain constructors who found ways of turning these new regulations to their advantage. In particular Delage and Talbot created entirely new cars in which the driver was enabled to sit extremely low because the engine and transmission line were offset to the left, the gearbox and propellor shaft passing through the space that technically was supposed to have been left for the mechanic. A seat of sorts was somehow fitted in above it, and so a striking new shape was created and a new fashion promoted: the cars built to the 1½-litre formula which prevailed in 1926 and 1927 were no wider than they had to be but very much lower than any of their precursors had been, so their projected frontal areas were remarkably small—much smaller than at any time in the past and scarcely greater than at any time in the future.

Both Delage and Talbot produced cars that resembled each other not only in this matter of general configuration but also in other fundamentals. Both had supercharged straight eight engines, both with two valves per cylinder seated in hemispherical heads at a wide included angle of about 100 degrees and actuated by twin overhead camshafts. Both were most generously endowed with rolling-element bearings, both were very powerful, both were very fast. Both, for that matter, could be said to cling to the fashion originally dictated by Fiat some years earlier, the most significant change being in the exploitation of the mechanic's absence.

In the case of the Talbot this was hardly surprising. It had been designed by Bertarione, who had now been joined by Becchia, another member of the original Fiat design team. The cars were produced at the Talbot works at Suresnes in Paris, but for Bertarione this was no more than an internal posting within the

49 Segrave and Divo in 1926 GP straight-eight Talbots at Brooklands during the British GP that year

international ramifications of the STD combine. As for the car, it was an immediate descendant of the immensely successful 1½-litre voiturette with which Talbot had campaigned in the subordinate class during the immediately preceding years, a car in which Bertarione had continued to refine the work that he had begun so much earlier in Turin and continued in Wolverhampton. The stroke:bore ratio of the cylinders had dropped somewhat to 1·35 in the quest for higher crankshaft rates, contributing to an output of about 145 bhp at 6,500 rev/min with a further 500 rev/min safely available beyond. The chassis of the Talbot was altogether more refreshing, its pressed side members being agreeably slender but impressively deep at mid-wheelbase, tapering to front and rear in recognition of those beam-building principles that Bugatti had already endorsed in his type 35 chassis. Indeed the same principles had been applied to the beam front axle, which displayed a progressive reduction in diameter away from its centre. The whole car was quite meritorious, but it was doomed to enjoy but little success due to the chill penury of STD suppressing what might have proved a most noble rage.

No such inhibitions appear to have affected Delage, who now enjoyed the services of Lory as designer of their new Grand Prix car. In the general arrangement of engine and transmission relative to the driver's seat, it was essentially similar to the Talbot. The engine was essentially similar too, even to the cylinder dimensions being almost identical; but Lory, who seemed to have had no reason to adhere too closely to the traditions established by Fiat, chose to base his engine upon a cast cylinder block rather than a welded fabrication. This casting was designed with such virtuosity, such sympathy for the task of the charge on its way through the induction system into the cylinder, and such solici-

50 (below) *Typical of the confusions caused by the international ramifications of the S-T-D combine, the Talbot was called a Talbot Special when in Britain*

51 (right) *In its original 1926 form, the straight-eight 1½-litre Delage was a merciless roaster of drivers' feet. Here Senechal takes over Benoist's car at San Sebastian*

1932-5 Alfa Romeo

EPITOMISING THE GRAND PRIX CAR of the early 1930s, from which indeed it emerged as the most successful example, the P3 Alfa Romeo was ingenious rather than iconoclastic. It was born to restore order where chaos reigned. The years following the demise of the 1½-litre formula in 1927 saw an unholy rabble of cars competing in events that might have been called Grandes Epreuves but were sad shadows of what they should have been; but Vittorio Jano, erstwhile member of the Fiat racing department, produced in 1932 an Alfa Romeo that would epitomise the best traditions.

In 1934 the car was enlarged, inside and out. Other developments were to follow: Bugatti-style rear suspension, Dubonnet independent front suspension (carried by the car in this picture, taken more than thirty years after its birth in 1935), bigger and bigger engines. But the Alfa Romeo could never be anything but classical, and it could not for long hold the might of the new German cars at bay.

1937 Mercedes Benz

IAM NOVA PROGENIES CAELO DEMITTITUR ALTO, as Virgil wrote, a new race now descends from on high. With the coming of the 750 kg formula in 1934 it did indeed seem as though a new breed of machines had suddenly descended upon the scene, to dominate motor racing with a display of wealth, power, and a rigorous focussing of every technological and human capability towards the aim of motor racing perfection. The new cars issuing from two German factories were like nothing that has been seen before: they were far more powerful, very much faster, considerably more comfortable, and were endowed with superior roadholding of the kind that enabled them to deploy their power to display acceleration of a new high order, even if their roadholding in terms of cornering ability was as yet suspect. None of their established opponents could hope to rival them, not even Alfa Romeo who were by now state-owned; but this was simply because the racing departments of Auto-Union and Daimler-Benz were encouraged in their expenditure by extravagant under-writing from the German government which (probably rightly) saw international motor racing as a most effective medium in which to publicise the technical and human superiority of the new National Socialist state. With authority from so high, these two German factories embarked upon a career in which no considerations of difficulty or expense might stand in the way of the resolve to come as near as possible to what was understood by technical perfection.

Extreme and extraordinary as the 1934 cars seemed when they first appeared, they were surpassed by a generous margin in all respects by the cars of 1937 and most particularly by the W125 car that was designed to carry the Mercedes-Benz star in Grand Prix racing for just one year, but to carry it honourably. This car mustered more power than any other Grand Prix racer before or since, obtaining it from an engine that was hardly at all unusual except in the superb workmanship and metallurgy that made its high performance possible. As for the rest of the car, it showed scant respect for established motor engineering practice: the chassis frame was made of thin-walled oval tubing, the springing was softer than any racing car had employed since the first decade of racing, the major components such as engine and transmission were arranged towards the longitudinal extremities of the chassis so as to contribute to a high polar moment of inertia, and the ingeniously concocted fuel blend represented no less than a triumph of chemistry over the supercharged four-stroke cycle. Even the tyres, bearing the brunt of more than 600 bhp in a car whose mean racing weight was a little less than a ton, had been studied by Continental technicians with a far more scientific approach than these over-taxed and under-privileged components had ever before received, so that it became commonplace to see the Continental technicians taking track temperatures before a race to decide on such matters as the appropriate inflation pressure for the huge nitrogen-filled tyres.

Only in one respect was the 1937 Mercedes-Benz noteworthy for its reversion to past practices; and this was something whereby it gained an enormous advantage over all its rivals (Auto Union included) and set a new fashion that was to be followed by virtually every successful Grand Prix car until 1959. This was the De Dion rear axle, conceived and patented as long ago as 1892 and subsequently falling into desuetude, until Daimler-Benz resuscitated it for the W125. By the use of a rigid dead beam axle to support the rear wheels, and of universally jointed drive shafts to carry tractive torque to them from the final drive unit located on the chassis and forming part of the sprung mass of the car, the De Dion suspension indulged the Mercedes-Benz with a combination of traction, cornering power, directional stability and immunity from torque

reactions that was far in advance of anything seen in motor racing since the demise of the chain-driven giants with which the Grand Prix story began – and the transmission used by those giants of old, though they weighed about the same as the laden 1937 Mercedes-Benz, could not have supplied the needs of its 646 bhp and 200 mph speed capability. By this one inspired move, Daimler-Benz enabled chassis design to catch up with more than twenty years of engine development.

52 Lory's beautiful 1¼-litre Delage engine shows strong Fiat influence, the main difference being the cast cylinder block of the later engine

tude for the numerous bearings which might be the source of a consumptive friction, that with the aid of a boost of 1·5 atmospheres, the same as that enjoyed by the 1925 Delage, this exquisitely constructed but otherwise hardly original straight eight contrived to produce as much as 170 bhp at 8,000 rev/min, corresponding to a bmep of 177 lb/in^2, at least as high as, and perhaps fractionally higher than, that of the 1925 V12. Such a power output and such a rate of revolutions could not safely be sustained, and the car very nearly broke new ground (being forestalled only by an occasional experiment with the V12 of the previous year) with a five-speed gearbox, the highest ratio of which was intended to serve as an overdrive in which the engine could sustain a continuous 6,500 rev/min, working in the process at 142 bhp which was equivalent to a bmep of no less than 190 lb/in^2. In fact, it took some little while for the Delage to be developed to this point, whereas the Talbot was realising a bmep of 194 lb/in^2 in 1926 and doing so at a piston speed which, at 3,230 feet per minute, was agreeably more modest than the 4,000 of the Delage.

Although the year 1927 was to be an excellent one for Delage, with all but one of the principal Grands Prix falling to it, 1926 was dogged with problems. Of these the most crippling was the liberation of so much heat from the exhaust pipe, where it passed close to the driver's compartment, that it sometimes actually burned through the bodywork; and even when it did not do this it so terribly overheated the drivers that they suffered agonies and had often to be replaced by substitutes in the course of a race. Relatively minor were the problems presented by the chassis, which was as inordinately flexible as its lack of substance and of cross-bracing suggested—one of the most obvious problems being rather violent front-wheel flap when the brakes were applied. It was, however, the roasting of the drivers that most handicapped

53 The 1927 Delage had its exhaust on the left. Benoist survived to win the British GP

54 By 1928 the racing rules were in disrepute and races were open to most comers. Here, in a view which captures the essential spirit of European motor racing between the wars, is a 1927 Delage competing for the Coupe Georges Boillot in 1928

the Delage in 1926, and the only race in which Delage was successful in that year (despite its regular demonstrations of greatly superior speed) was in the rather unrepresentative English Grand Prix held at Brooklands, where Segrave put in the fastest lap in a Talbot.

Fate has often displayed in racing that perversity which condemns those who have tried hardest to prosper the least. What had not been anticipated was that Bugatti, retaining the chassis, running gear and even the bodywork of the type 35, retaining even

the greater part of its engine, should, by merely altering its internal dimensions to suit the new regulations and by fitting a supercharger, produce a car that was to enjoy such success as to leave it completely dominant by the end of the year.

At the beginning of the year its domination of events was complete and not altogether welcome. For the first and last time the French Grand Prix was to be held at the new Miramas Circuit in Provence, whither teams from Delage, STD, OM, Sima-Violet, Alvis and the gifted Leyland engineer J. G. Parry Thomas should have travelled for the race. Alfa Romeo had already announced that they would not be engaging in Grand Prix racing. When in June 1926 the time came for the race it seemed that all the others must have been similarly disposed, for only Bugatti turned up, his three cars constituting the entire field for what must have been the most boring and lacklustre Grand Prix of all time.

At this stage the Bugatti had been reduced to $1\frac{1}{2}$ litres merely by reducing the cylinder-bore diameter, but before long Bugatti substituted a short-stroke crankshaft which gave better results. With a large number of faithful customers ever ready to absorb his output, Bugatti could always sell his prototypes.

Much more significant than the cylinder dimensions of the $1\frac{1}{2}$-litre straight-eight Bugatti was the supercharging system. The design and development of this was master-minded by yet another Italian engineer, of the name of Moglia, who had played a part in the design of the Talbot and of the intimidating and generally irrelevant Djelmo, built specifically to attack the world's land speed record. Moglia's work on supercharging was particularly successful: he contrived a version of the Roots supercharger in which the rotors were triple-lobed (two lobes in a figure-of-eight style were the general fashion) and kept the rest of the induction system neat and short, which may have had something to do with its efficiency. Bugatti himself, who did not always produce efficient engine wares but was a master of ingenuity and an unrivalled exponent of simple but extremely precise manufacturing techniques (of which his built-up crankshaft, with all parts fully interchangeable and perfectly balanced in any permutation, was a splendid example), was probably responsible for the detailed nicety of rotor gears that ensured precise meshing of the rotors without the usual Vernier coupling with which to make adjustments. At any rate the supercharger made a great difference to the type 35, and with the solitary exception recorded above it won every Grand Prix of 1926.

What is of equal interest is that in a number of other important races that were not run to the $1\frac{1}{2}$-litre formula, Bugatti enjoyed similar successes with larger versions of the supercharged type 35, either in 2-litre or 2·3-litre form, and these cars frequently succeeded in holding at bay formidable and unquestionably faster cars, such as the supercharged V12 2-litre Delage which had to give best to the superior roadworthiness of the Bugatti in the Targa Florio (actually won by an unblown 2·3 Bugatti), the Spanish Grand Prix, and the Milan Grand Prix. In events such as these

55 Less superb restoration could not
do justice to the beauty of the Delage
engine, though the supercharger
carries a non-standard SU carburettor

the Bugattis continued to fare well in 1927; but by then the Delage
was as perfectly fettled as the single-minded tradition of the factory might have led one to expect (their motto was *Ne faire qu'une
chose, mais le bien faire),* and they enjoyed as complete a domination of the Grandes Epreuves (the races counting towards the
World Championship, theoretically but not practically including
the Indianapolis event) as had Bugatti in 1926—which is to say
that every race but one fell to the French car.

The exception was the Milan GP, a short event run on the same
day and at the same venue as the Italian Grand Prix at Monza, as
always in the first week of September. Delage entered and won the
Italian, but abstained from the Milan, and to this event came Fiat,
with a completely new car. It had been known for some time that
Fiat had been experimenting with a $1\frac{1}{2}$-litre supercharged opposed-
piston two-stroke, an engine configuration that had attracted
those greedy for power ever since it was pioneered as a gas engine
by Ochelhauser in the nineteenth century. Even today when a
number of high-speed diesels successfully exploit the obvious
advantages of this layout, they do so only after painstaking attention to lubrication and cooling of the piston which controls the
exhaust port. In the 1920s there were neither the oils nor the metals,
nor even the sparking plugs, necessary to sustain the high temperatures and severe heat gradients concentrated around the
exhaust ports and the crown of the exhaust piston; and although
the engine could be made to produce a power output almost as
beyond belief as its noise output, Fiat soon recognised that it was
not a practical proposition. Their engineer Zerbi thereupon set
about the confection of a more conventional four-stroke alternative to this 170-bhp fulminator, but after that he was clearly conditioned to interpret conservatism somewhat liberally. The result
was a 12-cylinder $1\frac{1}{2}$-litre engine with two valves per cylinder, two
built-up crankshafts, eight main bearings of the plain journal

type (an important departure from the roller bearing convention that Fiat themselves had established), one-piece connecting rods again with plain bearings, three camshafts, and one Roots supercharger. In fact, the engine was two in-line sixes mounted side by side on a common crankcase with their crankshafts geared together, and with the banks of exhaust valves placed on the outer flanks of the cylinder heads, the banks of inlet valves thus being adjacent and operable by a single camshaft bearing twelve lobes.

Here was the quest for ample piston area and freedom to run at high crankshaft rates pursued further than ever before. The cylinders were of 50 mm bore, the piston stroke a mere 63, so that the stroke:bore ratio was only 1·26:1, lower than that of almost every racing car since the far-off days of the giant bores before World War I, lower than that of all contemporaries save the 60 x 66 type 39 Bugatti. In comparison with that significantly successful 1½-litre straight eight, the twelve cylinders of the Fiat engine gave it more piston area, almost as much as that of the 2-litre V12 Delage, while its inlet valve area was actually greater by 10 per cent. In other words, Fiat had contrived to fit larger valves into smaller cylinders, whereby the better to transmit the massive charge delivered by a supercharger pressurising the inlet manifold (which passed between the two banks of cylinders) to 1·9 atmospheres, a degree of boost rivalled only by the 1926 Talbot. What with the short stroke of the pistons, the stiffness of the one-piece connecting rods, and the punctilious construction of the crankshaft (built up on the Hirth principle of crankpins mating with webs by radial serrations and locked together by through-bolts, yet another novelty in racing but one which was to be revived quite frequently in the future, especially by German

56 Raced once before the Fiat retirement from motor racing in 1927, the type 806 car which won the Monza GP had an engine (type 406) that was tantamount to two in-line six-cylinder machines coupled in parallel. These diagrams of crankshaft and auxiliary drives display the basic simplicity of Zerbi's design

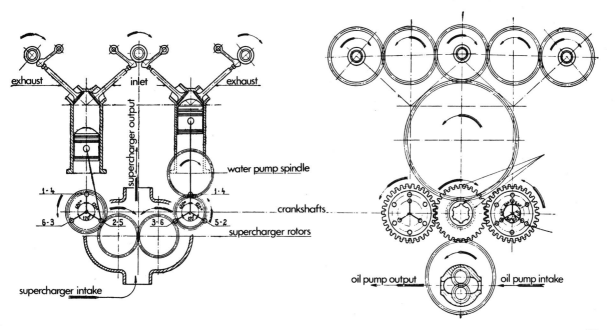

manufacturers), the twelve-cylinder Fiat type 406 engine could run happily up to 8,000 rev/min without exceeding a mean piston speed of 3,320 feet per minute, and this rate could be sustained in circumstances where the straight-eight Delage had to be given immediate relief by its extra high fifth gear. Thus while realising a peak power bmep of 190 lb/in^2 (177 for the Delage, remember) but with its pistons burdened to the tune of about 4·75 bhp per square inch (compared with 5·6 in the Delage) the Fiat generated no less than 175 bhp. Indeed it was run up to 8,500 rev/min and 187 bhp on the Fiat dynamometer.

Was this undertaken merely as a technical exercise? Or were Fiat still smarting with the recollection that they had fared badly on their last public appearance in racing, back in 1924? We cannot really tell; but in either case they must have judged their objects well and truly achieved when the low and light type 806 racer powered by this engine scored a runaway win on the rain-soaked Monza track. Thereafter Fiat and their car disappeared from the Grand Prix scene and were never to be seen there again.

This final abstention of Fiat from racing at the end of 1927 marked the beginning of a period in which, from the engineering point of view, Grand Prix racing went into a decline, so that in the next six years only one development of any technical value—the transmission of the 1932 type B Alfa Romeo—caused any stir amid the general stagnation. The period was also one in which the administration of the sport fell into disorder, the governing body finding itself powerless to control the active participants. Indeed it was this very dissension that contributed to the obstruction of of technical progress. Whether paradoxically or as a direct consequence of this, the sport enjoyed a rise in popularity *qua* sport, and the frequency with which races were held increased markedly during 1928 and 1929. In the first of these years it had been intended that a new set of regulations should supplant the 1½-litre formula which, in its brief two years of life, had demonstrated fairly conclusively that any attempt to limit increases in performance by imposing more severe limitations on engine size would only lead to intensive development of more complex and highly tuned engines so that racing would not become necessarily any slower, nor essentially any safer, but inexorably more costly. It was therefore proposed that engine capacity should be unrestricted, but that it should be related to a sliding scale of minimum weight limits ranging from 550 to 750 kg for the empty vehicle, and that races should be over a distance of at least 600 kilometres.

The manufacturers of racing cars responded to these proposals with a studied indifference; and, in the absence of any cars built to comply with the new formula, race organisers promoted instead a series of races which, profiting by the spectacular example of a few similar events in 1927, were open to racing cars of any size or types. There had once before been a *formula libre*, in 1912, when Henry of Peugeot seized the opportunity to create a new dynasty. This time it was rather Bugatti who made the most of the anarchy to strengthen an existing dynasty, and throughout 1928 his type 35

57 *The 2¼-litre 8C Maserati was the first really stylish and competitive example of the new breed of GP cars which were derived from sports cars in 1928 and after. A road-equipped version won the 1929 Targa Florio*

was almost everywhere successful. Most of the important exceptions were races won by Talbot, resuscitated after their year of purse-pinching and wound-licking, and showing just as much speed and more stamina than when they first appeared in 1926.

The 1928 formula having been stillborn, another was created for 1929, to fail even more abjectly: for, while still leaving engine capacity uncontrolled, it imposed a fuel consumption limit of 14 kg of commercial fuel *and oil* (an intimidating inclusion at a time when oil consumption was generally very high in racing engines) per 100 kilometres. The governors of the sport were in fact trying to ensure that the machines raced would bear some resemblance to those sold to the public and might serve in the development of features that would be applied to the latter's benefit; and in the pursuit of this idealism they stipulated two-seater bodies with a minimum width of a metre, carrying a spare wheel and uncovered fuel tank of non-streamlined shape (a reactionary move that must have been as unpopular as it was untimely), and of considerable weight. In general the race organisers remained aloof and the general free-for-all continued unabated. The pattern of results remained much the same, Bugatti continuing consistently to enjoy a well-earned success and the stable reputation of one whose cars were held by a majority of drivers, amateur and conductitious alike, to represent the pinnacle of achievement in racing car construction, whether practical or aesthetic.

95

This is not to say that the Bugatti was the fastest of those in contention. The Talbots, sold to Italian entrants for the 1928 season, had been able to give the Bugatti 500 or 800 cm^3 and still give it a run; and when they suffered a relapse in 1929 there were new Maseratis and Alfa Romeos to take up the challenge. The brothers Maserati had taken their independence from Diatto in 1926 and created a $1\frac{1}{2}$-litre car that, with its straight-eight engine, plain bearings, low chassis, and dashing good looks, might be judged either a cut-price racer or a natural evolution from the hyper-sportscar; but from it there sprang a line of straight-eight twin-overhead-camshaft racing cars, all with plain bearings, that was to emerge from the pack and prove by 1930 to include the fastest road racing machine yet seen. Meanwhile the Alfa Romeos continued to represent the ideal of the pure-bred specialised racing car, being the 1925 P2 models resurrected; but they did not have the temerity to venture beyond the confines of Italy.

Elsewhere the racing circuits of Europe reverberated not only with the capital scream of the compact and purposeful Bugatti but also to the borborigmal thunder of the stoutest sportscars that the enthusiasts of England and Germany could put into the lists. The second place earned in the French Grand Prix of 1930 by the late Sir Henry Birkin, Bart, in a supercharged $4\frac{1}{2}$-litre Bentley was an isolated example of this distinguished make being successful outside its intended domain, but there were many occasions when stripped versions of the big supercharged 36/220 and 38/250 Mercedes-Benz sportscars provided not only a useful leavening of the field but also threatened opposition that the driver of a thoroughbred racing car might despise at his peril.

The full and really considerable weight of this opposition was naturally most felt on their home ground at the Nurburgring, where the first German Grand Prix dating from 1926 had been for sportscars; but in 1928 one of the big 7-litre six-cylinder cars finished third behind two Bugattis, in 1931 the Mercedes-Benz team was victorious there, while (back again in 1929) by the most convincing display of driving virtuosity as well as of mechanical stamina, that outstanding driver Rudolf Caracciola finished the extremely strenuous and informative exercise in labyrinthine navigation known as the Monaco Grand Prix in third place in an SSK Mercedes-Benz, a position he was holding again in the same race in 1931 when clutch slip forced his retirement. It was considered axiomatic that so large and lusty a car should be able to conquer the smaller and more specialised racing machines on circuits with a preponderance of very fast straights, for by 1931 the power of the SSKL Mercedes-Benz was nearer 300 than the nominal 250 bhp which justified the 38/250 type designation, so that it must have profited from a ratio of about 17 horsepower per square foot of frontal area to reach an appreciably higher maximum speed than, say, the type 35B Bugatti, which could muster but 10·8.

That a car of such mass and magnitude could compete effectively with the legendary agility and precision of handling of the Bugatti on circuits so replete with corners and gradients as Monaco or the Nurburgring was proof either that in the 38/250 Mercedes-Benz had produced a car with a roadworthiness as admirable as that of their earlier small four- and eight-cylinder racing cars had been execrable, or that Caracciola was one of those very rare drivers to whom it is given to upset accepted notions of what is possible. Probably both explanations were contributory to the brief success of the big German cars, before they were forced for financial reasons temporarily to withdraw from racing: for the 38/250 was renowned for the quality of its steering and its superb balance, while Caracciola was probably the greatest driver of the period between the two world wars. It is, of course, easier to deliver such a judgement than to explain the *ratio decidendi,* and I am aware of the claims that could properly be made on behalf of Tazio Nuvolari; but there was only one occasion when these two drivers met in matched cars, and this was in 1932 when Caracciola was a member of the Alfa Romeo team and simply outdrove Nuvolari at Monaco, finally waving him by to victory as a concession to polity.

The cars that the two drove on this occasion were Jano's lovely type 8C 2·3-litre Monza, which first appeared in 1931. Any study of the regulations offered by the AIACR to govern Grand Prix racing will reveal a complete want of conformity by this car: the formula set up for the period from 1931 to 1933 banned superchargers (except on two-strokes), permitted up to 5 litres engine displacement, added a sliding scale of minimum weights working up from a basic 794 kg, and further stipulated dimensional limits for wheel track and body width. Their motives were the same as before, and their authority even less; and once it had been made clear that the

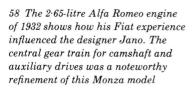

58 The 2·65-litre Alfa Romeo engine of 1932 shows how his Fiat experience influenced the designer Jano. The central gear train for camshaft and auxiliary drives was a noteworthy refinement of this Monza model

59 *Bugatti developed the type-51 from the type-35, the outstanding advance being in cylinder head design*

formula would be boycotted by every interested party, the governing body withdrew every stipulation save that cars must have two-seater bodies, and added a rider requiring that each of the Grandes Epreuves should endure for at least ten hours.

The stamina necessary for success in races of such inordinate length makes it a matter of particular interest to study the two cars that appeared in 1931 to do battle. One, the Monza Alfa Romeo, was a straight eight contrived in two cast iron blocks of four cylinders each, between which rose a gear train to drive the supercharger, the two overhead camshafts, and sundry auxiliaries, along lines pioneered earlier by the Salmson designer Emil Petit who created an 1,100-cm^3 racing voiturette of a similar disposition in 1927 to compete with the then new and successful Amilcar. The crankshaft of the Monza was likewise in two halves, bolted together at the middle; and like the engines of the Maserati and of the type 806 Fiat before it, it ran in plain bearings. Indeed there were no rolling-element bearings in Jano's Alfa at all, which was easily capable of sustaining 5,400 rev/min to yield 160 bhp. This was the product of a piston area of 41 square inches and a bmep of 165 lb/in^2 at 10 lb/in^2 boost, figures indicating that this engine was by no means highly stressed and might therefore be expected to maintain its vigour for as long as was necessary. The 88 mm bore kept the maximum mean piston speed down to little more than 3,000 feet per minute, as in the straight-eight 2-litre type 35 Bugatti; but by this time the Bugatti had had its own power unit

drastically revised, and the type 51 version which likewise began racing in 1931 offered the same power as the Monza Alfa Romeo at a slightly higher crankshaft rate (5,500 rev/min), and because of the more old-fashioned stroke:bore ratio of the engine this involved a piston speed of 3,650 feet per minute. The supercharge pressure was the same as in the Alfa Romeo, and the similarity was carried further by the one and only important new feature of the type 51, the twin-camshaft cylinder head bearing two large inclined valves at an included angle of 90 degrees in each hemispherical combustion chamber.

Bugatti had finally bitten the bullet—but he made no other concessions to the changing times, retaining his unique method of crankshaft construction with its proliferation of roller bearings, and continuing to rely as much on the road-holding and handling of the car as on its power. In these respects the Alfa Romeo was more nearly the Bugatti's equal than any other car of the time, for its chassis incorporated a number of detail refinements; and throughout 1931 the two makes fought tooth-and-nail battles occasionally relieved by the intrusion of the Maserati, which was still more powerful than either of them.

For those ultra-fast circuits such as Monza and Avus, all three firms proposed cars in which the provision of ample power took priority over all other considerations. Alfa Romeo and Maserati contrived this by coupling two engines by means more or less untidy, while Bugatti adapted the 4·9-litre engine of his type 50S sportscar, this engine being the first he made with the new twin-camshaft head. All these were fast and very difficult, not to say dangerous, to drive: they proved nothing save that the chassis of the day were incapable of dealing with such high speeds and such high power:weight ratios, confirming in particular that the torque reaction manifested through a live rear axle when the full might of such an engine was summoned made it virtually impossible for the power to be transmitted through the tyres to the road. Here was yet another influence at work forcing suspension to become firmer and firmer—as coincidentally did a marked improvement in the quality of brake-lining materials as produced by Ferodo and making a discernible contribution to the improvement in lap speeds to be noted in this period.

The intransigence of the traditional rear axle was a problem of forbidding proportions, and it was one which afflicted the Americans in their track racing as much as the Europeans in their road racing. The clever Miller dealt conclusively with the problem by adopting rear suspension and final drive of the de Dion type, such as he had employed for some time at the other extremity of his earlier front-wheel-drive racing cars. This development appears to have passed unnoticed by European designers, but in the following year Jano had created a new kind of transmission which did a lot to abate the problem.

In fact he created practically a whole new car, known as the type B officially and the P3 popularly. This again had a straight-eight engine, similar in essentials to that of the Monza but with a 100-mm stroke which increased its capacity to 2·6 litres. This time it had two superchargers in parallel, and although the boost remained the same (as did the piston area, of course, and the permitted rev/min, surprisingly) the power output rose in greater proportion than did the stroke and piston speeds, to a useful 190 bhp. Some other authorities have quoted 180, while Mr Hull has recorded that the factory claimed 215; but this was at a time when the Italian manufacturers in particular had learned the psychological value of making extravagant claims. At any rate, the type B was more highly stressed than the Monza in terms of piston speed, of bmep, and of bhp per square inch of piston area. Either Jano had found that the Monza was unnecessarily mildly tuned

61 *So long as the live rear axle remained in use, traction and roadholding remained at odds with new increases in engine power. Torque reaction was responsible for more oversteer in the racing cars of the late 1920s and early 1930s than any other single design feature*

(it had been up-rated for the earlier races of 1932 when the type B was not yet ready), or this was a reflection of the relaxation of the rules which now contented themselves with races which lasted a mere five hours and, at long and possibly overdue last, permitted single-seater bodies. More probably Jano was simply prompted by the fact that the Monza had been hard pressed by the type 51 Bugatti and by the 2½-litre Maserati throughout 1931, and he sought to confer upon his latest car that superiority which the P2 had enjoyed in its heyday.

Having created a Grand Prix car blessed with more power than any before, saving only those scarcely dirigible monstrosities to which we have made brief reference, Jano needed to ensure that this power could be conveyed to the road. This he did in the type B by removing the differential from its time-hallowed position in the middle of the rear axle, and placing it within a spherical jointed thrust housing immediately behind the gearbox, whence two propellor shafts diverged in torque tubes to communicate with simple pairs of bevel gears at the extremities of the rear axle casing, one adjacent to each wheel. By these means he saw to it that the rear axle was relieved of torque effects, and incidentally by increasing the polar moment of inertia of the axle reduced its tendency to patter. He also cleared the centre line of the car of the propellor shaft, making it easier to locate the driver directly behind the engine in the new *monoposto* body, where he was described by a distinguished writer as 'sitting in the middle of a conflict of forces'. In fact, the various forces were resolved into a modest gyratory moment about the spherical joint embracing the differential, and this was the more easily constrained because the unsprung weight of the axle and its related structures was sensibly reduced. The beam was a tubular light-alloy body, the halfshafts

101

62 *The last (and perhaps most?)*
beautiful classical Grand Prix car,
the type-59 Bugatti, driven by Varzi
and Dreyfus at San Sebastian in 1933

were no longer than was necessary to reach from the hubs to the bevel gears a few inches inboard thereof, the propellor shafts could be light because they each carried no more than half the total torque, and the differential unit with its heavy cage and the customary stout casing to contain it had been moved right out of the axle to a point where it became sprung weight. Thus the rear springs did not have to be as harsh as had been the case with a conventional rear axle, and the road holding of the type B Alfa Romeo profited accordingly. Similar attention was paid to the front axle, which was located longitudinally and restrained in torsion by a pair of radius arms, leaving the half-elliptic leaf springs free from brake torque effects so that they could be shackled at both ends, their only supernumerary duty being to locate the axle transversely. Thus the Alfa Romeo type B had the makings of a car whose obvious powers of speed and acceleration (it was commendably light) should be matched by roadholding, handling and braking of appropriate standards.

And so it proved: the car was one of the last and the most lastingly successful of the large generation of Grand Prix cars whose descent could be traced by direct or indirect line from the type 801 Fiat at whose birth Jano had assisted, and even to earlier cars whose influence could still be traced.

Bugatti, too, was to produce yet another racing car of classic beauty and orthodox morphology, relieved, as might be expected,

63 (above) *Although their 3-litre 8C was still enjoying development in 1934, Maserati returned to their old 6C34 and raced it in 3·7-litre form. Nuvolari had a couple of minor successes with it; here he is on parade at Monza*

64 *The regulations governing GP racing under the '750 kg' formula stipulated a minimum width of bodywork. The 8C Maserati accordingly had to be widened for racing in 1934*

by touches of that free-thinking stressmanship which made every Bugatti an object of wonder and delight even when its performance justified no especial admiration. This was the type 59, which embodied a few surprises; the straight-eight engine, originally 2·8 litres but subsequently 3·3 and eventually even larger, had plain main and big-end bearings; the front axle was split at the centre within a sleeve which allowed the two halves a degree of relative rotation and thus prevented the axle beam from acting as a prodigiously stiff anti-roll torsion bar; and the wheels were once again wire-spoked, the wire being thin and the spokes being radial since torsional loads were transmitted from the hub by way of radial serrations at the perimeter of the brake drum engaging with corresponding serrations on the inboard edge of the wheel rim. It was a surpassingly beautiful car, but it cannot be said to have achieved any real success. The *monoposto* Alfa Romeo did, earning its place at the pinnacle of Grand Prix car development and retaining it against all challengers (of which the enlarged Maserati with a 2·9-litre engine and hydraulic brakes was the most formidable) until 1934.

And then it was toppled from its pinnacle. Perhaps it was time for a new fashion to supplant the old. Perhaps Grand Prix racing cannot progress for a decade without *hic jacet* being inscribed to a few monumental constructions. The counterswing of the pendulum was due; and fugacious honour, spurning further Latin hospitality, sought a new alliance. On the other side of the Alps, an old people, a young nation already broken, was being forged anew; and in their conative zeal they included the highest form of motor racing among the media whereby they sought to befriend, impress or intimidate the neighbours with whom they had so fatally been at odds. In the process they were to introduce new fashions to motor racing, to revive old ones, and to raise that pinnacle to an elevation so remote that only they could aspire to climb to it. And then . . . why, then it would be time for them to topple in their turn.

chapter four

1934 to 1953

The size of engine which could be used within the framework of the 750 kilo formula was amazing—the last model had a cubic capacity of 6,330 cc. Yet no case had ever come to light, neither at Daimler-Benz nor at Auto Union, when faulty material had brought about an accident. This shows clearly that the designers had worked with great care and tremendous conscientiousness, since the weight in relation to the engine size was so very low.
Richard von Frankenberg

Es irrt der Mensch so lang er streht, wrote Goethe, Man errs so long as he strives. The heavy despair and pessimism of this may be relieved by the complementary observation of Samuel Smiles who wrote somewhat later: 'We often discover what will do by finding out what will not do; and probably he who never made a mistake never made a discovery.' The validity of both these statements was illustrated in the years from 1934 to the outbreak of World War II in 1939 by the motor racing activities of the Germans, whom candour cannot admit to having engaged in the sport for motives other than the demonstration and propagation of their technical and personal superiority; but so far from entering the lists with cars of such advanced and even revolutionary conception and such faultless execution that their rivals should forthwith be reduced to defeat and disorder, the Mercedes-Benz and Auto Union teams only arrived at a joint domination of Grand Prix racing after some early setbacks which might have seemed a very welcome reprieve for the drivers of the Alfa Romeo, Bugatti and Maserati cars which sought to hold off this new challenge from cars that made their own appear hopelessly outmoded—even if the style in which the Germans went campaigning allowed the others no cause for long-term optimism. Jointly the two German teams achieved an adequate subjection of their opponents during 1935; severally they needed some time more before the expenditure of much money, much effort, much material, and some blood, should show a return in the consolidation of new design principles which confirmed this period as the beginning of an era of technocracy. In this epoch entirely new schools of chassis design, and accelerated emancipation of the metallurgist and the fuel chemist, created a generation of cars revolutionary in design and flabbergasting in performance, the most powerful ever seen in Grand Prix racing; and the lessons learned by the two great German teams during the second half of the 1930s and applied by them with convincing results by the end of that decade were to endure as precepts for a further decade when motor racing was resumed after the war.

The circumstances in which this programme of discovery and conquest was conducted deserve comment before embarkation on a survey of the new engineering patterns it produced. Mainland of Europe, within which sub-continent all true enthusiasm for and understanding of road racing was confined, had been ridden since the 1919 Treaty of Versailles by social disorders and political controversies whose resolution was often sought by violence and seldom effectively conjured by other means, even though the equilibrium thus attained was unstable. It is probably little more than coincidence that the rise of Italy and the decline of France in the fortunes of Grand Prix racing may effectively be traced to the year 1922, in which Mussolini became dictator of Italy and developed a foreign policy calculated to reduce the influence of France. Undoubtedly the Fascist government that he headed encouraged the Italian motor industry in its efforts to overthrow the old regime and crown the alleged emancipation of the Italian people with laurels plucked in the field of Grand Prix racing; but it is doubtful whether this encouragement took any very substantial form in specie. On the other hand when Hitler came to power in Germany in 1933, he was already a confirmed and knowledgeable motor racing enthusiast, so when his Nazi commissariat urged the German motor industry to play a vigorous part in the extension of German prestige abroad and by their technical accomplishments to represent (or, if you will, misrepresent) the beneficial consequences of adopting the National Socialist ideology, the encouragement was made manifest in the allocation of considerable sums of money. A prize of £40,000 was put up for the most successful German racing car of 1934, an annual subsidy of £20,000 each for Auto Union and Mercedes-Benz was proposed, and more important in view of the very considerable sums that were soon to be lavished upon the cause (amounting to a quarter of a million pounds per annum then, and equivalent to approximately 1·3 millions in 1973 values) they were allowed to offset their racing costs against rearmament contracts. To Mercedes-Benz, whose racing department had been feeling the pinch of the company's financial controllers as lately as 1931, and to Auto Union—a consortium of the interests of Audi, DKW, Horch and Wanderer that had but recently been established—such tangible encouragement was understandably welcome. It may, however, have been accepted with a slight uneasiness, for the terms in which it was expressed were not so much hortatory as peremptory. The directed

66 In 1934 the W25 Mercedes-Benz got the 750 kg formula off to an unexpectedly vigorous start with no less than 354 bhp from 3·36 litres

technicians of the German motor racing axis, whose poles were at Stuttgart and Chemnitz, must have felt some misgivings when reading the following passage from *Mannschaft und Meisterschaft:* 'The Führer has spoken. The 1934 Grand Prix formula shall and must be a measuring stick for German knowledge and German ability. So one thing leads to the other: first the Führer's overpowering energy, then the formula, a great international problem to which Europe's best devote themselves, and, finally, action in the design and construction of new racing cars.'

Lest those who allow their political sensibilities to cloud their judgement of other matters infer too much from the foregoing, it must be recorded to the credit of Mercedes-Benz and Auto Union that the racing cars with which they entered this new era were laid down some time before the accession of Hitler to power on 30 January 1933. There is some doubt as to the exact date when Auto Union took the firm decision to proceed with the design, which had been finalised in the autumn of 1932. That elegant writer and generally infallible historian Cyril Posthumus has questioned this, saying 'It argues remarkable boldness and prescience on their part if they did actually plan a full onslaught on GP racing in the same year—1932—that their future rivals Mercedes-Benz had to give up racing, even on a shoe string . . . .' But what Mercedes-Benz told their drivers at that time (the evidence upon which Posthumus based this argument) may have been designed to disguise the reasonable commercial acumen with which Mercedes-Benz may have calculated that to commit themselves to a full motor racing programme in the free-for-all era of the early 1930s might be a much less profitable undertaking than to retrench and prepare for the new formula that must in due course restore some order to the chaos.

Such a formula was published by AIACR in October 1932, and was shortly followed by a board meeting of the company at which the directors discussed the design of a pure racing car with which to restate their interest in the sport. On the other hand we know that the final decision to compete was not taken until March 1933.

The formula in question reflected, as was now usually the case, the desire of the governing body to produce racing in which the speeds involved and the cars themselves should not get out of hand. Perturbed at the very high speeds and visible lack of controllability of the ultra-high-powered track cars produced by Alfa Romeo, Bugatti, and Maserati, they recognised that their previous attempts to inhibit performance by limiting engine size had been foiled. Further, they noted that the cumbersome engines adopted by those three manufacturers for those occasions where sheer speed was at a premium and roadworthiness at a discount produced cars that were considerably heavier than the accepted contemporary classics (such as the type 51 Bugatti or the type B Alfa Romeo, both of which weighed less than 800 kg ready to race) and were ill-balanced into the bargain. So it was reasoned that to lower the dangerously high level of speed then being reached, a weight limit of 750 kg should be imposed for the complete car—

less driver, tyres and fluids, which was a most important exclusion—and further stipulations sought to forestall reductions in frontal area by requiring the body width to be at least 85 cm and its depth at least 25 cm, these dimensions being taken at the driving seat. Further, to encourage reliability and discourage the production of unreasonably frail cars in which lightness had been pursued too ruthlessly, they required a minimum race distance of 500 kilometres. This formula was to take effect from 1 January 1934 and endure until the end of 1936, it was announced.

The reaction to the announcement by the manufacturers then engaged in racing was unimaginative and perfunctory. The type 59 Bugatti has already been mentioned: ravishingly beautiful, it was also mildly self-contradictory in that it was wholly characteristic of Bugatti without being typical of Bugatti. Miserably unsuccessful when it first appeared in 1933 as a 2·8-litre car, it showed to much better purpose in the following year, earning some meritorious third places as well as actually winning the Belgian GP—from which the German teams absented themselves on the unusual grounds that they were being dunned for exorbitant Customs duties on the large quantities of special fuel with which they presented themselves and their cars at the Belgian border.

Alfa Romeo, encouraged by the fact that their existing cars were well within the terms of the new weight limit, contented themselves with enlarging them in most directions and revising the suspension by fitting reversed quarter-elliptic springs at the rear (in imitation of Bugatti) and Dubonnet independent suspension at the front. Actually this programme of modification was only completed during 1935, by which time the greater torque of the engine (which had been considerably enlarged from 2·9 litres to 3·2, 3·5 and eventually 3·8 litres) proved too much for the strength of the gearbox, whose choice of forward speeds was reduced from four to three so as to make room for wider gear teeth. It was in one of these fully modified P3B cars that Nuvolari scored his celebrated win in the German Grand Prix at the Nurburgring in 1935.

As for Maserati, they made their car somewhat bigger without making it in any respect better, and they went into full eclipse. As in the case of Bugatti, the fortunes of the Maserati company were founded on the economical design and modest production of racing and sports cars for sale to private customers, and they simply did not have the resources to compete with larger and wealthier organisations.

The complete contrast to the situation enjoyed by Auto Union and Mercedes-Benz went a long way to explaining the iconoclastic designs that they produced. Each of these firms created a racing car that was, despite visible ancestry in each case, really like no other that had ever been seen before. Each of them was in some respect a bold contrast to the other. Each of them was characteristically German in its engineering style. Both of them had a number of features in common, features which were most

111

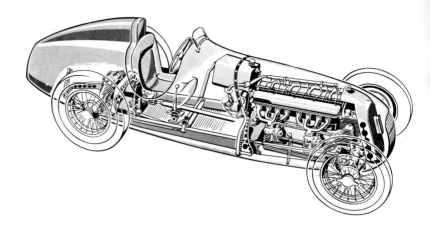

important in distinguishing them from the common herd of racing cars that they were calculated to put to rout. Thus we find that both cars had engines very much larger than can have been within the expectations of the committee that formulated the regulations according to which they were constructed. Both of them enjoyed an excess of power even greater than the size of their engines might suggest, due to the refinement of their design. Both of them employed fully independent suspension of all four wheels, large hydraulic brakes, some semblance of bodily streamlining and all the advantages of strength, stiffness, lightness, durability or thermal stability that could be conferred upon a machine by an engineer having at his disposal the most punctilious and capable artificers of a renowned manufactury and the most sophisticated products of metallurgical research.

Nevertheless they both gave trouble, albeit in different ways, for they were conceived, designed and constructed in different ways. Thus the Mercedes-Benz had a straight-eight engine with two overhead camshafts and a one-piece crankshaft, while the Auto Union had a V16 with but one camshaft high up between the two banks of cylinder heads and its crankshaft was built up from no less than thirty-three component parts. The Mercedes engine had four valves seated in each combustion chamber, the Auto Union had but two. Indeed the cars varied considerably in a large number of details such as their suspension geometries, their supercharging techniques, their use of bearings of one sort or another in their engines, and so on; but all these details were subordinate to the principal contrast that in the Mercedes-Benz the engine was in front of the driver and in the Auto Union it was behind him.

How the persuasions of individual men affected this refractoriness affords scarcely less interesting a study than the dispersal of Fiat engineering philosophy during the preceding decade, discussed in a previous chapter: for such was the conjunctive action of the corporations and the migratory movement of the individuals concerned, in the years which anticipated this development, that it could easily have come about that the Mercedes should have been rear-engined and the Auto Union the more conventional.

The chief designer of the latter was the late Doctor Ferdinand Porsche, who had been responsible for the design of the cars which had carried the names of Mercédès and Mercedes-Benz into racing up to 1931. Setting himself up thereafter as an independent consultant, he had been joined by Adolf Rosenberger, a wealthy amateur racing driver who had worked with Dr Rumpler on the design and development of the Benz Tropfwagen which we have noted as competing in the Grand Prix at Monza in 1924, and which Rosenberger also drove with no little success in hill climbs and sports car events. Indeed his driving was of such quality that he could rival the great Caracciola when both were competing in the big six-cylinder Mercedes-Benz that Porsche designed, finishing second to Caracciola at the Nurburgring in 1927 and even beating him at the Freiburg hillclimb in that same year. He was therefore unquestionably competent to advise Porsche on the feasibility of

68 More astonishing than even the Mercedes-Benz: Auto Union began racing in 1934 with this all-independent car bearing a V16 engine behind the driver

the rear-engined racing car and, having the technical perception to recognise its theoretical advantages, he strongly influenced Porsche in the evolution of the original racing Auto Union. He was also blessed with what might in a more temperate time or place be considered the advantage of being Jewish; and by a timely recognition of the policies that Hitler would implement, he fled the Nazi jurisdiction a matter of hours before the dictator was confirmed in power, and went to live under an assumed name in America. That his part in the creation of the Grand Prix Auto Union was not thereafter advertised is scarcely surprising.

Nor was it surprising that experience with the Tropfwagen had also filtered into the Daimler-Benz ménage, where the technical direction of the racing programme was led by Dr Hans Niebel (who had originally been with the Benz company before the amalgamation) assisted by another Benz inheritance in the form of Wagner, who had been directly concerned with the 1924 racers.

It was therefore to be expected that the advisability of a rear-engined configuration was earnestly discussed when the design of the new Grand Prix Mercedes-Benz was being considered. In the light of what Auto Union were to achieve, and with the wisdom of hindsight which reveals things not known at the material time and which, it must be admitted, can too easily lead the historian to be unnecessarily censorious, it is interesting to examine the reasons for which Mercedes-Benz rejected the idea of a rear-engined car.

First, they argued that rear engine mounting did not result in any weight reduction. This, of course, must have been the first consideration, the new formula being couched in terms that accorded weight-saving the utmost priority; but it is hard to see how the Mercedes-Benz engineers could ignore not only the weight of a propellor shaft capable of transmitting massive torque but also the fact that the apposition of the engine with the housings for the clutch, gearbox and final drive would confer upon the assembly a natural stiffness in which was implicit the possibility of reducing the weight of each and all. In fact, the weighing-in sessions which preceded each Grand Prix demonstrated that Auto Union were comfortably within the stipulated weight limit, whereas Mercedes-Benz sometimes qualified by the narrowest of margins.

Second, it was assessed that the drag factor would be much the same in either type of car. It is tempting to accept this, since it was based on wind tunnel tests; but although the coefficients of penetration of the different types might have been sufficiently similar, the elimination of the propellor shaft which must pass beneath or alongside the driver of a front-engined racing car allows him to be seated lower and thus permits a sensible reduction in the projected frontal area of the car. Now we have seen that in 1926 and 1927 the elimination of the riding mechanic allowed Delage and Talbot to offset their engines and transmissions so that the propellor shaft passed alongside the driver, who could therefore be seated very low with commensurate reduction in scuttle height and frontal area. The very fact that the 1934 formula stipulated a minimum body width that was sufficient to allow the passage of a transmission shaft alongside the driver's feet without incurring any penalty in the front area might have justified the conclusion that Mercedes-Benz drew; but in fact they did not avail themselves of this possibility, and the driver of their new car sat above the propellor shaft—so that although Auto Union did not fully exploit the possibility, seating their driver eleven inches above the ground and so placing him three inches higher than the driver of the 1926 Talbot, they nevertheless produced a car whose projected frontal area of sixteen square feet was 6 per cent smaller than that of the Mercedes-Benz.

Third, it was argued that if the engine and transmission positions were well arranged, the propellor shaft running between the engine and the rear axle would present no design problems. This must be considered in relation to the preceding paragraph: there may be no problems if the crankshaft and propellor shaft are co-axial, whereas additional gear trains or deflected universal joints would have to be employed—and the frictional losses occasioned by them would have to be suffered—if the shaft were to be moved out of the way of an ideally located driver. Not until 1938 did Mercedes-Benz produce a transmission which satisfied all requirements, but if this cure was vaguely homeopathic, Auto Union's simple elimination of the propellor shaft was decidedly allopathic.

Next to be considered was the effect on roadholding and handling. The smaller polar moment of inertia characteristic of a rear-engined car was thought beneficial in its action about the vertical axis but detrimental in relation to the longitudinal axis and the suspension of the car, and it was expected that adhesion to the road would be impaired. In the absence of the original minuted wording, this translation permits certain ambiguities; but it appears that the Mercedes-Benz designers, while welcoming the high pitch frequency and small pitch amplitude that could be achieved with a low polar moment of inertia, did not relish the directional instability that it might also be expected to promote. In fact it seems that they recognised that they were going to build an oversteering car, and that if the driver's capabilities were not to be unreasonably strained it would be advisable to employ a fairly high polar moment to mollify the twitchiness that they evidently recognised would stem from the proposed independent rear suspension. With what unjustified confidence and lack of foresight Auto Union approached these related matters we shall later see.

Finally, Dr Niebel and his colleagues concluded that the weight distribution of the rear-engined car was inimical to that first-class adhesion for the front wheels that they considered particularly important in a fast car. This would be most apparent when the car was in the accelerating mode, when the opposition of immense tractive effort at the rear wheels and the inertia of the car's mass acting through its centre of gravity would produce a transfer of load on to the rear wheels and off those at the front. This transfer would be sufficient in a front-engined but reasonably well-balanced car such as the proposed Mercedes-Benz to ensure an adequate coefficient of friction (or adhesion) between the rear tyres and the road so as to permit full-power acceleration without wheelspin at the higher speeds general on most racing circuits; at lower speeds the greater load on the rear tyres of the inherently tail-heavy Auto Union would give it the advantage, and it was usual to see the Auto Union out-accelerate the Mercedes-Benz on the exit from a slow corner—an effect which was only partially attributable to the weight distribution, for the larger and more lightly stressed engine of the Auto Union disposed of more low-speed torque than did the Mercedes-Benz, whose engine during the first two or three years of its life suffered a noticeable drop in bmep below about 3,000 rev/min. In this context we should note that the cars of this period were capable of accelerating from standstill to 60 mph at

69 1934 Mercedes-Benz engine, with supercharger delivering air to pressurised carburettors—an inefficient system

an average rate of about 0·7 *g*, with peak instantaneous rates considerably higher at some stage in this exercise and not necessarily much lower even after the driver had changed up into second gear which would carry the car well beyond 100 mph.

In fact the accelerating abilities of the cars were limited by wheelspin at such speeds even on dry roads, and the value of weight transfer or indeed static load on the rear tyres may be appreciated from the fact that the value of adhesion between the driving tyres and the road increases in proportion to the vertical load on those tyres. Of course, the converse of all this is true when the car is in the decelerating mode: when the brakes are applied there is a forward transfer of load on to the front tyres, increasing their grip and permitting greater braking coefficients to be realised. Even when the car is merely in the overrun condition this forward load transfer may be detected, though its magnitude is naturally less. It has been estimated that the cars now under review spent about one-third of their racing time in being accelerated, about one-third on the overrun, and the remaining third in braking; but on the other hand it was not the practice of the drivers to brake very heavily, for in the course of a 500-kilometres race such treatment could easily cause overheating, fade and rapid wear of the brakes. The normal practical maximum rate of retardation was generally about 0·3 *g*, which may informatively be compared with a rate of acceleration already quoted.

Despite the increased work they were called upon to do in checking large cars from speeds much higher than had previously

116

been reached, brakes did not enjoy much development at this time apart from the adoption of hydraulic operation, a change prompted more because of the convenience with which it could be reconciled with independent suspension than from any improved performance that it might offer. An exception to this may be remarked in the abortive Sefac, in which the former Salmson designer Petit conceived the idea of a multiplicity of small brake shoes instead of the conventional pair of large ones, and introduced what must stand as the record number of six shoes within each drum. It was entirely characteristic of the unbalanced design of this car that these components should have been cable operated, as it was that the generally crude chassis should carry a fairly refined eight-cylinder engine consisting of two in-line fours set side by side and geared together, the transmission being aligned with one crankshaft and a large supercharger with the other.

The complete antithesis was provided by the Germans, who developed large and supremely powerful engines only after satisfying themselves that the chassis that would bear them were of such advanced design as to permit a reasonable utilisation of the power thus made available. Noteworthy though their engines were, it is their chassis which were all-important, especially from the historical point of view. Right from the beginning of their studies Auto Union and Mercedes-Benz accepted as a design postulate that the proper utilisation of great power depended on the relief of the rear suspension from the torque effects introduced by the final drive bevels reacting to input by trying to twist their casing about its longitudinal and transverse axes. To resist this effect the final drive casing would have to be anchored firmly to the chassis and convey its output through suitably articulated half-shafts to independently sprung wheels; and in order to avoid any distortion of the frame and thereby of the suspension geometry through loads imposed either by the engine or by the movement of the wheels on the road, it was especially necessary that with independent suspension the basic chassis frame should be considerably stiffer than what might pass as satisfactory in a stiffly sprung beam-axle car.

The means to this end adopted by Auto Union was a frame consisting of two parallel tubes of chrome–molybdenum steel, 105 mm in diameter, connected and braced transversely by four tubes of the same chrome–molybdenum stuff. Mercedes-Benz employed an assortment of tubes and fabricated box sections for the cross-members of their chassis, the longitudinals of which were pierced box sections (with every hole, of course, properly swaged) and tapering to each extremity from a section more than six inches deep at mid-wheelbase. Both these frames were very light in relation to their strength and also in relation to their stiffness, which was undoubtedly greater than that of any earlier racing car. Auto Union sought to save further weight by employing the main tubes of their frames as conduits for the cooling water which had to be carried from the engine in the rear of the car to the heat exchanger in the nose and back again; but they were frustrated by minute fissures in the welds by which the tubes were joined, these cracks not being serious enough to impair the structural functions of the chassis but sufficing to allow the escape of water, so that in some of the early races of 1934 the cars were in severe trouble from overheating; and eventually the coolant was re-routed through separated pipes.

The nub of the matter was undoubtedly independent suspension. The Germans might well exploit all the industrial and scientific resources at their command to produce cars of sufficiently low weight and tremendous, even superfluous power; but it would avail them little without the revolution in suspension design that permitted this power to be used with some semblance of control. The Italians and French had found themselves unable to utilise 300 horsepower in traditional chassis, the Germans were more or less successful in using considerably more, and the difference was accounted for by, and entirely justified, the new fashion they had created in chassis and suspension design.

Independent suspension was not itself a novelty. In the very earliest days of racing, Sizaire-Naudin and Bollée cars had independently sprung front wheels, while Doctor Rumpler's 1923 Benz had independently sprung rear wheels. The Benz, as we have mentioned in recording the exploits of Adolf Rosenberger, was also built in sportscar form, and the basis of the design was adopted by Tatra in Czechoslovakia when Benz abandoned the model upon their amalgamation with Daimler in 1926. The gifted Tatra engineer Ledwinka added independent front suspension to the independent rear, to produce a car which rode the rough highways of Czechoslovakia better than the conventional models; and observation of this prompted Mercedes-Benz to introduce two low-powered touring cars similarly endowed (one of them incidentally being rear-engined, which confirms that in their rejection of the principle for their racing car the Mercedes-Benz designers were being rational rather than merely reactionary).

The need for front wheels to be steered led to a variety of independent front suspension systems as designers interpreted in their different ways the objects of independence. Its main purpose was generally held to be that the movement of one front wheel riding over a bump need not be communicated to the other, so that although the effects of gyroscopic precession might be evinced by the former they need not be transmitted to the latter—and indeed it was the object of most designers to secure substantially vertical movement of the wheels so that precessional movement would not be generated, while at the same time the track would remain constant and thus lateral scrubbing of the tyres on the road prevented. These motives inspired the design of the Dubonnet system used by Alfa Romeo (in which the rise and fall of each wheel was accompanied by a variation of the steering castor angle) and the twin trailing arm Porsche system used by Auto Union (in which incompatibility between the suspension motion and the geometry of the steering linkage caused variations in toe-in or toe-out to occur with vertical movement of the wheels, unless they were directed straight ahead). Others experimented with pairs of equal and parallel wishbones, a transverse leaf spring sometimes replacing one of them, with which perfect steering geometry could be obtained at the expense of slight lateral tyre scrub of negligible importance.

Mercedes-Benz, in choosing wishbones, introduced some variations to the basic principle by pivoting the whole of each suspension assembly on a vertical axis about which it could swing so as to give the wheels complete freedom of movement forwards and backwards through a total distance of about half an inch before the motion was checked by stops. This was a technique that they had already employed on their touring cars, the object being to damp out steering shimmy, this longitudinal compliance having been found effective in the SSK beam-axled car where the compliance was provided by hanging one of the front springs on two shackles so as to give a limited horizontal freedom, the idea having originated in the United States, where Packard exploited it effectively. To this extent the suspension of the Mercedes-Benz was ingenious and effective; but on the Grand Prix car the geometry of parallel wishbones was modified slightly by making the upper one somewhat shorter than the lower, with the object of keeping the track constant at road level and thus minimising scrub. In the process some variation of wheel camber was introduced, the camber increasing towards the full bump position; and a corollary of this was that when the car was in a one-wheel-up one-wheel-down attitude, as when lateral load transfer in cornering caused it to tilt or roll outwards, the upper or outer wheel might, because of its positive camber relative to the car, remain more or less vertical relative to the road, and thus maintain its cornering power, while the lower or inner wheel would add its negative camber to the tilt of the car and thus have its cornering power sensibly degraded, although, being relatively lightly laden, this might not be a serious matter. In fact, the springing of the car was so stiff and the suspension movement so limited (less than two inches from static laden height to full bump) that the angular variation was very slight. Now the tyres of the period, although they had grown somewhat larger in section than those in use at the beginning of the decade, were still fairly narrow in relation to the load they bore and, more important, were based on a carcass of approximately circular cross-section which entailed a tread crown of appreciable convexity: and it is a characteristic of such tyres that they are not unduly sensitive to camber variations, although the loading of them at a marked negative camber would introduce a palpable degradation of cornering power.

Nevertheless, camber variation could be sufficient in the early German racing cars to interfere with the handling and stability of the car, especially in the case of the rear tyres whose sensitivity to camber would vary greatly according to the amount of tractive torque they were transmitting, and this, of course, was exceptionally high in their case. So if it was unfortunate that the ground-level roll centre of the Porsche suspension of the Auto

119

Union's front wheels caused them to tilt through the same angle as that to which the car rolled, and nearly as unfortunate that the wishbone front suspension of the Mercedes-Benz had nearly the same effect (reduced only because of the disparity in the lengths of the wishbones), it was doubly unfortunate that both cars employed swinging half-axles as a means of securing the independent rear suspension that was to them of crucial importance. Not only does such a system locate the rear roll centre very high (in their case more than two inches above hub level at static deflection) and thus encourage a large roll couple to increase load transfer to the outer wheel in cornering, but also it has been shown by numerous careful studies of the system (which achieved a certain notoriety in the 1960s in a passenger-car application) that there can be a jacking effect which, in raising the tail of the car, allows the outer rear wheel to droop or tuck under to a very extreme degree of positive camber, such as may be guaranteed to degrade its power to sustain the cornering forces that it alone of the two rear wheels is sufficiently laden to accept. For these two reasons, both the Auto Union and the Mercedes-Benz suffered from troublesome over-steer, and the consequent difficulty of driving them made them somewhat slow into and through corners compared with their old-fashioned rivals. This handicap was generally set at nought by the ability of the German cars to accelerate out of the corners much faster and more profitably, their independent rear suspensions allowing much more engine power to be turned into effective tractive effort.

All of this does not, alas, complete the list of geometrical solecisms by which the German cars were betrayed in their suspension systems. Mercedes-Benz, who could easily have arranged things otherwise, inexplicably chose to ignore the desirability of the steering linkage tracing the same arc as the rest of the suspension, with the result that slight variations in toe-in were prescribed by the track rod halves as the front wheels rose and fell. Already the very short travel of the wheels has been recited, and it was this paucity of movement that made the navigational aberrations of the steering small enough to be of little consequence; but Auto Union permitted themselves the much more serious folly of a rear suspension geometry describing similar deviationist tendencies. Whereas Mercedes-Benz swung their half axles about trunnion joints that were parallel to the longitudinal axis of the car (and of course were horizontal), Auto Union swung theirs about part-spherical bearings on each side of the final drive, leaving tractive and torque reaction to be fed into radius arms fixed to the outer extremities of the half axles and feeding their loads into ball and socket joints on the chassis alongside the engine. Thus the rear wheels moved about an axis passing through the forward pivots of the radius arms and the inner pivots of the half axles, with the complicated result that as the wheels rose and fell they were made to exhibit variations in camber, in track, and in toe-in. Any one of these could be detrimental; the concatenation of all three was deplorable; and when the capacity of the tyres to accommodate

1939 Mercedes-Benz

ORTHODOXY IS MY DOXY, as Bishop
Warburton once observed,
heterodoxy is another man's doxy.
Daimler-Benz had a reputation for
adhering to their own individual
tradition, a reputation established
as early as 1914 and strengthened
by every subsequent one of their
products. By 1937 it was clear that
one of the Stuttgart traditions to
which they adhered, reluctant to
admit any serious objections, was
the use and indeed the rightness
of the straight-eight engine in
racing cars. Many commentators
were therefore not a little
disturbed to find in 1938 that the
new Mercedes-Benz Grand Prix
car had a V12 engine; but they
should not have found this so
surprising, for the true tradition
at Daimler-Benz was one of clear,
cool scientific judgement
unclouded by any considerations
of tradition for its own sake.
The terms of the formula
introduced in 1938 lent emphasis
to the usual demand for the
highest practicable rate of
crankshaft revolution and the
largest possible piston and valve
areas. Simple morphological
study showed that for the
purposes of the new formula a
straight-eight engine did not lend
itself to such development,
whereas a V12 did; and so it came
about that the 1938 GP Mercedes-
Benz was, in its engine as well as in
every other respect, considerably
more complex that the essentially
simple W125 that had preceded it.
It was a successful car, even
though it was not as good as
theoretical forecasts promised;
but by dint of two-stage
supercharging and some detail
revisions to the chassis and body
the 1939 version proved to be the
fastest racing car yet seen. With
two superchargers in series
pressurising its induction system
to 2·65 atmospheres absolute, the
W164 car of 1939 was given 483
bhp with which to urge its
maximum laden weight of 1·2 tons
at speeds up to 195 mph while
consuming expensive fuel at the
unparalleled rate of about 1 mile
per gallon. The fuel necessary to

1939 Mercedes Benz (continued)
satisfy this thirst accounted for a quarter of the car's total weight on the
starting line; but it was weight that would be shed rapidly, and to good
purpose, so that the value of two stage supercharging impressed itself so
firmly upon the motor racing world that for more than a decade no proper
Grand Prix car would be considered complete without it.

1950 Talbot

THE CHILL PENURY OF FRANCE after World War II forbade any return to the
motor racing fray which that nation had once so nobly adorned, Grand Prix
racing gradually revived under the terms of a formula which permitted
supercharged cars of 1½-litres engine capacity or unsupercharged cars of three
times greater displacement; but the only machines to carry French colours
convincingly were unsupercharged six-cylinder Talbots owing their origins
to a pre-war sports car design. They could never hope to compete for the lead
when the Alfa Romeo team was running; but against any meaner opposition
the Talbot was always a force with which to reckon, simply because its modest
consumption allowed it to run non-stop through a race at a respectable speed
while the faster supercharged cars were forced to stop for refuelling.

The importance of the Talbot was not what it achieved but what it inspired:
it was the example of this car that persuaded Ferrari to embark upon the
development of a series of unsupercharged cars designed *ab initio* to rival the
performance of the Alfa Romeos without suffering their dipsomaniac thirst.
Little or nothing else in the Talbot encouraged any emulation: its Wilson
preselector gearbox, controlled by a lever moving in a quadrant beneath the
plane of the steering wheel, had featured in other cars, but thereafter only the
Connaught would win a Formula I Grand Prix thus equipped. Its leaf-sprung
live rear axle was a superannuated inheritance from the past, as indeed was
the pushrod actuation of its engine's valves. It was a handsome car, even a
beautiful one; but the lesson it taught was strictly economical, and was well
learnt.

1951 Alfa Romeo

The last successful supercharged Grand Prix car was a synthesis of most of the successful principles learned in the decade of racing immediately preceding World War II. Indeed it was born in that decade, in response to the demand for a class of Voiturette racing such as might be conducted much more cheaply than the now extravagant and expensive Grand Prix category – and, which was more to the point, might be free from the attentions and inevitable domination of the Germans. The type 158 Alfetta was created in 1938, its straight-eight engine like a pup out of the bigger racing Alfas except that it had only one supercharger and all its camshaft and accessory drive gear was at the front. By the end of 1961 the type 159M (or Maggiorata) was developing over 400 bhp and running at 9000 rev/min; but it was to no avail, and Alfa Romeo withdrew from Grand Prix racing. It was the end of more than the Alfetta, of more than the noble line Grand Prix Alfas. After thirty glorious years the reign of the supercharged engine was over.

them was sharply modulated by the application or withdrawal of tractive or braking effort, the natural symptoms were aggravated into a culminative disorientation which the drivers were often unable to parry.

In fine, the Auto Union was a car that very few people could drive effectively; and only one man, Bernd Rosemeyer, whose previous competition experience was on motor cycles and who was therefore able to drive the Auto Union with his judgement unclouded—for all he knew, all racing cars were like that—was able to drive it so fast as consistently to extend the Mercedes-Benz opposition. The Auto Union oversteered wildly and often unpredictably: all its designers' care in endowing it with what was conceived to be an ideal weight distribution was valueless in face of the dynamic peculiarities of the suspension. Even the pains taken to ensure consistent handling and constant weight distribution by locating the fuel tank (whose contents amounted to more than 16 per cent of the car's starting-line weight) at the centre of gravity bore little fruit, the most remarked effect being to force the driver's seat even further forward. There were many who proclaimed that his position in the car explained his difficulty in controlling it, arguing that if he sat further to the rear he would be better able to detect the onset of oversteer; but this argument overlooked the fact that the angular acceleration to which he would be subjected (and which may be measured in radians per second per second) will be exactly the same no matter where he may sit, within or indeed without the wheelbase. Discussion with drivers who were racing in the 1930s has strengthened Setright in his view that what they call 'driving by the seat of the pants' in fact involved a sensitivity to angular acceleration; linear acceleration (which may be measured in feet per second per second of displacement, and was the kind the aforesaid critics were considering) need not vary appreciably during the onset of oversteer. Given a less aberrant kind of suspension there is no reason why the

Auto Union should not have been eminently controllable and far more successful than it was.

Instead, it was the Mercedes-Benz that, after the teething troubles that beset both teams in 1934, emerged as the dominant car in 1935. This was despite the fact that the Auto Union had a larger engine, a smaller frontal area, and a five-speed transmission (in which they had been anticipated by Delage in 1925 and 1927) and could achieve a higher performance on a straight road. Its engine followed no fashion and set no fashion, and perfectly reflected the sentiments of Doctor Porsche who had said that a formula that imposed no limit on engine size was the most stimulating and that it encouraged the design of an engine as large and light as might be, and as moderately stressed as was consistent with its giving the necessary power. Thus the Auto Union began with a V16 of 4·36 litres displacement and yielding its full 295 bhp at a mere 4,500 rev/min. For all its size and immense piston area (90 square inches, far more than any Grand Prix car since the 14-litre Fiat of 1912) it was astonishingly light, not merely because of the extensive use of aluminium alloys but also through the ingenuity with which, for example, one camshaft was arranged to serve all thirty-two valves, the cylinder-head castings arched together over the centre of the V so as to constitute a duct leading from the supercharger to the inlet ports and making a separate manifold redundant, and the revival of the inserted wet cylinder liner simplified the block structure considerably.

Concerning the inlet passage, it must be expected that the casting which constituted its walls must have done much to heat the mixture travelling through it. This was delivered by a Roots supercharger which was on the suction side of the carburettor, so that the latent heat of evaporation of the high alcohol content in the fuel had a countervailing cooling effect and so helped to ensure that the cylinders had delivered to them a charge of moderate temperature and fair density.

Mercedes-Benz, on the other hand, persisted in their traditional technique of drawing air through the supercharger and delivering it pressurised to the carburettors, suffering thereby all the penalties of high charge temperature and low density that are associated with superchargers of low adiabatic efficiency. This circuitry also demanded a further complication in the throttle linkage, which had to be coupled to a relief valve between the blower and the carburettors through which surplus air could be vented to the atmosphere when the carburettor throttles were partially or wholly closed. This feature, which was unaccountably to persist until 1937, was responsible not only for the most impressive noise of these cars but also for the failure of the engines to develop as much power as they might otherwise have done. Nevertheless, in the M25, which made its debut in 1934 and continued until the end of 1936 with its succession of engine enlargements and up-ratings, Mercedes-Benz made better use of high revolutions, bmep, and mechanical efficiency than Auto Union did of high piston area and displacement. In 1934 when we have seen, Auto Union began with 295 bhp from 4·36 litres at 4,500 rev/min, Mercedes-Benz began with 1 litre less and 1,300 rev/min more to achieve 302 bhp on a 50:50 benzole mixture and as much as 354 using an alcohol-rich fuel. The following year Auto Union, in search of more power, enlarged their engine to 4·95 litres by increasing its bore (and incidentally its piston area to 102·5 square inches), also raising its speed to 4,800 rev/min at which 375 bhp were yielded; but in that year Mercedes-Benz had enlarged their engine to 3·99 litres and raised its power output to 430 bhp without increasing the rate of revolutions. This superiority magnified the other disadvantages that the Auto Union was already suffering, with the result that the Mercedes-Benz team conquered nearly everywhere.

The tables were turned in 1936. Mercedes-Benz enlarged their engine to 4·3 and then to 4·74 litres from which, with alcohol fuel, they obtained as much as 494 bhp, still at 5,800 rev/min; but Auto Union, this time increasing both the stroke and bore of their engine and raising the permitted crankshaft rate even higher, emerged with a full 6 litres and a mighty 520 bhp at 5,000 rev/min. Add to this the poor controllability of the new short chassis adopted by Mercedes-Benz and the virtuosity of the young Rosemeyer, whom Auto Union had acquired to lead their team of drivers, and it is easy to see why the fortunes of the latter team were as favourable to them in 1936 as they had been unfavourable in the preceding year.

71 Rosemeyer at the 'Ring again, in the 6-litre 1937 Auto Union

While the Germans were setting a new and matchless pace they were also setting new fashions which appeared sufficiently clearly stated for other manufacturers to follow. The configuration of the Auto Union was popularly dismissed, the car being considered something of a sport (in the biological sense) and its engine location a mutation that would doom it to eventual extinction. The couturier after whose style other manufacturers would cut their metal was Mercedes-Benz, and there accordingly emerged some other cars complying with the basic pattern of a fairly stiff chassis endowed with independent suspension of all four wheels and carrying as large as possible an engine whose cylinders should number at least eight and would be supercharged at about 1·6 atmospheres absolute. Behind this engine the driver would sit, astride the transmission shaft and therefore still fairly high in a body whose contours no longer betrayed the basic functional shapes of radiator or petrol tank but was now functional in its own right as a lightweight envelope containing virtually all the mechanical parts except the wheels and the outermost elements of the suspension, and ensuring the least possible aerodynamic drag.

The general shape of this body was derived from the work of Freiherr König von Fachsenseld, an aerodynamicist who had been responsible for turning the angular SSKL Mercedes-Benz of 1932 into a well-faired aerodyne which won a race at the Avus track at an average speed of 120·7 mph. Nevertheless, the fuselage of the Auto Union was, when considered in isolation from the protruding suspension and wheels, probably the best shaped of them all, its drag coefficient being a mere 0·057. Unfortunately the protruding suspension and the huge wheels and tyres were in close enough proximity to this hull to create considerable interference in the air flow around it, which added to their own considerable drag to raise the overall coefficient of penetration for the complete car to 0·61; and this was in every respect typical of what the other manufacturers were achieving. Such interference effects were carefully studied by Auto Union and were substantially eliminated in their superbly streamlined record-breaking car of 1938, which was required only to go very fast in a straight line and could therefore be faired according to the dictates of aviation practice. Aircraft techniques were employed in the road-racing Auto Union to a limited extent; the side panels of its body, being structurally redundant, were made of doped fabric so as to be as light as possible.

Another to emulate aircraft practice was Count Trossi, an eminent Italian driver who had the idea of building a Grand Prix car that was virtually a small aircraft fuselage with a supercharged air-cooled radial engine in the extreme nose coupled to front-wheel drive with independent suspension all round. This was a most refreshing piece of unorthodoxy, probably hampered by its engine being a sixteen-cylinder two-stroke, and was reported to have gone quite quickly in testing although it was never submitted to the proof of a race.

More consonant with the newly established fashion was an Alfa Romeo which was gradually evolved during 1934 and 1935. Various components, such as the swing-axle rear suspension, were operationally tested on adaptations of the late type P3B car, whose chassis was, of course, not really stiff enough to be associated effectively with fully independent suspension. When finally the whole car emerged it was with a new frame, with

72 The pedals, front suspension and other nosegear of the 6-litre Auto-Union make an interesting study in weight-saving

73 Even in its engine the Auto Union was exemplary in its economical use of material. With a more suitable kind of rear suspension, what might it have achieved?

independent front suspension by Porsche trailing links and rear by swinging half-axles, with a new four-speed gearbox and eventually with a V12 engine of 4·06 litres displacement for which 370 bhp were claimed at 5,800 rev/min. In general the car was no match for the Germans, but on slow and particularly twisty circuits it could give them some opposition when handled by that exceptional driver Nuvolari. However, Auto Union had their own exceptional driver and there was little that Nuvolari (or for that matter Caracciola) could do to prevent 1936 being Rosemeyer's year. As for Bugatti and Maserati, they could not effectively compete and they knew it, withdrawing more and more from racing though occasionally toying with some half-hearted concession to modernity.

Alfa Romeo were at least trying, but they left their efforts rather late. The 750-kg formula was due to expire at the end of 1936, to be superseded by one which admitted supercharged engines of not more than $3\frac{1}{2}$ litres displacement or unsupercharged engines up to $4\frac{1}{2}$ litres, the actual capacity in each case being related to a sliding scale of minimum weight. It took some time to arrive at the final terms of this formula which were only published in February 1936, which left insufficient time for the design, manufacture and testing of new cars in time for 1937, so it was eventually conceded that the 750-kg formula would endure for a further year, after which the new formula would take effect in modified terms which limited a supercharged engine to 3 litres.

This remission was accepted by Auto Union, who made only slight changes to their 1936 car, modifying the steering and introducing two-leading-shoe brakes in what was already an extremely fast and thoroughly reliable car; but it was exploited by Mercedes-Benz, who had already profited from the hard lessons they had learned in designing a new chassis for the anticipated $3\frac{1}{2}$-litre formula, and this was rapidly adapted to take an entirely new engine larger than any they had previously thought feasible within the terms of the 750-kg formula. Like their earlier ones, it was a straight eight, constructed as ever along the lines that they had pioneered in their aero engines and which in turn had been inherited from Panhard at the very dawn of the century. That is, the cylinders were individual steel forgings upon which ports, plug bosses and the like were superimposed by welding, the whole being girt about with a welded water jacket of thin steel sheet. Split roller bearings were conceived for the big-end and main bearings, permitting a one-piece crankshaft to be turned from a solid billet; and the practice of using five main bearings in the M25 engine current from 1934 to 1936 inclusive was modified only to the extent of increasing the number of main bearings to nine. In all these respects—number and layout of cylinders, their constructions, the number and type of crankshaft bearings, and kindred details—the engine was a direct continuation of Fiat practice established in 1921 when their type 801 car first appeared to challenge the traditions established by Henry; but in their cylinder heads and valve gear Mercedes-Benz preferred the Henry pattern of four valves seated in a pent-roof combustion chamber at an included angle of 60 degrees and, of course, operated by twin overhead camshafts. These communicated with the valve stems almost directly, subject only to the interposition of finger followers to take the side thrust—just as Henry had used fingers interpolated between the cams and tappets of his 1913 Coupe de l'Auto Peugeot.

The alimentation of this engine, at least in its early stages of development, strictly followed Mercedes-Benz tradition with a Roots blower supplying two carburettors which in turn fed the cylinders by way of branched tubular manifolds. It seemed as though somebody influential at Daimler-Benz was obsessed with the evils of mounting the carburettor on the suction side of the blower—most notable of which, especially with a rich fuel-air mixture, is the tendency for fuel to be deposited by condensation and agglomeration on the inner surfaces of the manifold—because at a time when other aero-engine manufacturers such as Rolls-Royce were earnestly developing supercharger systems of such a kind, and exploiting to very good purpose the cooling effect of the fuel upon the compressed charge, the Daimler-Benz series of aero engines were supercharged with pure air, the fuel dosage being administered by direct injection into the cylinders.

In at least one detail, however, the M125 engine prepared for the 1937 Grand Prix season endorsed Rolls-Royce aero engine practice, though this in turn was something borrowed from America: the sodium-cooled exhaust valve was invented by the late S. D. Heron in 1922 when he was a civilian employee of the US Army at their McCook Field Aero Engine Center. This, though used extensively and enthusiastically by American aero-engine manufacturers thereafter, only materialised east of the Atlantic in the Rolls-Royce R Schneider Trophy racing aero engine in its developed 1931 form.

With due respect to such minor details, the M125 engine can be seen as constituting an amalgam of French, German and Italian practice in the creation of racing engines during the preceding quarter of a century. In it, all existing and earlier fashions, or all that was best of them, were reconciled and crystallised; and in it their lines of development can be seen to terminate. It is true that at a later stage in the history of Grand Prix racing, engines generically similar to this one were again to figure; but as we shall also see, this was more a case of opportunism than of *ad hoc* development, in that they merely emerged from established voiturette classes when the Grand Prix formula was changed in their favour:

The 1937 Mercedes-Benz M125 engine could therefore be considered the culminating work of a classical school that had developed over thirty years. The remainder of the W125 car (M stands for *Motor,* W for *Wagen* in the Mercedes-Benz lexicon) was, on the contrary, the first statement of new theories that were to hold sway until 1960. It demonstrated the importance, and constituted the means, of doing something that Mercedes-Benz and Auto Union in particular had been trying to do for three years: to make a car capable of utilising effectively the unparalleled power which could be put at its disposal. *Es irrt der Mensch so lang er streht*—and it is facile to agree when considering the errors of commission or omission in the cars of 1934 to 1936; but perhaps a

74 The great leap forward. . . .
Mercedes-Benz W125, the most
powerful GP car yet. The freedom
conferred by de Dion rear suspension
to have softer rear springing than ever
before was matched by a new
arrangement at the front of the W125.
As always in the weight-conscious
'750 kg' cars, details such as the
wishbone construction offer rewarding
study

better parallel may be found in the musicologist Hans Keller's description of the sketch-book technique of Beethoven and especially of Brahms in composing his C Minor Symphony—'years of muddle, errors, and stupidities, and then the great leap forward into genius'.

The new theme so triumphantly stated by Mercedes-Benz in 1937, and subsequently taken up by every other manufacturer instrumental in Grand Prix racing during the next generation, was that a racing car of sufficient power to be able to induce oversteer on demand could be built basically as an understeering vehicle with good directional stability. We have seen that at about this time Mercedes-Benz were inimical to the low polar moment of inertia championed by Auto Union. Instead they took particular pains to make the W125 with a high polar moment by arranging the two principal masses—the engine and the combined gearbox and final drive—at opposite extremities of a car of generous length. Of these the engine was inevitably the greater, a new one whose displacement was no less than 5·66 litres but whose weight was still only 494 lb, a mere 45 more than the weight of the original 3·36 engine of 1934. However, with the driver and the considerable fuel load massed around the rear of the car, the desired object was achieved. To a lesser extent this had been done in the W25 of the preceding years, and it was in the entirely new rear suspension of the W125 that its special significance resided. Mercedes-Benz did what Horch had done in a touring car two or three years earlier, what Miller had done in an Indianapolis car in 1931, and what de Dion had done in the nineteenth century: they tied the rear wheels together by a transverse tubular dead-axle beam which ensured that they would remain perpendicular to the road surface at all times, driving them from the chassis-mounted differential through universally jointed shafts that conferred complete freedom from transverse torque reaction. The axle beam, located longitudinally by radius arms and laterally by a peg or roller engaging in a vertical slot at the back of the transmission casing, was given a slight degree of torsional freedom by a central joint that prevented it from acting as an immensely stiff anti-roll bar, but was nevertheless so light that the total unsprung mass of the rear suspension was only a very little greater than that of a fully independent system. By this means all the exaggerated angular changes typical of the old swing axle motion were eliminated, and now it was possible to exploit the low ratio of unsprung to sprung mass by using springing much softer than before. This having been done at the rear, it was done at the front so as to produce properly matched springing, and there the total wheel movement was half as great again as in the W25. This, of course, made it imperative that the inaccuracies of the original steering gear be eliminated, and a great improvement was made in this respect.

It followed from this softer springing and more accurate suspension and steering geometry that the car's adhesion, roadholding, steering and handling should be appreciably better than what had gone before. So it proved: the W125 set completely new standards in its ability to make ample and effective use of prodigious power. And the power really was prodigious, for when after some early 1937 races Mercedes-Benz finally did away with their system of blowing air into the carburettor and substituted a suction carburettor on which the Roots supercharger drew to fill a new and uncharacteristic straight inlet manifold, the output of its engine rose to 545 bhp at 5,800 rev/min. This was with a basic testing fuel comprising equal parts of petrol and benzole; but the general practice was to race with a fuel rich in alcohol and laced with acetone, nitro benzine, and ether, which raised the peak power output to 572 bhp at 5,500 rev/min and produced even greater increments at lower engine speeds. Moreover, by the development of a special carburettor offering full-throttle mixture enrichment such as only alcohol fuels can tolerate, the final maximum power figure was elevated to 646 bhp at 5,800 rev/min.

This was power the like of which had never been known in Grand Prix racing before and has never been since. This was power that made it possible for the car to achieve 200 mph, and made it seem quite reasonable that it would be timed at 193 while racing in the Belgian GP at Spa. This, above all, was power that demanded no more valour of the driver than in previous years (possibly less, since the car as a whole was so much more roadworthy) but demanded the utmost discretion.

It is hardly necessary to rechronicle the events of 1937, to show with what imperious sway Mercedes-Benz dominated events, their ambitions frustrated only occasionally by the indifference of

75 *The type 145 Delahaye was a V12 GP car built in 1937/8, here with a two-seater body*

capricious misfortune and the spirited virtuosity of the indomitable Rosemeyer.

Having been admonished of the necessity of a very powerful racing car being conveniently dirigible, and of the desirability of high specific power output in the engine of such a car, Auto Union could reasonably be expected to reduce in 1938 the technical lead extended by Mercedes-Benz in 1937. While the 750-kg formula had endured, it had been open to them to pursue the theories of Porsche by making their engines even bigger, so that by the end of 1937 the C-type Auto Union disposed of 6,330 cm^3; but its power was still inferior to that of the 5,660 cm^3 M125 Mercedes-Benz and, as we have seen, its pernicious handling constituted a further handicap. For 1938, however, with a new formula in effect postulating supercharged 3-litre and unsupercharged 4½-litre engines, both these formidable German contenders for international honour would have to start again from scratch as far as their racing engines were concerned, and this might well prompt fundamental revisions to the rest of the cars' specification. They might, in fact, have been expected to fight hard for individual supremacy in 1938; and indeed the similarity of their solutions to the fresh problems imposed by the new formula ought to have ensured a year of particularly well-matched performances. But whereas Mercedes-Benz had nothing but time and metal to contend with in readying themselves for the new season, Auto Union had human problems of which the most important were the departure of Dr Porsche from the design office and of Bernd Rosemeyer from this world. As Auto Union were less wealthy than Mercedes-Benz, so they were slower in the development and final readying of the cars for serious racing, and both these personnel losses aggravated the delay.

Nevertheless it very soon transpired that both of the German firms had reacted in the same, indeed in the obvious, way to the constraints of the new formula, by recognising that when power per litre is the enforced criterion then success would be best assured by deploying high supercharge pressures and generous valve areas which in turn required large piston areas contributing to short stroke and thence a high rate of crankshaft revolution, from which followed a high rate of consumption of air and of fuel in unit time and therefore the utmost transformation of chemical energy into mechanical power. Thus directed along the road already well sign-posted by Fiat, Delage and Miller, both Auto Union and Mercedes-Benz arrived in 1938 at similar solutions. Each furnished a V12 engine with Roots superchargers boosting the induction to about 2 atmospheres, while a generous attention to mechanical refinement permitted crankshaft rates to exceed 7,000 rev/min. The eventual differences between the two were slight but significant: Auto Union contented themselves with a slightly longer stroke:bore ratio and therefore about 6 per cent less piston area than Mercedes Benz; they employed a higher geometrical compression ratio within their cylinders, which entailed a more modest boost pressure (1·9 atmospheres) than the 2·2 of the Mercedes-Benz; and while a greater adiabatic efficiency of the supercharger might be inferred from this, it was offset by a sacrifice in valve area consequent upon the continuation of established Auto Union practice in having but two valves per cylinder whereas Mercedes-Benz persisted with their four. The result of these differences was that while the Auto Union mustered a respectable 420 bhp at 7,000 rev/min, the Mercedes-Benz prevailed with 468 at 7,800.

In other respects the two appeared to borrow from each other. Mercedes-Benz adopted a five-speed gearbox in emulation of Auto Union and Delage before them, while Auto Union were at some pains to replace their independent rear suspension by a de Dion apparatus of refined design, immediately finding handling qualities greatly improved—a fact that the drivers were possibly better placed to appreciate now that the lateral fuel tanks allowed them to sit further aft than previously.

This change to the Auto Union did not suffice to give it parity with its rival in roadholding; for Mercedes-Benz, while retaining the 1937 chassis fundamentally unchanged, had the wit to offset the engine and transmission at an angle to the car's longitudinal

76 *Maximal piston area and minimal frontal area were pursued by Daimler-Benz in the 1938 W154 Mercedes-Benz 3-litre V12*

axis, thus bringing the propellor shaft alongside the driver whose seat could be lowered in consequence. With the regulations governing body width remaining unchanged, the reduction in overall height and in the height of the centre of gravity (to both of which the shape of the new engine contributed) reduced the frontal area and increased the stability of the car. The merits of this expedient were not lost upon the drivers, who found that the cars were not as much slower than their predecessors as the reduction in engine size might have suggested (certainly not as much as the sport's legislators presumably intended) while the improved road-holding allowed them to utilise a greater proportion of the engine's power for a greater proportion of the race distance, so that their lap speeds were only about 2 per cent lower than in 1937.

With all these factors in their favour, Mercedes-Benz enjoyed an exceptionally successful season in which Auto Union failed to win a race until the Italian Grand Prix in the autumn of the year.

This success disguised a deterioration in reliability which was the inevitable consequence of imposing greater loads on the engines. The thermodynamic measure of this increased stress was a deterioration in fuel consumption from about 4·5 to about 3 miles per gallon, so that the 3-litre Auto Union had to leave the start of a race carrying 66 gallons of fuel whereas the 6-litre machine was burdened by only 45. Even this provision could not exempt the cars from the need of attention during the course of a race: rapid and highly disciplined pit work therefore remained a feature of races, although the extravagant consumption of tyres that had reached desperate levels in 1937 became less of an embarrassment thereafter.

This dypsomaniac thirst of the highly supercharged 3-litre cars was to betray them at the beginning of 1938, when Mercedes-Benz suffered the shock and ignominy of defeat in the traditional open-

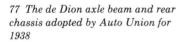

77 The de Dion axle beam and rear chassis adopted by Auto Union for 1938

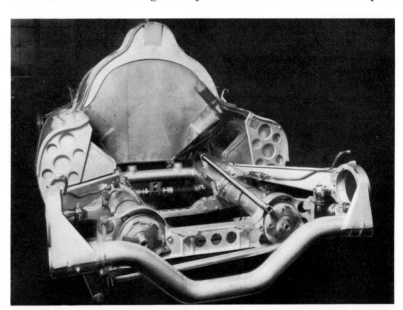

78 Although much lower, the 1938 Mercedes-Benz projected as much frontal area as the 1937 car, and weighed rather more

79 Caracciola during his winning
drive in the W154 during the 1938
Coppa Acerbo at Pescara. Alas, motor
racing in such natural conditions will
probably never be seen again

ing event of the season at Pau, victory going to an unsupercharged
Delahaye. On the intestine convolutions of the urban circuit the
Mercedes-Benz could not demonstrate much greater speed than
the far less powerful French car, which trailed the leading
Mercedes-Benz of Caracciola by only six seconds at half distance.
The need to refuel then took the German car into the pits for 50
seconds, during which it lost a lead that it was unable to recover.

As was the case with Talbot, Delahaye had been active in sports
car racing in the preceding years, evolving unsupercharged
4½-litre cars which—more by coincidence than foresight—were
technically acceptable in Grand Prix racing under the new formula even if they held no great promise of competitiveness. However, Delahaye were sufficiently encouraged to build a chassis of
some ingenuity, notably in its de Dion rear suspension where the
axle beam was located longitudinally by pairs of equal radius rods
at each side of the car, constituting parallelogram linkages which
relieved the axle beam of torsional loads and thus simplified its
construction. Into this chassis with a somewhat clumsy single-
seater body there eventually went a V12 engine with pushrod-
operated overhead valves and dual ignition, *prima facie* a feeble

device mustering only 250 bhp but, as we have seen, capable of running non-stop throughout a full-length Grand Prix.

If this Delahaye, supported by the six-cylinder Talbot and occasionally by new versions of the type 59 Bugatti, were all that could be expected of France at the time, some positive response to the German challenge might have been expected from Italy. Surprisingly, the most aggressive representative of that once supreme nation was a new Maserati, new in that it had a 3-litre supercharged engine but otherwise of hoary age. Its eight cylinders were in effect a duplication of the four-cylinder 1½-litre car's, its rear axle was still of the live variety controlled after a fashion by half-elliptic leaf springs—but on sporadic occasions it displayed an altogether unexpected turn of speed, so that in the hands of Villoresi and Count Trossi it sometimes challenged the German cars, albeit briefly and at great cost to its staying power.

Alfa Romeo were far less convincing: with some overt pride they produced three new engines satisfying the requirements of the new formula, all of them supercharged and every one of them a bitter disappointment. One was a straight eight giving 300 bhp from cylinders whose stroke:bore ratio of 1·45:1 was by this time positively antique. Another was a V12 giving 320 horsepower; the third a V16 giving 350. These three engines had one extraordinary thing in common: every one of them was rated at a mere 6,000 rev/min, suggesting that Alfa Romeo designs suffered from an impediment that the progressive reduction of stroke from 100 mm to 70 could do nothing to overcome.

It is possible that this impediment was political rather than technical, and that these cars were put up as a deliberate false front to dispel rumours of a movement that was gathering force in Italy with consequences that we shall shortly see were of lasting if

80 Alfa Romeo 308 driven by Sommer at Pau in the GP of 1939

135

81 *The 1½-litre voiturettes had a profound influence on the sport in the late 1930s. Here Villoresi drives the 6C Maserati at Monza in 1938*

varied effect. We have already seen that from 1935 onwards the Italians and all others had fallen back before the regimented onslaught of the newly inspired and materially encouraged German firms, so that the faint echoes of what once had been a great rivalry between nations remained only as an indistinct accompaniment to the rivalry between the German teams. The want of sport, of support, and of international interest, was to some extent supplied by lesser teams such as the French and by individual amateur entrants driving whatever inadequate machines they could procure; but there was a general tendency to decry the luxury, the professionalism and the quasi-military organisation of the two teams who were then supreme and virtually unchallenged. 'But it is always easy as well as agreeable,' as the historian Gibbon told us, 'for the inferior ranks of mankind to claim a merit from their contempt of that pomp and pleasure which fortune has placed beyond their reach.' The virtue of those who affected to disdain the achievements of the conquerors was very frequently guarded by poverty and ignorance.

These would-be participants, whom a common and ineluctable austerity had welded into a dissident majority, organised a revival of interest in the 1½-litre class which had on a number of previous occasions provided a second class of racing. These voiturettes, constrained by enforced economy to abjure the costly privileges of engineering radicalism, were not the less elegant for being relatively simple, and their growing popularity was assured when the Italians conspired to take their own course without reference to the impositions of international regulations. The first steps

82 *The Alta had sliding-pillar independent suspension in 1939 and by British standards was a moderately successful voiturette. Its engine led to greater things after World War II*

83 *One start, one win—a racing record equalled by one other 1½-litre GP car, the 1927 Fiat 806—made the W165 Mercedes-Benz V8 politically very successful. Note the two compressors providing two-stage supercharging, introduced earlier in 1939 by Daimler-Benz in the W163*

84 *The W165 looked very much like the W163 Mercedes-Benz*

towards this were taken in 1938, when Alfa Romeo withdrew from their arrangement with the Scuderia Ferrari that had looked after their racing interests for so many years, and resumed control of their own racing fortunes, setting the engineer Colombo (with Ferrari to assist him) to design a 1½-litre racing car that was in many respects a scaled-down version of their last Grand Prix car. In common with that it featured swing-axle rear suspension, Porsche-type front suspension, a tubular chassis, hydraulic brakes, and a gearbox integrated with the final drive. The engine was a straight eight, and was tantamount to one bank of cylinders from the V16 Grand Prix engine. Altogether it was a little car of great promise which was eventually to be fulfilled, and it was not alone: for Maserati also took the trouble to perfect a very fast 1½-litre car. In Britain ERA sought to do likewise with their hitherto

85 *Extensive tankage was vital to the W163: its two-stage supercharged V12 used alcohol-based fuel at an unprecedented rate, and the driver had to sit almost surrounded by fuel*

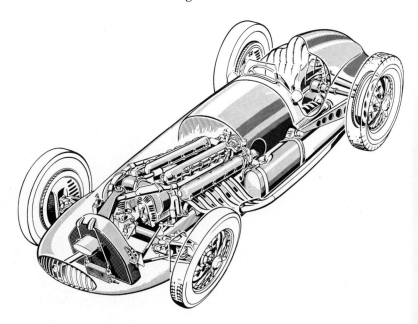

rather tall and square-rigged six-cylinder cars, but this was probably not at all material in influencing the Italian Federation when they announced that all races in Italy would be confined to 1½-litre cars in 1939.

As a means of ensuring some Italian victories, such a scheme seemed assured of success; but it did not entirely have the expected results. Auto Union, recognising a probable future trend from which they were unlikely to profit, seriously contemplated abandoning Grand Prix racing; but they were persuaded to continue, and in fact they began the design of a 1½-litre car against the eventuality of it being necessary. Mercedes-Benz were in no doubt about their continuing in Grand Prix racing, and they responded to the Italian challenge with fine vigour and spirit, designing and building in the space of six months a 1½-litre V8 engine which, mounted in a chassis essentially similar to that of the 1938 Grand Prix car, qualified them to give the Tripoli Grand Prix the support which they had always given it, despite its inclusion within the terms of the Italian national ruling. The fact that this car, the W165, scored a runaway win in this, the only race of its career, gave the Italians humiliating confirmation of their despair.

Auto Union, who were to win only two of the seven events regulated by more authentic Grand Prix rules in 1939, nevertheless had some cause for satisfaction with the performance of their cars, and indeed with that of the driver Nuvolari whom they acquired late in 1938 to step into the breach left by Rosemeyer. Yet it was Mercedes-Benz who continued to prevail in engineering merit, in race results and in general esteem. Both the German teams had subscribed for 1939 to the aviation doctrine of two-stage supercharging, an idea that was certainly not novel inasmuch as the American Chadwick had employed three-stage supercharging as long ago as 1908. It is never too late to mend: by setting two Roots

86 Auto Union 3-litre V12 driven by Hasse in the 1939 Belgian GP

87 The 1939 Mercedes-Benz probably had the best roadholding of any pre-war GP car. Here von Brauchitsch drives in the French GP . . .

88 . . . and Caracciola in the German GP. With better roadholding and braking than ever before, the W163 created new lap records that were to stand in some cases for nearly two decades

blowers in series, Mercedes-Benz and Auto Union realised inlet manifold pressures of 2·6 and 2·65 atmospheres respectively, pressures that could not have been achieved by single-stage supercharging except at great cost in adiabatic efficiency and power consumption. As it was, they were able without increasing the crankshaft rate of either engine to raise bmep to unprecedented levels, with the gratifying result of 483 bhp for the former and 485 for the latter. The difference between these figures is so slight as to be within the margins of experimental error, but it should not escape notice that Auto Union had overcome what had in the previous year appeared a severe handicap in that they retained two valves per cylinder while Mercedes-Benz had four.

This parity of power was not attended by equality of execution. The Auto Union presented less frontal area than the W163 Mercedes-Benz, which now aped it in the use of side tanks which dictated an increase in body width. However, Mercedes-Benz contrived a body of better shape, more completely enclosing the suspension and evidently inducing less drag since the outright maximum speeds of the two cars were virtually identical. Moreover, they had now perfected their steering geometry, whereas that of the Auto Union's Porsche front suspension was necessarily imperfect; and perhaps most important of all, they had developed new brakes of a size, power, and thermal stability that combined to make them at once more efficient and more durable than those of any other. The most distinctive feature of these was the provision of helical cooling fins around the periphery of each drum, the turbine-like blading being shrouded by a flimsy band of aluminium to ensure the most faithful possible flow of air over the surfaces of the fins, the flow thus induced also drawing air through the interior of the drum so as directly to cool the friction linings. In fact, some later calculations by the Auto Union designer Eberan von Eberhorst admit (somewhat elliptically) that a 10 per cent improvement in braking would produce a greater increment of lap speed than a like increase in engine performance; and since the improvement in the braking of the Mercedes-Benz appears to be of at least this order, whereas their other performance factors differed merely in the matter of a 6 per cent larger frontal area for the Mercedes-Benz, it is not difficult to infer a compelling reason for the superiority of the Mercedes-Benz. We also know that the refinements of its suspension design, coupled with the improvement in the ratio of sprung to unsprung masses favoured by the high minimum weight demanded by the prevailing formula, allowed the W163 to enjoy softer springing than ever before, springing that was lower in rate and more profound in amplitude

89 Even the supple long-travel springing of the 1939 cars was not always enough. This picture was taken during the Belgrade GP on 3 September 1939, the day war broke out

90 The last GP of the 1930s was won by a V12 Auto Union at Belgrade, driven (as here) by Nuvolari. The Mercedes-Benz team having had such a good season, it was a rare treat

than any racing car had enjoyed for a very long time, if indeed ever. The benefit of this would be manifest as improved roadholding, which we know to be of even greater value than improved braking in increasing lap speeds. Whatever the justification, the W163 was generally regarded as having the best-developed roadworthiness of any racing car then current or superseded; and it is demonstrable that on any circuit reasonably taxing all the properties critical to the viability and success of a road racing Grand Prix car, the W163 was the fastest yet seen when racing came to an end in 1939—even though the last word went to Nuvolari with an Auto Union in the Yugoslav Grand Prix, held in Belgrade on the very day that war was declared.

In 1945 when the official state of war was replaced by a shocked and troubled peace, sporadic attempts were made to reassemble the scattered remains of Europe's motor racing inheritance and weld them into a coherent whole. The international governing body of the sport was formed anew, and in February 1946 agreed the terms of a new Grand Prix formula. In arriving at these they listened attentively to restatements of the opinion that had been gaining ground in the late pre-war years, to the effect that it was demonstrably unreasonable to equate a 3-litre supercharged car with an unsupercharged $4\frac{1}{2}$-litre, and that the supercharged $1\frac{1}{2}$-litre machines as exemplified by the machines current in the voiturette class of 1938 and 1939 were at once more comparable with the unblown $4\frac{1}{2}$-litre car and more practical, economical, realistic and safe than the blown 3-litre. While the evidence available lent strong support to this view, it was an inductive rather than a deductive logic which confirmed it: simple engineering reason was less persuasive than the necessity of catering for cars that were known to be available.

The $1\frac{1}{2}$-litre V8 Mercedes-Benz cars, the type W165 of Tripoli fame, were known to be in Switzerland, having been interned there during the war; but there were legal barriers to their owners recovering them, and in any case the German manufacturers were not being permitted to belong to the FIA for the time being. This was of course an entirely political decision, but temporarily of no moment since neither Auto Union nor Mercedes-Benz could afford to go racing yet. Italy was more fortunate in still having the $1\frac{1}{2}$-litre straight-eight Alfa Romeo cars that had competed so successfully in the subordinate races of 1938 and 1939. Indeed they had continued racing into 1940, for it was not until the summer of that year that Italy was drawn into the war; and in the Tripoli Grand Prix of that year they won at a higher speed than that of the W165 that had beaten them in 1939.

There were also a shoal of Maserati cars about, most of them the four-cylinder model of 1939, although there were some of the old six-cylinder $1\frac{1}{2}$-litre cars in circulation as well. The 1939 car, the type 4CL, had single-stage supercharging and a simple chassis whose channel section side members were braced by a substantial cast alloy cross-member which served as oil tank and seat substructure. Independent front suspension by wishbones was sprung by torsion bars, reflecting an increase in the popularity of these media in the late 1930s, while the simple live rear axle was located by radius arms and sprung by quarter-elliptic leaves emphasising the Maserati tradition of simple construction such as an independent entrant could maintain. This did not, however, mean that its engine was lightly to be dismissed: for by virtue of a stroke:bore ratio of unity it boasted a piston area only $6\frac{1}{4}$ per cent less than that of the eight-cylinder Alfa Romeo, while as a result of four surprisingly large valves being fitted into each combustion chamber it was not inferior to that car in inlet valve area. In most of its mechanical details it resembled the 3-litre straight-eight Maserati of 1938, the principal alterations being in the use of finger followers for the cams instead of the piston tappets of the earlier and larger engine.

For real crudity one could look to the $1\frac{1}{2}$-litre ERA, of which several examples existed in Britain. The shapes and chassis of most of these represented very little advance over the typical Italian cars of 1932, although a good deal of praiseworthy detail improvement had been applied—much of it by the consultant Reid Railton, who had already amassed considerable experience working on privately owned Maseratis in the years immediately preceding 1934 when the first ERA chassis were laid down. It was, however, the engine of the ERA which wanted refinement, stemming as it did from a road-going Riley of overrated quality: a six-cylinder design of long stroke and small bore, its pushrod valve actuation and its ill-supported crankshaft (belying the rigidity of the deep crankcase) and the sheer weight of cast iron in the main engine block condemned it as generically inferior to almost all its rivals. It had in some cases been supercharged by a vane-type compressor, the efficiency of which allowed high boost pressures and respectable power output; but reliability demanded the use of a Roots blower at necessarily lower boost for any event such as a Grand Prix in which stamina was essential, and in this case the engine was reckoned to be doing well if it generated 190 bhp.

An improved version of this engine, with bigger bore and shorter stroke, higher boost and lower reliability, was installed in a chassis of much more modern concept in 1939, this being the E-type ERA of which two examples had been made and were still in circulation. The chassis was generally an imitation of the late pre-war Mercedes-Benz, save that the independent front suspension was of the Porsche type as first tried on the C-type ERA and earlier, of course, on the Auto Union. As much as 260 bhp was claimed for this car, and it ought to have been reasonably competitive; but the times when it went well were distinguished by their infrequency rather than by their duration.

No better executed and not much better conceived, the Alta was the only other British example of a car complying with the new formula. Designed in 1939, it had a tubular frame with independent suspension of all four wheels by wishbones and rubber blocks in compression—an excellent idea, in that the rate of such a spring can easily be adjusted to suit virtually any requirement, while the dynamic hysteresis of rubber can provide a good deal of inherent damping, but an idea that was a trifle precocious. The engine of the Alta was more promising, with twin overhead camshafts crowning its four cylinders in which the bore, stroke and piston area were the same as in the 4CL Maserati —though the number of valves was only half as great and the power output appreciably less.

Opposed to all these supercharged 1½-litre cars were the French contingent, which were unsupercharged machines derived from sports cars and therefore generally rather heavy and ungainly. The V12 Delahaye has already been mentioned, but more important in the post-war period were a number of six-cylinder Talbots. Most of these were 4-litre machines, with two inclined valves in each hemispherical head being operated by rockers (of extremely disparate size) with which the single low camshaft communicated by pushrods. With one exception the bodies were offset single-seaters betraying their sports car origin, but that one had lapped the circuit at Reims in 1939 at 105 mph, which was almost as fast as the average speed maintained by the winning Auto Union for the full race distance, pit stops and all. In this, however, lay a clue to the supposed virtue of the Talbots, this being their ability to run throughout the longest race without the need to stop for more fuel or tyres. The cars might not be very fast, but they had a most

91 *Voiturettes promoted: the Alfa Romeo team of type 158 straight-eight 1½-litre cars at Berne in 1948 for the Swiss GP*

agreeable ability to keep on keeping on, which was to stand them in good stead on a number of occasions.

Such was the motley assortment of cars that could populate the starting grids of early post-war races. The events of 1946 are best dismissed as unco-ordinated and unrepresentative. Already, however, Alfa Romeo were at some pains to develop the engine of their type 158 car, adopting two-stage supercharging to raise its power output to 254 bhp at 7,500 rev/min. For 1947 they raised the boost pressure further and fielded the car with 265 bhp, while Maserati also embraced two-stage supercharging. So did the French government Arsenal, which began work on a blown 1½-litre car commissioned by the government and designed by that same Lory who had developed the early V12 Delage of Plancton and then gone on to create for 1927 the memorable straight-eight Delage. He now devised a V8 of no great style but quite considerable power, 270 bhp being claimed at 8,000 rev/min and 2 atmospheres boost. The chassis was all independently sprung and set about with many solecisms, the majority of which never became fully apparent because the organisation was not equal to its task

92 San Remo model Maserati, the 4CLT/48, driven by Gonzales

93 (above right) Anthony Lago's Talbots had six cylinders, three carburettors, and two camshafts communicating with the valves by pushrods and rockers

and the cars were never raced. Nevertheless the design is of interest in confirming the current trends of thought, which were all directed towards the use of two valves per cylinder rather than of four, Maserati being the notable exception. As an inevitable corollary of a limited displacement formula, designers were endorsing the principle of large piston area, high crankshaft rates and fairly high boost pressures, accepting the penalties of severe mechanical stress, poor thermal efficiency and the limitations imposed by the current state of the art among providers of lubricants, spark plugs, ignition systems, bearings, and so on. No more thoroughgoing demonstration of the potentialities and hazards of such a philosophy was ever presented than by the V16 $1\frac{1}{2}$-litre hypercharged BRM, the design of which was begun at this time and the future of which was to be plagued with more bad luck, bad management, empty patriotism, and ill-judged publicity than any other racing car ever suffered before or since.

If the BRM as it eventually turned out was to constitute a particular from which inductive logicians could argue the general fallacy of the small supercharged high-speed engine, the type 158 Alfa Romeo was evidence from which the deductive kind could show that the general principles of such a design had been particularly well validated. Alfa Romeo concentrated on raising manifold pressures all the time, so that during the 1948 season they arrived at 310 bhp, still at the original 7,500 rev/min. This made a vivid comparison with the 225 obtained from the single-stage version at the end of 1939, and the 190 (at 6,500 rev/min) given when the first tests were conducted on the engine in 1938.

By the end of 1948 it was clear that there was nothing capable of competing with the Alfa Romeos. They ran easily, usually to team orders, and displaying a reliability the like of which has no peer in Grand Prix racing. The best of their rivals, the Maseratis, were forced to pursue them at a respectable distance, though the introduction of the San Remo version at that particular circuit in 1948 gave them a new lease of life and credibility. This model, otherwise known as the 4CLT/48, was developed after the departure of the Maserati brothers from their company, which they left in the hands of Orsi, who continued the development of the tubular frame, increased two-stage boost, and added a new form of independent front suspension featuring inboard helical springs worked by cantilevered wishbones, for which the designer Alfieri could claim the credit. These emendations resulted in a very handy car disposing of 260 bhp at 7,500 rev/min and 2·6 atmospheres boost, a figure which might well have been considerably higher had the valve timing not been so modest as to afford only 50 degrees overlap. By contrast, the Alfa Romeo had the most ferocious valve timing, not so much to ensure good cylinder filling as to secure internal cooling of the engine by a generous blow-down of scavenging air heavy with alcohol. This, of course, made its fuel consumption extremely heavy, even worse than that of the 1939 3-litre cars.

Meanwhile Anthony Lago of the Talbot company, now solely French but enjoying the services of designer Becchia who, it will be remembered, originated from the Fiat design office in the early 1920s, was encouraged to pursue his notions of fuel economy and his hopes of victory by staying power, and in 1948 produced a 4½-litre car whose engine differed principally from its slightly smaller ancestor in its much improved valve gear: there were now two camshafts set reasonably high on each side of the cylinder block, communicating via fairly short push rods with simple rocker gear to operate the two big inclined valves in each hemispherical head. Nevertheless it remained a pushrod engine and in other respects a decidedly old-fashioned one, for its stroke:bore ratio was 1·13:1, its 250 bhp were produced at a mere 5,000 rev/min, and the modest peak-power bmep of 144 lb/in² belied the impression of good breathing given by three Solex carburettors drawing from a cold-air plenum chamber.

Against such opposition the Alfa Romeos were so easily able to prevail that the Italian firm felt justified in withdrawing from racing in 1949 in order to save money that, had it been spent on a racing programme for that year, could hardly have caused any more to be proven than had been already. As it happened, this abstention coincided with the first appearance of a Grand Prix Ferrari that could be taken seriously—as distinct from the under-powered oversteering miniaturised monstrosity of 1948—so that Italy's contribution to the sport remained the most important.

The original GP Ferrari of 1948 had been based by Colombo on his design for a 2-litre sports car which had appeared in 1947. The idea was to make everything very small—not least the cylinders, which would make up in number what they lacked in size. So he created a beautiful little V12 with overhead camshafts and

single-stage supercharging, and the first stroke:bore ratio of less than unity since the 1939 W165 Mercedes-Benz. Despite this short stroke (52·5 mm) the engine was not allowed to run at high revolutions, peak power being set at 7,500 rev/min. In spite of this evidence, which points to a weakness somewhere in the design, most of the engine components were obviously only lightly stressed, and it is possible that if the light weight and low frontal area resulting from the car's smallness had not been accompanied by diabolical handling qualities from a chassis of deplorable mediocrity, the original GP Ferrari might have been effective as a rival for the San Remo Maserati, if not for the type 158 Alfa Romeo. Matters were improved greatly for 1949 by an extension of the wheelbase and detailed revision to the independent rear suspension; but the swinging half-axles at the rear continued to exercise their usual disorientating effect and the car was still very difficult to drive. It was nevertheless fairly successful, mainly due to the want of worthy opposition.

Far more successful, and deservedly so, was the new Ferrari which appeared in time for the Italian GP at Monza in the September of 1949: this had a new chassis (still welded from oval-section tube), two-stage supercharging, and de Dion rear suspension, and with it Alberto Ascari made the most of improved roadholding and 305 bhp to win convincingly, albeit at a lower speed than the Alfa Romeos had displayed on the same track in the previous year.

Ferrari himself was not a man to be deluded by an easy victory of this nature. He was not convinced that the blown 1½-litre solution was the correct one, and he had been impressed by the threats often presented by the big unblown Talbots whenever his own cars had to stop of refuelling. Surely a proper modern and efficient unsupercharged car could match the thirsty little blown machines? This became a matter of some dissension between Ferrari and Colombo, something that Ferrari could seldom, if ever, tolerate. He had a splendid design team in Colombo and Bazzi, who had also come from Alfa Romeo and was yet another of the original 1921 Fiat school; but he had rid himself of good men before and was quite prepared to do it again.

Colombo went and Lampredi came—a young but not entirely unblooded designer who had been responsible for an iconoclastic Isotta-Fraschini project that never reached fruition through lack of funds and/or company enthusiasm. Lampredi was convinced that a big unsupercharged engine would be a success, and worked quietly on a new engine which made a surprise debut in 1950 for the Belgian GP, where it was two seconds slower than the two-stage 1½-litre Ferrari. At this point in its development, however, its displacement was only 3·3 litres, and by 30 July when it had been increased to 4·1 it showed at Geneva that it could match the pace of the Alfa Romeo. It reached its full 4½ litres in time for the Italian GP in the September of the year, when it shattered the existing lap record in practice and was again faster than all the Alfa Romeos except that driven by Fangio.

Many and varied were the pointers to the great merit of Lam-

95 *The Dunlop tyres on this well-restored V12 Ferrari are anachronistic*

96 *The Talbot-Lago had a Wilson preselector gearbox: four forward ratios and marche arrière*

predi's design. Not the least was the fact that the type 158 Alfa Romeo had been so much further developed by Alfa Romeo for the 1950 season that it had been renumbered the type 159. The breathing of the engine (both in and out) had been laboriously studied, and the valve gear had been modified, so that the crankshaft could now run at 8,500 rev/min, at which 350 bhp coincided with 3,900 feet per minute piston speed and 360 lb/in² mean effective pressure. As for the fuel consumption, it was worse than ever, about 1·5 miles per gallon, and the level of stresses within the engine were such that it had to be given a complete overhaul after every race. Firms such as Ferrari could hardly afford to conduct their affairs in this indulgent way, and the unblown Ferrari was much less demanding. If anything it represented the triumph of light weight and vast piston area over high power and mechanical complexity: for its piston area in the final full 4½-litre form amounted to no less than 93·6 square inches, rivalled only by the C type Auto Union in all the racing years since 1912. This was the result of the V12 engine following the already established fashion of large bore and short stroke, its cylinder dimensions allowing such an ample valve area that stresses in the valve operating train could be minimised and one single camshaft deemed sufficient above each cylinder head. Thus, although it was a big engine, it could be made a light engine; and it was actually lighter than the much more compact 1½-litre BRM, which also showed up in Grand Prix racing for the first time in 1950.

On paper the BRM should have out-performed the Ferrari and the Alfa Romeo and indeed anything else that might have offered itself for comparison, pre-war cars included. Here was a design in which nothing but bad management and incompetent workmanship had been allowed to stand in the way of theory, in which a chassis little more advanced in concept than that of the E-type ERA (from the drawing board of the same designer, Peter Berthon) carried an engine intended from the outset to have as many cylinders, as much piston area, and as little frontal area, as feasible, and

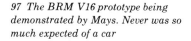

97 *The BRM V16 prototype being demonstrated by Mays. Never was so much expected of a car*

to operate at crankshaft rates and manifold pressures perhaps even higher than had been thought possible. If the utmost power were to be derived from an engine of limited displacement, there could be no doubt but that this was the way to achieve it. Here was an engine with sixteen tiny cylinders, the bore and stroke merely 49·5 and 47·8 mm respectively so that the piston area was nearly 48 square inches. Cylinders were arranged in two banks set 135 degrees apart, and the potential hazards of torsional vibration of a long and perhaps slender crankshaft were held at bay by the simple expedient of taking the drive from the middle of the crankshaft— not only for driving the camshaft and other auxiliaries as Alfa Romeo and Salmson had done many years earlier, but also the power output to the transmission. There were two valves to each hemispherical combustion chamber, operated by twin camshafts above each cylinder head and finger followers.

Here was an engine that ought to be capable of running up to 12,000 rev/min, a figure that was to seem modest when compared with the astronomical figure of 39,000 of the centrifugal supercharger impeller. This component, a two-stage device designed for BRM by Rolls-Royce, was a vital feature of the engine which was expected eventually to give 600 bhp, which would be equivalent to a peak-power bmep of 435 lb/in². Alas, this was never realised, though in its later days when any hope of Formula 1 victories had perforce been forgotten but development continued, the engine did produce an amazing 525 bhp on the test bench. In practice it never gave more than 485 in a car, nor indeed was it expected to, for shortage of power at peak revs was a complaint never levelled against it. This was true even in 1950 and 1951, when its output was 430 bhp at 11,000 rev/min. Not that it raced very often, a deplorable series of failures to start and several failures to finish making the car an object of almost universal ridicule, much of which may well have been deserved since many of its shortcomings appeared then and still appear to have been the result of petty ineptitudes on the part of those building or preparing the car.

Undoubtedly its greatest handicap in racing, however, was imposed by the induction system. Much has been made of the

98 BRM V16 losing the Spanish GP at Barcelona in 1951

unsuitability of the centrifugal compressor for a road racing car, based on its delivery characteristics which involve an increase in boost pressure proportional to the square of the increase of rotational speed. As applied to the BRM, this meant that the bmep and torque curves rose throughout the engine's effective operating range, so that if the accelerator were depressed while negotiating

151

a corner with the engine turning at a modest rate—say 8,000 rev/min—then as the engine speed built up the surplus horsepower available might increase with speed until the point could be reached when the limit of tyre adhesion would be passed and wheel-spin of a furious and incorrigible nature would intrude, robbing the driver of control. Because of this handicap it was not possible for the BRM to be driven through corners under power in the four-wheel-drift style that was accepted at the time as being the fastest way to get through a corner, and one that had been developed most impressively in the late 1930s. So the BRM was slower than its rivals through corners, and since it developed so little torque at anything less than about 9,000 rev/min it often lagged behind them on acceleration out of corners as well.

For all this the centrifugal supercharger was held responsible, ignoring the fact that as designed by Rolls-Royce it embodied a system of vortex throttling which would have held the boost pressure virtually constant above 10,000 rev/min, enabling it to be elevated at lower speeds without becoming excessive at higher, and thus correcting the unsuitable basic characteristic of the blower. The engine would then have been left with the inestimable advantage of operating at a manifold pressure considerably higher than could be achieved by any other type of mechanically-driven supercharger, the centrifugal kind being considerably more efficient than those commonly employed in racing and having in particular been developed to an incomparable level of efficiency by Rolls-Royce. There is, or should be, no doubt that in specifying this type of supercharger Berthon made the right decision; but there is equally good cause to deplore the fact that it was never furnished with its vortex throttles—and even more that a decision was taken to limit maximum valve acceleration to only 52,000 feet per second per second (only one third of the acceleration suffered by the pistons!), with the result that valve lift was limited to only a quarter of an inch and the breathing of the engine unreasonably and unnecessarily stifled. This was why, when certain empiricists argued that the way to improve the power output at low speeds was to increase the supercharger drive ratio and thus the low-speed boost, the improvement in realised power did not match the increased supercharger performance. The drive ratio was increased by 24 per cent, resulting in a delivery of 485 bhp at 10,000 rev/min; but by the time this was done, Grand Prix racing had passed on and left the BRM to find minor events in which to live out its last active years.

Deeply though it was felt in Britain, the tragedy of the BRM's failure was but a small part of the drama that was being played out on the motor racing circuits of Europe as the unsupercharged 4½-litre V12 Ferrari went from strength to strength. The type 159 Alfa Romeo was holding its own, but by the barest of limits, and by 1951 it was being squeezed so hard as to render over 385 bhp at 9,500 rev/min and 3 atmospheres boost, and no less than 404 at 10,500 rev/min. It was not recommended to the drivers that they avail themselves of this final increment, for it represented a

1954–5 Lancia

THE EXPRESSION OF TECHNICAL PROGRESS enjoyed no greater variety or excitement in the history of Grand Prix racing than in the period which began in 1954, under the rules of the new formula which permitted unsupercharged engines of $2\frac{1}{2}$ litres and supercharged engines of 0·75 litre. The number of different solutions offered at this time made the sport more interesting than ever before or since. Unquestionably the supreme example was the $2\frac{1}{2}$-litre Mercedes-Benz; but the D50 Lancia, which appeared late in 1954, was in fact as fast and in some ways more prophetic. It has been conjectured that the D50 might, if adapted to modern tyres, have served as the basis of a competitive Grand Prix car a dozen years after its introduction; but its tragedy was not that it was too soon for its time, but that it was too late for its purpose. The Lancia firm found themselves unable to sustain the expenditure necessary to keep their cars competitive, and the D50 was disposed of lock, stock, and barrel to Ferrari whose own cars had failed miserably in the face of much more modern exotic designs; but the Lancia was in many ways very modern indeed. In some respects, as in its rejection of the popular high polar moment of inertia, it was at least individual; in others, such as its use of the V-8 engine as a structural contributor to the chassis, it was ahead of its time, while the outrigger fuel tanks carried between front and rear wheels recognised possibilities that were not explored again until the late 1960s. Even its suspension was intriguing, notably in the location of the De Dion rear axle so that its suspension was undamped in roll. Only in a few details did it display any shortcomings, as for example in the rudimentary design of its original exhaust system; but it was in more than detail that it was revised when it came into Ferrari's hands.

1954-5 Mercedes-Benz

THERE WERE CARS REPLETE WITH INNOVATIONS before the W196, and more innovators that came later; but there can seldom have been a first-class racing car so full of heterodoxies as the 2½ Grand Prix Mercedes-Benz, and never such a car so successful. Defeated only twice in 1954 and only once in the following year, the Mercedes-Benz dominated Grand Prix racing during both seasons. That it did so in a form that bore little superficial relationship to the great racing cars that had preceded it, whether from its parent factory or from others, indicates the value of the original thinking that it represented; that it did not in fact go as fast as might be expected betrays the lack of really effective competition during much of the time that the car was current; and that the other constructors of racing cars were reluctant to follow the Daimler-Benz example may be explained in some cases by their almost frantic lack of money, and in others by their almost resentful lack of imagination.

The writer can find no better words than these, his own, culled from a previous work, to summarise what was outstanding about the car with which Daimler-Benz celebrated their return to Grand Prix racing. Whether as a dramatic streamliner or a matter of-fact bare-wheeler, the W196 remains the most outstanding racing car yet seen. Yet, successful though it was, it was apparently not as fast as it should have been. The explanation of this is that the car had been originally intended to enjoy a longer competitive life than it was permitted, being designed with a view to progressive development over a span of four years. The car pioneered a large number of features that were to pass out of currency when it was withdrawn, only to be adopted afresh by other racing car constructors later; and indeed the plans that Daimler-Benz had for its development included features that have to be explored by others.

99 Alfa Romeo 159 at last losing a race—the 1951 British GP at Silverstone . . .

100 . . . where Gonzales broke the run of the supercharged cars with this 1950 model V12 4½-litre Ferrari

101 The 1951 Ferrari beat the Alfa Romeo team in the German and Italian Grands Prix. Here Ascari leads a Gordini over the Monza cobbles

*102 It took the BRM five years to
attain mechanical reliability. By then
it was prodigiously fast, wonderfully
noisy, and too late—Grand Prix racing
could not wait for it*

piston speed of 4,750 feet per minute, but undoubtedly they made good use of the power available at 9,500 rev/min and 4,300 feet per minute. However, sheer power was not enough, and improvements to the chassis were recognised as long overdue. In earlier years the Alfa Romeo team had never been hard pressed to win, and they drove circumspectly, never taking risks on corners since they could easily gain all that was necessary on the straights. Setright vividly recollects seeing three Alfa Romeos, in line ahead, braking early and cautiously for an impending corner while a 4½-litre Talbot (driven, so far as memory allows, by Giraud-Cabantous) passed the whole lot and skimmed through the corner ahead of them, after which the whole lot repassed the Talbot and went on their way serene and uncatchable. That was in 1950; in the following years things were very different, and the Alfa Romeo drivers needed all the new stability and control afforded by the de Dion rear suspension lately acquired in order to maintain lap speeds that would keep them in touch with the V12 Ferrari, now mustering 380 bhp and terrifying them with its promise of running a non-stop race. Eventually, at the British GP in 1951, the inevitable happened: try as Fangio might in the fastest of the Alfas, taking the bends at Silverstone in great drifting swathes of precarious virtuosity, he could not prevent his compatriot Gonzales from winning with a Ferrari that was, in fact, a 1950 model.

This was the beginning of the end. In the German GP Ferrari again defeated Alfa Romeo, as they did in the Italian GP; and although in races at Bari and Barcelona the Alfa Romeos managed to win again, everybody recognised that the supertuned supercharged small-capacity engine had shot its bolt. Thirteen years after it was designed, the Alfa Romeo had met its match, and it offered no scope for further development. Its manufacturers got out while the going was good, having amassed just enough points to assure themselves of the World Championship for 1951, and generally making it known that since they had won this yet again they might just as well withdraw from racing. They had good cause to be proud of their achievements, which will bear a statistical comparison with those of any other car, but they were good enough strategists to know when to stop. They had, in fact, already designed and built later and more modern cars, including a rear-engined flat 12 and a most intriguing front-engined four-wheel-drive car whose pilot sat in the extreme tail; but their run of past successes could scarcely be bettered, and it would be all too easy for some unforeseen difficulty to impair their good reputation.

There had been hopes that others might step into the breach vacated by Alfa Romeo. Mercedes-Benz were known to be working on a new 1½-litre car, Cisitalia had built one to the designs of Porsche and it was conceivable that funds might have been found to support it, and there was still the possibility that the BRM would soon justify itself. All these were examples of the highly supercharged 1½-litre car, the large unsupercharged engine being an alternative taken up only by the brothers Maserati who, now working under the Osca logotype, built a V12 of orthodox chassis and sober mien, its cylinders evidently being based on those of the 4CLT Maserati and its inadequate power bearing witness (as did the AJS Porcupine in motorcycle racing a trifle earlier) that an engine designed for supercharging will not work very well when unsupercharged.

All hopes of new blood in Formula 1 racing were dealt a fatal blow when in October 1951 the FIA announced that the then current Formula 1 and Formula 2 rules would remain valid for a further two years, pending the introduction effective from 1954 onwards of a new Formula 1 which would permit unsupercharged engines of 2·5 litres displacement and supercharged ones of only 0·75 litres. Collapse, as Mr Punch used to say, of interested party — nobody was going to spend money building and developing a new racing car that would be useless in two years' time.

Formula 2, for what used to be called voiturettes, stipulated unsupercharged 2-litre engines. For Formula 1, what remained? The Ferraris were flourishing, the BRM faltering, the Talbots and Maseratis superannuated and uncompetitive. Finally, when BRM disappointed a race promoter once again by deciding that they were not sufficiently fit, the fears and expectations of all were rapidly confirmed, as race organisers throughout Europe scrambled to revise the regulations for their meetings so as to cater for Formula 2 cars instead of Formula 1.

Naturally less expensive and less esoteric, Formula 2 was thriving and there were many different and in some ways quite interesting cars competing. Most of these made a brave show in the early part of 1952, but it soon became clear that of them all, it was Ferrari and Maserati who were doing all the real racing and Ferrari doing most of the winning. Thus although some of the others had significant lessons to teach us, they tended to be dismissed as incompetent also-rans simply because the majority of

155

*103 The Bristol touring-car engine
was developed into a remarkably
efficient racing unit in the early 1950s
and powered several British Formula
2 cars that were popular—if not
successful at GP level—during the
2-litre period of 1952–3. The Cooper
was one of the best known*

them used proprietary engines that were inevitably less effective than the purpose-built power units of Ferrari and Maserati, not forgetting Gordini, who was always a respected rival. For example, the G-type ERA, designed by young David Hodkin, had far and away the best chassis and suspension of them all, incorporating a main frame of large-diameter Elektron tubing which endowed the car with the greatest torsional stiffness of any open car yet (or indeed for some time afterwards), suspension of which the most remarkable feature was a linkage to the de Dion rear axle permitting adjustments to be made for oversteer or understeer to suit the requirements of a given circuit or the preferences of a given driver. It had withal softer springing than had been believed possible for a racing car, so soft as to secure outstanding road-holding and tyre adhesion, with the consequence that its brakes could be made very powerful and used to good purpose—harder, in fact, than the racing drivers of the time were prepared to use them, so conditioned had they been to sparing their brakes for fear of failure. Thus, despite Hodkin's demonstration of a 1 g stop from 100 mph in the G-type ERA, those who drove it in competition were reluctant to try more than the 0·6 g or thereabouts that was customarily treated as the limits of prudence.

A severer handicap than this was that no proper racing engine

156

was available. ERA were no longer able to make an engine (if, indeed they had ever been) and the best they could obtain was the 2-litre six-cylinder 18-pushrod Bristol—which, despite its outstanding quality and efficiency, was nevertheless no more than a modified version of a touring car engine. It was therefore unreasonable to expect that it should be able to offer serious competition to a new and purpose-built racing engine such as the Italians enjoyed, and this handicap affected not only ERA but also an unholy rabble of other small manufacturers, all proprietors of chassis of considerably less merit than this one, such as Cooper, Frazer Nash, HWM, Connaught, Veritas and AFM. Of all these only Connaught deserves to be distinguished for excellent chassis design, and AFM for commissioning a new engine design, an eight-carburettor V8 to replace the six-cylinder engine (based on the BMW 328 sports car, as was the Bristol) with which the former BMW exponent Alex von Falkenhausen achieved some domestic success. As for the rest, they were all specious devices powered either by the Bristol engine or some other power unit of more humble origin and obscure future.

The Gordini was in a somewhat different case. Its constructor Amedée Gordini admitted the use of certain Simca parts, which were really Fiat components made in France under licence; but they were surprisingly few, and by the time his tiny Roots-blown four-cylinder 1·5-litre Formula 1 car had grown into an unblown six-cylinder Formula 2 machine, so much of it was his own work that Gordini was entitled to claim the entire credit. As always, the car's principal virtue was in light weight and small size, these advantages being obtained by expedients that were often surprising and sometimes quite elegant. Even so, the car was hardly in the

157

class of the Maserati or a Ferrari, and for two long and frankly rather boring years the motor racing world settled down to forget about the spectacle of cars weighing more than a ton, deploying more than 350 bhp, and reaching speeds of more than 170 mph to the accompaniment of noises rich in power and kaleidophonic variety. Instead they had to content themselves with watching—or perhaps not watching—events in which mild-mannered little motor cars mustering perhaps 160 bhp but seldom much more, and weighing perhaps 0·6 tons, proceeded in a fairly orderly fashion at speeds not exceeding 150 mph and lap times generally inferior by about 6 per cent to those achieved by the Formula 1 cars of 1951. Some of those earlier cars had been said to sound like the ripping of vast sheets of calico; by comparison, the noises made by these new and depressingly democratic little Formula 2 cars might be likened to the gentle unravelling of a piece of knitting.

For those who could ignore the dramatic and sensual elements of motor racing, the machines of 1952 and 1953 were not without their attractions and merits. In their engines, designers learned to explore and exploit the improvements in volumetric efficiency made possible by providing separate inlet tracts for each cylinder and by adjusting the lengths of these and of the exhaust systems so as to harness the pulsations that could be stimulated therein. Pioneered by Miller in the early 1920s and then forgotten in motor racing circles until the idea was revived by HWM and Connaught, these principles had long been known and profitably employed by the makers and tuners of racing motorcycles. In 1952 and the following year the practice became common, being put to best use perhaps by Aurelio Lampredi whose four-cylinder 2-litre Ferrari engine generated a peak-power bmep of 165 lb/in^2, then an excellent figure for an unsupercharged engine. Taken in conjunction with a crankshaft rate of 7,000 rev/min, this gave the engine a power output of 180 bhp, while Colombo's six-cylinder Maserati offset greater piston area against lower bmep to develop 190 bhp in 1953.

Thus we see that the power of the best cars of 1953 was merely half that of the corresponding machines of 1951, and while their weights stood in very nearly the same proportion there was comparatively little disparity in their frontal areas. It may therefore seem a matter for comment that the reduction in lap speeds was as slight as the 6 per cent already noted; and this may be explained by the considerable improvements in braking and cornering power effected by the designers of the Formula 2 cars. The years 1934 to 1939 had been an edifying period in which chassis and suspension design had been forced to improve tremendously because the cars had so much power that they could not otherwise be adequately controlled. Now in 1952 and 1953 chassis, suspensions, and running gear were once again subjected to furious improvements because the cars had so very little power that they could not otherwise achieve a satisfactory performance.

106 Pau in 1953: Ferraris, Gordinis, Maseratis

chapter five

1954 to 1960

How long halt ye between two opinions?
1 Kings 18:21

The temporary decline of the Formula 1 racing car after 1951 may have caused the excitement of Grand Prix racing to abate somewhat, but it left a useful interim period of two years during which designers could consider with more than usual care to what state their art had so far been elevated and to what purpose they should seek new solutions to the problems that were presented by the new formula due to take effect from 1 January 1954. The value of such an hiatus is apparent if we look to history for other examples: the years 1909 to 1911 inclusive, 1928 to 1933, and 1952 and 1953 all represent periods when Grand Prix racing, although nominally continuing, did so in a state of suspended animation in which prevailing schools of design were run down, crystallised, weighed in the balance, and generally found wanting. The two earlier periods were followed by years in which new theories were stated with considerable conviction and supported by emphatic demonstration: 1912 gave us the remarkable new Delage and Peugeot, 1934 the no less astonishing Auto Union and Mercedes-Benz. War and its aftermath did not necessarily produce the same effect, presumably because racing car designers had other things with which to occupy their minds and because future requirements could not reliably be anticipated; but the lacuna of 1915 to 1920 was followed by the epoch-marking Fiats, while after the interruptions of 1940 to 1945 it was only the circumstantial survival of the type 158 Alfa Romeo that artificially delayed the downfall of the supercharged engine.

At other times in the history of motor racing when one formula has given away to another, it has been found that many of the cars competing in the first season under the new rules are very closely related to and not seldom little developed from those racing in the final years of the preceding formula. As racing has become more popular, more widespread and more commercialised in the years since 1950 so has the pressure on participants increased so as to give them less opportunity for reflective thought and exploratory design studies. Thus we find that when the new formula arrived in 1954, the manufacturers who were to provide the greatest technical stimulus and novelty were those who had not been engaged in racing immediately before. Ferrari and Maserati on the other hand had been busily engaged in supporting the Formula 2 events promoted in the preceding two years, so it was not unexpected that their new Formula 1 cars should strongly resemble their latest Formula 2 designs.

They were, in fact, typical of the majority of serious contenders in Grand Prix racing for the next five seasons, and they confirmed several moratoria in engineering fashion as applied to the racing car. Already by the end of 1953 we had seen the disappearance not only of the supercharger, which had been the *sine qua non* of any serious racing car since 1924, but also of the four-valve head, the beam front axle, the gearbox in unit with the engine, and the long-stroke small-bore cylinder. Both in engines and chassis, the latest cars were newly improved.

The typical chassis frame, as in the case of the 1954 Ferrari and Maserati cars, was a multi-tubular construction which, while not a genuine space frame, still offered many of the advantages of that type while being much easier to make and maintain. The front suspension was by unequal wishbones, the de Dion rear axle beam was located by a pair of parallel radius arms linked to the chassis on each side of the car, and anchored in the chassis adjacent to this beam was the combined final-drive unit and four-speed gearbox. The engine itself might be a four-cylinder as in the case of the Ferrari or a six like the Maserati, but in either case it would have a cast block (not a fabricated one in the old Fiat/Mercedes tradition), twin overhead camshafts, two valves per cylinder, a one-piece crankshaft running in plain bearings, and a large-bore carburettor serving each individual cylinder. From this engine there might be 240 or 250 bhp available, testifying to the effectiveness of its motorcycle-inspired breathing system.

Now that 100 bhp per litre had been demonstrated from an unsupercharged engine, there was little probability of any manufacturer pursuing the option of a small supercharged engine, the terms of the formula making 333 bhp per litre necessary if a supercharged engine were to reach parity; and of all the supercharged engines hitherto seen, only the BRM had ever attained such a specific output, and then only on the dynamometer. Mercedes-Benz were rumoured to have been studying the possibility of an effective supercharged engine, but in fact the only supercharged car ever fielded under this formula was a modest little machine entered by Taraschi in the Rome Grand Prix of 1954: this was the Giaur, its engine developed by Giannini from a production Fiat, supercharged by a Roots blower. The car's tubular chassis relied on Fiat front suspension and live rear axle, with the driver sitting to the left of the transmission. It was

107 The crankshaft of the 2½-litre Mercedes-Benz was built up with Hirth joints to allow one-piece connecting rods and roller bearings. Drive is taken from the central spur gear, and torsional vibration dampers are hung on each end

108 W196 Mercedes-Benz, probably the most complex GP car ever raced

probably enormous fun, and undoubtedly sounded beautiful, but it was hardly a car to be taken seriously.

A little later in 1954, at Reims for the French Grand Prix, Mercedes-Benz at last revealed their new car, which everybody had properly anticipated was one that had to be taken very seriously indeed. Hardly anyone, however, seemed prepared for something of such originality and complexity. Its engine was unsupercharged, a straight eight with power taken from the centre of the crankshaft (as in the V16 BRM) in order to minimise the effect of torsional vibrations, but instead of carburettors it had direct fuel injection into the cylinders. There were two valves to each cylinder, huge ones, operated by twin overhead camshafts through a desmodromic linkage that provided positive mechanical closure of the valves as well as normal opening thereof—a

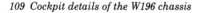

109 Cockpit details of the W196 chassis

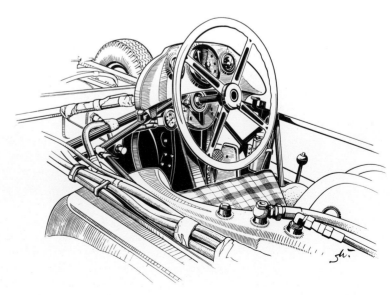

revival of the principle followed by Delage in the years before World War I, but ingeniously refined by the simple expedient of leaving out the little supplementary springs that were supposed to be necessary to ensure final closure of the valves: instead, the cam and its attendant mechanism brought the valve to within about half a millimetre of its fully closed position, after which the valve's own inertia and gas pressure within the cylinder did the rest.

No less beautifully engineered was the chassis, based upon a proper space frame of small-diameter tubing, with independent rear suspension of a geometrical refinement that belied the swinging half-axle concept upon which it was based, dead half-axle beams being mounted on a low central pivot so as to bring the rear roll centre within a very few inches of the ground. The brakes were inboard, not only at the rear, which a few cars had already featured (the earliest was the 1924 Benz) but also at the front, where the space available allowed drums of immense width and obvious power to be located.

All these features came as a shock to the preponderantly conservative elements of the motor racing world, but even cumulatively they were scarcely as shocking as the body of the Mercedes-Benz, which was an all-enclosing streamlined shell whose low bonnet line had been made possible by the engine being canted over on its side until its cylinders were almost horizontal. Such a shape was eminently suitable for the long straight roads which made up the very fast Reims circuit, and despite hectic efforts by the drivers of the Italian cars it was the German ones which dominated both practice and the race. The fact that the lap times they achieved were only faster than their rivals by the narrowest of margins should not be taken as proving anything other than that the cars were driven as circumspectly as befits a first outing, for the Mercedes-Benz pair had exploited a sprinting bottom gear in their five-speed transmissions (at a time when all but Gordini made do with four) to establish a substantial lead before the first corner, and thereafter they were never seriously challenged.

The W196, as the new German car was coded, was not the sole repository of all innovative engineering. The years of the $2\frac{1}{2}$-litre formula were to prove one of the most fruitful eras in motor racing technology, and the pace of technical development was already evident even as early as this midsummer of 1954. Thus there was an HWM running with fuel injection, as well as the W196, while a Maserati privately entered by the Rubery Owen organisation (now proprietors of the BRM) sported 'corners by Dunlop'—an expression then understood as implying tyres, light alloy disc wheels, and disc brakes, all manufactured by that firm. The car was virtually a mobile test bed for ideas that might be embodied in a new BRM, and had already raced with another form of fuel injection, as indeed had the Formula 2 Connaught in 1953.

These were tentative essays in progress. The W196 was more of a manifesto for the future, a statement of what was possible and what ought soon to be common practice. Indeed, most of its features eventually earned general acceptance in racing cars, including the space frame, fuel injection, the eight-cylinder engine, independent rear suspension, and fairly soft springing. Of these perhaps the most surprising at the time was the rear suspension, for virtually all other manufacturers had accepted that there was no effective substitute for the de Dion axle, and those who did not see their way to incorporating this in their cars were strongly tempted to persevere with the live rear axle rather than risk the geometrical vagaries of any independent system.

For that matter, it was general at this time for racing cars to be contrived to display a basic understeering characteristic. Indeed it is not unreasonable to declare that the general pattern of racing car construction in the early 1950s was substantially inherited from, and was in some respects a slavish imitation of, what Mercedes-Benz had introduced in 1937. Now in 1954 it was again the German firm that was striking out in new directions; but it seems that they were not quite original enough. The desirability of understeer was accepted by them, as by the others, almost without question; and bearing in mind the oversteering proclivities associated with swinging half-axle rear suspension, they took steps firmly to eradicate any such tendencies in the W196. The rear roll centre was lowered as already described, the rear wheels were set with considerable negative camber at static deflection, and the wishbones of the front suspension were connected by a strong torsion bar to resist roll and increase lateral load transfer in cornering. All these features contributed to a degree of understeer so marked that when the cars came to Silverstone for the British GP they found it so difficult to negotiate some of the corners in the wet weather there obtaining that they had to resort to extremely untidy driving techniques calculated to produce some unsatisfactory sort of oversteer; and while they were thus engaged, two Ferraris and a Maserati led them to the chequered flag.

Such disgrace and embarrassment was insupportable, and before the German GP at the Nurburgring Mercedes-Benz had traded the 20 per cent reduction in aerodynamic drag offered by the original streamlined body for the lightness, compactness, low frontal area, and good visibility for the driver, offered by a more conventional slipper type body wrapped as tightly around the very wide frame.

The connection between body design and excessive understeer may not be immediately apparent but it is likely that in the streamlined W196, as in the sports-racing cars of the time, drivers found that untoward changes in handling characteristics were occurring at high speeds. In fact, it was common for cars boasting aerodynamic bodywork (as understood in the 1950s) to suffer an increasing tendency to oversteer as they went faster. Mercedes-Benz had studied the problem in relation to their passenger cars as early as 1939, but by 1954 the only firm to have resolved the problem was Bristol, who in their sports-racing cars had perfected the idea of bodywork shaped to give aerodynamic understeer combined with a chassis set up to give dynamic oversteer. All the

other constructors of the time were content to combat aerodynamically induced oversteer by suspension-induced understeer, two
conflicting tendencies that could be properly balanced only at one
speed, usually at or near the maximum at which the vehicle was
capable. At lower speeds, therefore, the understeer tendency would
predominate, and all the evidence suggests that in the streamlined
W196 it was severe.

Free from the threat of spurious handling defects associated
with the streamlined body, Mercedes-Benz could revise their
suspension settings for the naked cars they took to the Nurburgring, and in one of these Fangio at last improved on the lap
record that had been set by one of the 1939 W163 cars, lending
further support to the suggestion (based on his record practice
lap at Silverstone a month earlier) that this new Mercedes-Benz
was probably the fastest road racing car the world had yet seen.
Further to support this contention, it duly won at the Nurburgring; yet for all its engineering sophistry it was still not all that
much better a performer than the comparatively primitive Italian
cars. In view of the theoretically excellent breathing provided by

111 Jano's Lancia D50 in its original form

its generous porting and unique valve gear, amplified by its free-dom to run beyond 9,000 rev/min, it should have far exceeded them in power; but in fact it did not, and when Ferrari raised the compression ratio and strengthened the bottom end of their $2\frac{1}{2}$-litre four-cylinder Lampredi engine for this race, it developed 250 bhp, only two less than the German engine, while its peak bmep of no less than 207 lb/in^2 at 5,000 rev/min indicated the excellence of its torque characteristics.

The six-cylinder Maserati, too, was proving to be a force with which to reckon. When the entrants gathered at Monza for the Italian GP in September 1954, many of them had put various re-finements and modifications into effect, and the confusing parity of apparently disparate cars noted earlier persisted, to delight the

112 Lancia D50 engine, with hairpin valve springs and asymmetrical cams

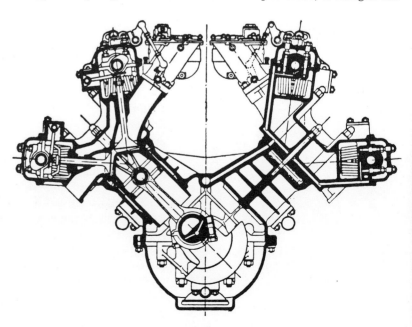

1958 Vanwall

THE APOTHEOSIS OF THE VINTAGE RACING CAR was reached in the years 1957 and 1958, when the Vanwell presented itself as the last front-engined car capable of dominating a Grand Prix season. Its origins were distinguished: the upper half of the engine was based on the geometry of the Manx Norton racing motorcycle engine, the lower half upon a Rolls-Royce military engine, and the chassis upon established Ferrari practice. The evolution of the car was painful, but no mistake was made without some useful lesson being inferred from it; and when eventually the design was extensively revised with chassis by Chapman and body by Frank Costin, the Vanwall emerged as not only one of the most beautifully made and finished machines ever seen, but also as one of the most effective of its time. In 1957, when alchohol-based fuels were still permitted, its engine was more powerful than any of its rivals; in 1958, when revised rules stipulated gasoline, it lost this superiority but gained so much in reliability and road-holding that it toppled the Italian factories from their accustomed supremacy and established Great Britain as the country from which the terms of racing car design would be dictated for a long time to come. As it happened, those terms were not in any way consistent with those to which the Vanwall designers referred. It is interesting to speculate on how the Vanwall would have fared in 1959, with due improvements and amendments such as might have been carried out during the intervening winter, in competition with a new style of car which set at nought the accepted tenets of marked understeer and high polar moment of inertia, and confirmed the superiority of a new breed of rear-engined racing cars.

The Vanwall was not the last front-engined Grand Prix car; but it was the last to be an unquestionable success, and so it stands as the culmination of fifty-two years of endeavour.

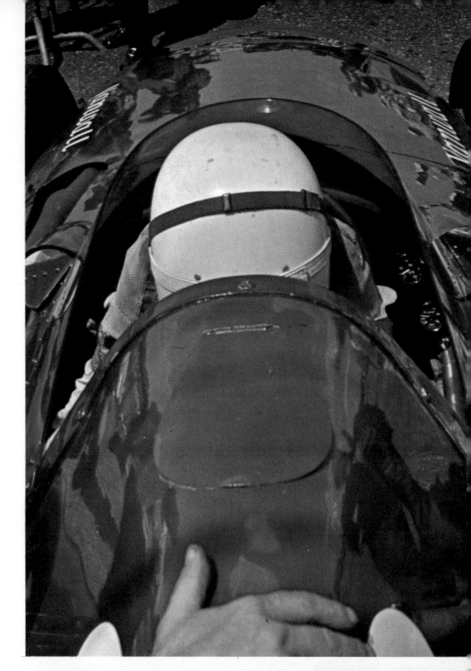

1963-6 Lotus

THE DELICACY OF PERFECTION is a very precarious thing; and the delicacy of the Lotus chassis, evolved in the mid 1960s so that it was undoubtedly the most perfect thing in existence, made its durability a very precarious thing indeed. There were times when suspension or steering components would come apart, or wheels would fall off; times when a driver noted for his courage grew very petulant about the relative chances of breaking records or his neck; and times when it all held together so that this beautiful fragile creation might demonstrate that ineffable superiority which declared Chapman to be the most intelligent, purposeful, and creative designer in Grand Prix racing. It was he who conceived the Lotus 25, the first GP car to have a stressed-skin hull.

The weight of this eggshell fabrication was but one-sixteenth that of the total machine, but its strength and stiffness were unimpeachable. All the ancillaries were studied with an eye resentful of every ounce, however – whence the habitual delicacy of appearance and occasional fragility of constitution which characterised not only the Lotus but also the many other cars that were created in its image.

It is not at all fanciful to aver that all subsequent Grand Prix cars have been modelled on the Lotus 25 or its even more refined derivative, the 33. By 1965 the 33 was established as the standard by which all others were judged and mostly found wanting.

By 1966 such brilliance was not enough without a suitable engine. On twisty circuits the little Lotus gave outstanding performances, but without scoring any victories. Nevertheless, the Lotus 33 is seen here (in the hands of Clark at Monaco) as the archetype of a new generation of racing cars.

1960 Cooper

BUILT ON A SHOESTRING WITH A HACKSAW, the Formula 1 Cooper encompassed a revolution greater than any that had ever been brought about by any of the great and famous organisations engaged in motor racing. It did what neither Benz nor Auto-Union nor Bugatti could do: it proved that a racing car with its engine behind the driver was superior to one with its driver behind the engine. In 1958 the presence of a few Coopers in the major Grand Prix had been little more than a source of amusement or irritation; but in 1959, with a Coventry Climax engine that had at last been enlarged to a full 2½ litres, the Cooper leaped into prominence, to become a source of amazement and confusion.

In 1960, with further improvements, it again emerged as champion – not merely of the racing season but also of a cause to which all future GP cars (save the short-lived four-wheel-drive Ferguson) would rally.

lay sportsmen and defy the engineering critic. Mercedes-Benz
took streamlined and naked cars to Monza, the former proving
appreciably faster on this essentially high-speed circuit, but the
Ferrari and Maserati were scarcely slower. In the race Moss in a
Maserati had a comfortable 20 seconds lead when on the 68th of 80
laps the severance of an oil line from the tank in the tail of his car
forced his withdrawal, leaving a faintly embarrassing victory to
Mercedes-Benz.

Disappointment in the showing of the W196 was justified. The
Mercedes-Benz team were campaigning in the grand manner, but
respect for such pomp and panoply can all too easily turn to ridicule if events do not justify the means. Despite their multitude of
supporting technicians, their fifteen cars that had been built to
keep three or four ready for the starting line, the tremendous
organisation at the factory and in the field dedicated to the maintenance and support of the racers, Mercedes-Benz were not doing
as well as they should. When they suffered defeat at the hands of
Ferrari at Barcelona a month later, and humiliation in practice at
the hands of the intriguing new Lancia, their discomfiture was
complete.

The D50 Lancia had been a long time in preparation, but its excellent performance and refreshing design made the delay seem worth while. Interest in it was bound to be strong, for it was only the second wholly new car to be built to meet the requirements of the new formula; and interest was sustained by the fact that, while it was nothing like the German cars, neither was it at all like the other Italians. It had eight cylinders, but they were arranged in a 90-degree V formation in an engine of great structural stiffness. This was utilised as an integral part of the chassis, the front suspension units being attached directly to it. The rest of the chassis was of a multi-tubular structure but not a space frame, and the rear suspension was a de Dion form that was conventional enough. The transmission was less so: in addition to an aggregate of final drive and gearbox at the rear of the chassis, Lancia had put the clutch there as well, thus improving the gearchange by relieving the gearbox input shaft of the additional inertia of the propellor shaft. This was an expedient that Lancia had already proved in their Aurelia production car—yet another example, like the 500K Mercedes-Benz, of the touring car of today that led to the racing car of tomorrow.

Another even older idea had been revived by Lancia for the D50, and this was the most striking of all: outboard pontoons or panniers served as fairings to fill what would otherwise have been an area of turbulent air between the front and rear wheels, at the same time constituting fuel tanks which would keep the disposable load at about the centre of the wheelbase throughout a long race which might be finished with the car weighing 300 lb less than at the start. These pontoons contributed to a very short and squat appearance and hinted properly at an extremely low polar moment of inertia, as confirmed in practice by the twitchy behaviour of the car. It was nevertheless faster than anything else at Barcelona, followed in order of practice times by a Mercedes-Benz, a Ferrari and a Maserati. Yet even the Lancia, driven by the masterly young Ascari, could not lap as fast as Fangio had done on this circuit three years earlier when he drove a type 159 Alfa Romeo. Perhaps the new $2\frac{1}{2}$-litre cars were not the world's fastest road racers after all?

If not, they were clearly on the brink of becoming so, and with a winter in which to carry out some development work it was to be expected that they would reappear in 1955 faster, more manageable and more reliable. So it proved: there was little further novelty, but a great deal of detail change and minor adjustments which added up to a considerable improvement in the cars' behaviour. Perhaps the most altered and the least improved was the Lancia, which by next season was to be withdrawn from racing as the firm found itself suffering financial strictures too severe to allow them to continue. Before this withdrawal, however, the Lancia showed itself as fast as the revised Mercedes-Benz, whether around the slow Monaco circuit or the very fast Spa roads.

The work undertaken by Mercedes-Benz in the intervening

period had been in the nature of enquiry into fundamentals rather than mere attention to detail. Scheduled development of the engine brought its power up steadily until by the end of 1955 it was giving 282 bhp at 8,500 rev/min, but it was clearly the car's indifferent handling in 1954 that had attracted the most attention. It had been understeering far too strongly. Perhaps Jano's Lancia showed them the way, but at any rate they revised the suspension so that the car acquired almost neutral steering characteristics, a trace of understeer remaining until shortly before ultimate breakaway when final oversteer prevailed. This enabled the drivers to control the cars with great precision while pressing them much closer to their limit. Years were to pass before all other racing car constructors accepted this as the new ideal, but the winter of 1954–5 must be marked as the time when the earlier theory of directional stability afforded by a high polar moment of inertia combined with dynamic understeer, as propagated by Mercedes-Benz with their 1937 cars, was invalidated.

Work on the W196's handling did not stop there. During 1955, versions of it appeared with front brakes removed from the chassis to the hubs, to the detriment of both braking power and of sprung:unsprung mass ratio, because there was no longer room in the chassis of this ultra-short-wheelbase car that was intended for the most sinuous circuits such as that at Monaco. Already the 92-inch wheelbase of the original streamlined Silver Arrow had been reduced to $87\frac{1}{2}$ inches for the slipper-bodied car that took its place for the rest of the subsequent races in that year; but to Monaco in 1955 came new cars whose wheelbase had been further shortened to 85 inches. At Spa, for the Belgian Grand Prix that followed, all three lengths of wheelbase were tried with the outboard front brakes, the two longer types being also tried with the inboard brakes, and even the effect of mounting the engine a couple of inches further forward was evaluated. The outstanding feature of this is that for the first time some effort was being made to provide a variation in the setting up of chassis and suspension to suit the handling demands of differing circuits and differing drivers. This was to lead ultimately to the universally adjustable suspension that has been an enduring feature of racing cars since 1960.

Not long after the Belgian Grand Prix there occurred the infamous Levegh accident in the 24-hour sports car race at Le Mans. A number of races were cancelled forthwith, and some were never to return to the calendar. Mercedes-Benz, one of whose cars made most of the mayhem at Le Mans, announced that they would withdraw from racing altogether at the end of the season, ostensibly because they had established all they had set out to demonstrate. Only one car had been fast enough in Grand Prix racing to challenge them, and this was the Lancia; but the racing organisation supporting it had been wound up and the existing cars, complete with drawings, spares and Jano as a job lot, were transferred to Ferrari. He had agreed to keep them racing and develop them with a free hand, but this was probably through need rather

114 The streamlined 2½-litre
Connaught

115 The B-type Connaught, first car
to win a Grand Prix with disk brakes
and the last to win with a Wilson
preselector gearbox

than charity, even in the biblical sense (the original Hebrew word
also meant justice); for his own cars, now christened Supersqualo
because they were more shark-like than ever with their long snouts
and bulbous flanks heavy with fuel, suffered consistently strong
understeer. The Lancias had also been offered to Maserati, but
this firm reckoned that their own car was better anyway—and
the way it was developing, they had some cause for so thinking.

All this time the British manufacturers continued weak and
ineffectual. This was in complete contrast to the health of the
sport in Britain, where its popularity had soared with incredible
rapidity in the past eight years, so as to become so entangled with
commercial enterprises that it was barely checked in its career by
the aftermath of the Le Mans tragedy which left such serious
repercussions upon European racing. Thus the British Grand
Prix was held in due course, and was in due course won by the
Mercedes-Benz team. It was, however, an occasion for British
manufacturers to show what they could do—apart from the four
Englishmen in privately owned Maseratis. There were two
Vanwalls, so far unconvincing but nevertheless a good deal quicker
than the four Connaughts, which were mechanically conventional by prevailing standards, their only oddity being the Alta

engine with SU fuel injection and Wilson preselector gearbox. Some examples also had a beautiful aerodynamic body which turned out to be impossibly bulky to manage in the pits, where it had been proposed that the entire envelope should be lifted clear of the car. Then there was the Cooper of a scarcely known Australian named Jack Brabham: this was the 1·1-litre rear-engined sports car chassis somewhat modified to accept a 2·2-litre Bristol engine but retaining the central seat and all-enveloping bodywork of the sports car. It was the slowest car there; but it was also the first rear-engined Formula 1 car to be raced in an international event since the passing of the days of Auto Union; therefore with Brabham as its driver, it accounted for two straws in the wind.

Towards the end of this rather dull year something rather significant happened, something which was to undermine the confidence already expressed in the virtues of the Maserati, to restore the confidence that had been signally lacking in British cars and drivers, and set one or two technical hares up, not to mention the odd red herring. At Syracuse in the last Grand Prix

116 The B-type Connaught cockpit

117 The 2¼-litre Alta engine of the Connaught

118 Good breathing was the forte of the Connaught's Alta engine

of the European season, which was expected to be a walkover for Maserati, the best of them were outdriven and outpaced by the latest version of the Connaught driven by a young, intelligent, and meticulously precise driver named Brooks, who had previously never even sat in a Connaught. Yet he won by over 50 seconds after establishing a new lap record for the circuit, becoming the first British driver to win a Grand Prix in a British car since the 1924 San Sebastian GP, when Segrave's winning Sunbeam was merely Bertarione's blown version of the 1922 Fiat. The occasion was also important in that it was the first Grand Prix to be won by a car equipped with disc brakes and the last by a car with a Wilson gearbox. One of the most valuable lessons it taught was that a full-bodied power curve was more useful than a peaky one, for Brooks established that he could allow the leading Maserati to outdrive him into and through the Syracuse hairpin, knowing that the Connaught could out-accelerate the Maserati on the exit from the corner. His car's Alta engine, now with carburettors instead of fuel injection, developed but 240 bhp and was seldom run higher than 6,500 rev/min—and this was a very modest rate for a racing engine whose bore and stroke of 93·5 and 90 mm were almost the same as those of the 1954 Ferrari type 625, and much less over-square than the 100 x 79·5 mm of the pot-bellied Ferrari type 555 engine (which was later to power the Super Squalo), both of which produced maximum power at 7,500 rev/min. What mattered was that the high bmep of the Alta engine was sustained over a very wide range, to produce a torque curve flatter than was characteristic of its rivals.

As far as Connaughts were concerned, the event proved to be a flash in the pan. Looking back, however, the occasion may be

119 *The first 2¼-litre BRM alongside a V16 Mark 2*

seen as beginning a period of more active and competitive participation by British manufacturers, as became evident the following year when BRM and Vanwall proved themselves to be in possession of uncommonly powerful and fast four-cylinder cars. The BRM was as unreliable as its last lineal predecessor, but was a lot simpler in concept. The engine was a four-cylinder type of extremely large bore, mounted in a frame built up from a number of fairly large diameter tubes, not all of them straight. The car was notably small and light, the body interestingly stiff through double-skinning of the section around the high-sided cockpit; and the engine, replete with extraordinary torque, gave it unrivalled acceleration for as long as its huge valves would stay in one

175

piece—which was not long, since they tended to resolve themselves into the two pieces from which they had been made. The designer, Berthon, was extremely stubborn in his retention of two valves despite the vast area they had to cover in the big combustion chambers; and he refused to accept the advice of the late Stuart Tresillian (whose distinguished career embraced service to both Rolls-Royce and Bristol, and who may one day be recognised as perhaps the greatest engine designer never to become famous in his own lifetime), who insisted that four smaller valves would have been better.

Less extreme in its stroke:bore ratio, the Vanwall was more adventurous in most other respects, and scored an encouraging victory against the Ferrari team in a minor event at Silverstone early in the 1956 season. Its chassis, originally a humdrum multi-tubular affair, had been completely revised by Chapman who, acting as a consultant, devised a genuine space frame with all its constituent tubes straight and sized according to the load they bore, just as he had done with his successful Lotus sports cars. The engine, ostensibly just another big four, had in fact some

121 Hawthorn in an early (1955, pre-Chapman) Vanwall

122 The Vanwall at Aintree, profiting from a Chapman frame and Costin body

claims to distinction: an amalgam of Norton, Rolls-Royce and Bosch experience, it was unusual in having exposed valve stems, hairpin valve springs, and high-pressure fuel injection. At least as important was the body design, the work of the aerodynamicist Frank Costin who had previously worked in association with Chapman: unusually smooth and bulbous, it had none of the scoops, louvres and miscellaneous enations that were common to other cars of the time, but properly shaped apertures let into the body surface at points calculated to be in regions of relatively high pressure, while low pressure areas were exploited to exhaust vitiated air. Thus the car suffered less aerodynamic drag than any rival, and since it had as much power as most it often showed itself to be the fastest car of the year in a straight line. Its handling was not yet completely satisfactory, however, and it was the Ferrari-modified Lancias that were the most consistently successful

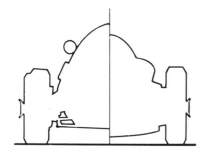

123 The Ferrari type 555 Supersqualo Ferrari had no less frontal area (right) than the earlier type 625, but was significantly lower

124 Supersqualo Ferrari at Spa, 1954

throughout the season. All sorts of modifications were applied to these cars, not a few of them being proved inferior to the original Jano design, but some fairly drastic revisions to the engine and in particular to the exhaust system gave it enough power to complement its good handling and allow the team leader Fangio to become world champion yet again.

This was in the face of considerable tyre troubles that beset Ferrari for years as the result of an unwise contractual engagement with Englebert, and probably despite rather than because of the modification of the car's handling characteristics so that it became a fairly strong understeerer. It was not perhaps as bad as the BRM, which went to such extremes that the driver had to back off the throttle quite a lot through a bend in order to hold the car on course, surplus power simply driving the nose of the car

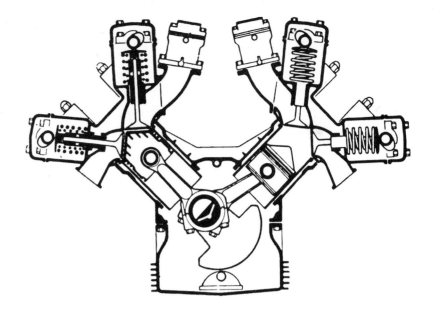

125 Ferrari altered the Lancia V8 substantially to make it his own: direct-acting cams, coil springs, new conrods and crankcase, and much besides

126 V8 Ferraris at the Nurburgring pits during practice for the 1956 German GP

straight on more or less regardless of where the wheels were pointing. As for those other violent understeerers the four-cylinder Ferraris, they simply vanished: they had established a pattern for racing cars which was to endure for several years, but Ferrari was so completely given over to the development of Jano's Lancia that Lampredi, who had designed the four-cylinder cars and done much of the initial modification of the Lancia, left to work for Fiat.

At this point we must recall his predecessor, who was dismissed from Ferrari's service when work was started on the big unblown V12 that was to put both Ferrari and Lampredi well and truly on the map. After going to Maserati to do some valuable work on their six-cylinder car, Colombo had eventually found himself designing a new car for Bugatti, a car which was more extraordinary than any of its contemporaries, more promising, and more abjectly a failure. Known as the type 251, this Bugatti made its first and only racing appearance at the 1956 French Grand Prix; and those who associated the name of Bugatti with beautiful but superficial variations on an orthodox theme must have found the fundamental heterodoxy of Colombo's car most disturbing. It was a short, bulbous, and curvaceous shape which revealed very little save that the engine was behind the driver, who sat at about mid-wheelbase. This was made possible by the transverse location of the engine, which was a twin-overhead-camshaft straight eight with central power take-off to a five-speed Porsche-synchromesh gearbox which was linked by further gears to the final drive. The frame was box shaped and properly triangulated in small-diameter tubing, with lateral fuel tanks to ensure that the centre of gravity did not migrate during a long race. The rear suspension was of the de Dion layout, somewhat odd in that each end of the dead axle beam was coupled by rod and crank to a coil spring on the far side of the chassis frame. Even more odd was that the same type of suspension was employed at the front, the Bugatti thus standing out as the only Formula 1 car to be built and raced with a rigid beam front axle since the last examples of the pre-war type 59 Bugatti, which were exercised in minor events immediately after World War II.

In 1956 the type 251 Bugatti was so radical as to appear ridiculous, and since its poor performance—always excusable on a first outing—was followed by disappearance into unknown but probably less sensitive hands, Colombo never had the chance of vindicating himself with it. Today it appears an altogether rational design. The disposition of engine and transmission is essentially similar to that of the demonstrably successful Lamborghini Miura and makes impeccable sense in a car whose body design affords sufficient width for a transverse engine, as so many modern racing cars do. Its use of telescopic dampers all round was prophetic in an age when rotary vane dampers were almost universal. It was not quite iconoclastic in having disc brakes, for by now all British racing cars had them, but the Bugatti ones were odd in that they were conical enough to create a negative servo effect and eliminate the danger of the brakes locking on, as had happened to some of the pioneer designs, and were properly fan cooled through volute casings. Finally, and perhaps most prophetic of all, the beam axle suspension would, with suitable increase of track to comply with modern standards, admirably suit the characteristics of the latest ultra-low-profile racing tyres—whose aerodynamic shortcomings would be overcome by the hammer-head frontal fairing of the Bugatti, which found an echo in the excrescent noses of the 1971 Matra, Tyrrell, Ferrari and sundry copyists. With the type 251 Bugatti, Colombo proved himself exceptionally clever; but alas he was not clever enough to recognise and accept that it is very dangerous to change more than one thing at a time, intelligibility depending on the gradualness of evolution within conceivable limits.

A useful way of explaining this impediment to progress is to make a comparison, which may be more than mere analogy, to language. Shakespeare, for example, would have difficulty with modern English, for in each generation the vocabulary changes and so to a less extent does the grammar: there is a limit to the changes that can be made in a given time without the language becoming incomprehensible. Thus at any given time, the design of the Grand Prix car has a certain formal vocabulary which can be used and even extended slightly in the manner of idiom or slang: the evolution of streamlining in the naked-wheeled racing car (as opposed to more thorough all-enveloping bodywork) is of this nature. However, there have throughout the history of Grand Prix racing been people such as Voisin, Rumpler, Grillot and in this instance Colombo, who have tried to change the grammar— that is, the conceptual sub-structure. Too great a change too soon is unintelligible, even though the statement may be important.

128 From top to bottom: BRM, Bugatti, Connaught, Ferrari, Maserati, Vanwall. By the standards of the early 1970s, the Bugatti is the most modern

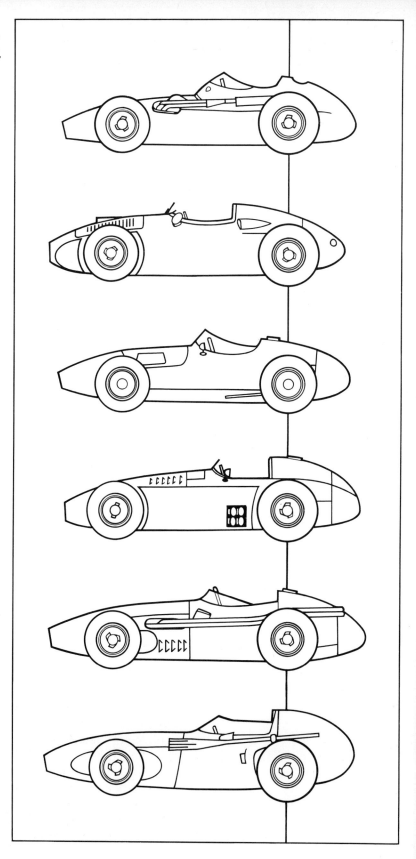

130 Another Maserati 250F with more
chassis bracing and ventilation

Conversely, it is possible to retreat a certain distance into the past and make statements that are distant enough to be romantic while not yet archaic. In this light may be seen the 2½-litre Maserati, which continued into 1957 as a faster car than ever, a better handling car than ever, yet in comparison with its rivals a more old-fashioned car than ever. Moving the propellor shaft alongside the driver allowed the car to be lower overall, more tubes might be put into the chassis to make it stiffer, minor tricks of the aerodynamicist's trade might be tried around the radiator duct to make it a little faster; but the Maserati trump card for 1957 was that they had Fangio to drive a car that had been brought *al punto* by Moss at the end of the previous season. It was evident then that the car had more than sheer power and speed to help it on its way, for it was visibly more controllable through corners than were its rivals. Profiting from reduced weight and increased power (derived largely from a fuel mixture that included nitromethane as well as the basic alcohol that was the normal racing

131 *Moss sliding the low-chassis Maserati at Monza, 1956*

132 *Behra in an earlier version at Aintree*

potion of the time) the best drivers could use the great reserve of power for controlling the car's attitude through fast bends in that interesting condition, so rarely achieved, known as stable oversteer, with the rear wheels held on breakaway point by judicious use of power while the front ones were directed some way towards opposite lock, all four of them running at a high slip angle in an excruciatingly beautiful drift that could subsequently be traced along the four black lines left by the tyres. This cornering technique was highly developed by Moss and in particular by Fangio in 1957, giving the lie to those remaining theorists who still held that a high polar moment of inertia and a good measure of understeer was the best combination of virtues—as perhaps it was for any but the most skilful of drivers.

The argument raged throughout 1957: for Fangio was driving a Maserati like a man possessed—which indeed he was—while Moss, now leading the Vanwall team, clearly had the fastest car in racing, and only an infuriating series of minor troubles such as injector pipe fractures and throttle linkage derangements prevented him from achieving personal success to match that of the car. The V8 Ferrari, now nothing like the original Lancia, could seldom offer a serious challenge to these two, and it was clear that Ferrari must soon produce something new.

In April 1957 he did so at Naples, where he brought his Formula 2 car to race for the first time. There was nothing special about its chassis, much of which was the work of engineer Bellantani who had come from Maserati to lead the design team which was responsible for this new car, which was called the Dino in memory of Ferrari's son. The real novelty of the car was its engine, the conception of which has been credited to Jano. It was a V6, the two slightly staggered cylinder blocks of which were spaced at the inexplicable angle of 65 degrees apart on a one-piece crankcase. In compliance with the Formula 2 regulations of the time, the six cylinders had a displacement of $1\frac{1}{2}$ litres, and with the pistons giving a compression ratio suitable for petrol the engine was reputed (though it was a dubious reputation) to produce 190 bhp at 9,200 rev/min. Abundant detail felicities included dual ignition, and the lightness and compactness of the car evidently

133 The Italians were reluctant to adopt disk brakes. This is the copiously ventilated drum of a Maserati

134 Ferrari V8 in full cry—a considerable noise, with each cylinder exhausting through its own pipe and megaphone

allowed the most to be made of its engine, since its best practice lap at Naples when driven by Musso was only 1·7 seconds slower than the new record established by Hawthorn in the $2\frac{1}{2}$-litre V8 car when hard pressed in the race itself. Again we have an example of a car from a subordinate class of Grand Prix racing

135 *Ferrari eventually got rid of the Lancia-style pontoons to leave the exhaust pipes of the V8 exposed*

136 *The Ferrari Dino V6 engine and chassis*

186

showing promise of revitalising the topmost class.

While Ferrari cultivated a balanced whole in the Dino, Maserati experimented with a powerful intransigent in the form of a V12 engine in an otherwise more or less normal chassis. This V12, notable for its induction tracts passing between the banks of opposed inclined valves and camshafts above each head (in the manner already used by Bristol and Mercedes-Benz) produced no less than 310 bhp, more than that of any other to be used during the currency of the $2\frac{1}{2}$-litre formula. But while it would run up to 10,000 rev/min, it would deliver little useful power at more modest speeds, and because of its peaky torque characteristics it was an extremely difficult car to drive effectively, albeit very fast on high-speed circuits such as Monza. Even there the car was scarcely impressive, for if it was somewhat more powerful than the Vanwall it was by no means as well shaped; and Fangio preferred his lightweight six-cylinder car for the race, having to content himself with an unwarranted fourth place in the starting order, the Vanwall team having dominated practice as effectively as they were to dominate the race.

Already the British cars had been doing some winning: the BRM eventually gained a victory in the Caen GP, an admittedly minor event as was the Pescara race where Moss in the Vanwall trounced Fangio in the Maserati. The Italians took their revenge on home ground in yet another minor event, the Modena Grand Prix in September 1957. Ferrari treated the event as an opportunity to give the Dino an airing, the engine having been enlarged to 1·86 litres as an earnest of their intentions to make it a Formula 1 car and not confine it to duties in Formula 2. Thus suffering a deficit of nearly a third of a litre, the V6 Ferrari established a new lap record that was only to be equalled by one of the Maserati team. In the following month when the Grand Prix circus came to Casablanca for the Moroccan GP, the process of enlarging the V6 Ferrari to the full $2\frac{1}{2}$ litres permitted by the formula was nearing completion, one of the cars having a capacity of 2,417 cm³. Ferrari had already announced that the Lancia-based cars were finished and that a $2\frac{1}{2}$-litre Dino V6 would be the team's future mainstay. What he did not emphasise, and what should not have needed emphasis to those competitors most worried by the car,

137 *The Dino cockpit*

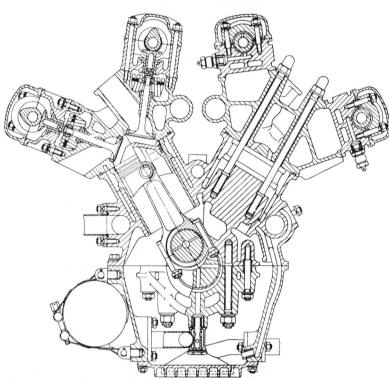

was that its engine had been designed from the outset to run on petrol. This played a significant part in minimising the car's all-up weight at the starting line, especially at Modena, because its fuel consumption was naturally less than that of an alcohol-fuelled car. In future its importance would be considerably greater: alcohol was to be proscribed.

The formula admitting unsupercharged 2½-litre and super-charged three-quarter litre cars to Grand Prix racing was intended originally to last only through the four years of 1954 to 1957 inclusive. When the time came to evolve a new formula there was little or no enthusiasm for any significant change, for race promoters, drivers and car constructors alike had found that racing had been as fast, dramatic and at least as profitable as at any time in the past. Only the oil companies were unhappy with the regulations as they stood, preferring for commercial reasons that all fuels other than petrol should be forbidden. They could then advertise a victory as having been won on fuel such as the public could buy from ordinary filling stations.

If there were any other objections of note to the continuation of the existing formula, they concerned only the length of the races. Motor racing was becoming more and more a kind of entertainment rather than a serious sport, let alone a proving ground for advanced technology; and many race promoters, recognising this trend and wanting to put on variety shows rather than simple, classical Grands Prix, argued that if races were made shorter, other races could be held on the same day to build up a supporting programme that would do manifold good to the box office.

These two demands were unintentionally self-compensating: the cars should be slower on petrol but, what with their inevitably more modest fuel consumption and the reduction in the length of the race, their fuel loads would be but half of what they had been in the full-length races of the era ending in 1957, so the cars should be quicker. In fact, the change in regulations, which was scheduled to remain valid until the end of 1960, created tremendous difficulties for some manufacturers while reviving the declining fortunes of others. Ferrari was profiting from extraordinary foresight and his petrol-burning Dino was ready. Maserati had no stomach (or perhaps literally no head) for the fight and withdrew from racing. Vanwall and BRM stayed to face obvious problems.

The readiest measure of their severity is provided by the Vanwall's power figures for 1957 and 1958: when it indulged its taste for alcohol and nitro-methane, its remarkable engine yielded 290 bhp (as installed in the car, though it had reached 310 bhp on the test bench), but when limited to petrol it could manage no more than 262—and even this was achieved only after the most concentrated work on the fuel injection system. As for the BRM, the loss of the evaporative cooling which was one of the most

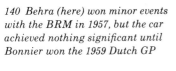

140 Behra (here) won minor events with the BRM in 1957, but the car achieved nothing significant until Bonnier won the 1959 Dutch GP

141 Late versions of the 2¼-litre BRM had an improved exhaust system

142 Vanwall mechanics at work in 1957, when the car relied on Pirelli tyres

valuable attributes of alcohol left it dreadfully susceptible to overheating and failure of its enormous valves. When it was going properly it might develop as much as 275 bhp on petrol, as it did in its final 2½-litre form in 1959, but it never kept it up for very long. By contrast the V6 Ferrari, now known as the Dino 246 (the 24 denoted the displacement in decilitres, 6 the number of cylinders), gave a good 280 bhp and was safe to 9,400 rev/min, although the usual recommended limit was 8,500.

Unusual though its engine was, everything else about the Dino

190

143 Moss sets out to win the 1957 Italian GP

was almost depressingly usual, typifying the orthodoxy of the preceding two decades. Thus it still had drum brakes because Ferrari hated the idea of appearing to copy any other manufacturer, especially a British one; and it was still an understeering car. Thus it found itself on a number of occasions, at fairly tight circuits including Monaco, pressed rather unexpectedly not only by the Vanwall and BRM but also by 2-litre rear-engined Coopers, derived like the Dino from Formula 2 machines. These Coopers, with their low weight, low frontal area, excellent handling and modest thirst, had already shown that they were to be taken seriously even on fast circuits; on slow ones they were an even greater threat.

While the seeds of dissension and revolution were thus being sown, Vanwall continued to develop and refine their car. The exhaust system was modified, cast magnesium alloy wheels replaced the old-fashioned wire-spoked variety (subject to the drivers' whims and fancies, for some chose to retain wire wheels

191

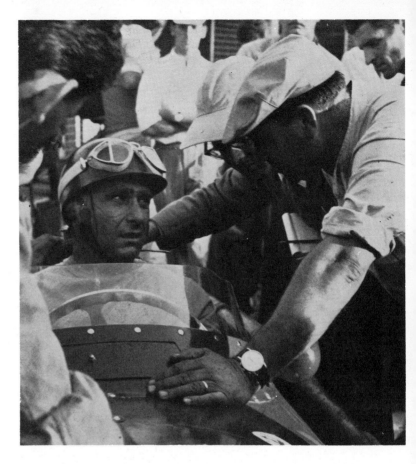

144 *Fangio, greatest Grand Prix driver in the world, with tears in his eyes. For the first time in years, he has been beaten in practice—by the Vanwall at Monza*

at the front), and the ideal of low sprung weight was pursued so far that the front hubs were eliminated, the bearings being located actually in the wheels themselves, to which the brake discs were bolted.

In the Lotus, yet another Formula 2 car that was finding its way into Formula 1, most of the ideas implicit in the design of the Vanwall could be carried to virtual finality. Unfettered by the need to reconcile his ideas with those of others, as he had to when acting as a consultant to Vanwall, Chapman was free to make his own car precisely as he wished; and in the new Lotus that he took to Monaco in 1958 we began to see that he was capable of designing structures of unequalled elegance, refinement and originality. The body design, again by Costin, was naturally similar in principle to that of the Vanwall, but improved thereon by projecting the least possible frontal area while retaining the extremely low drag which was one of the twin ideals that Lotus sought to attain. The other was lightness, assisted in this case by the fact that the car was strictly a Formula 2 chassis fitted with an oversize four-cylinder Coventry-Climax engine. This reposed in the front of an extremely light space frame built up from small-diameter tubes, the engine being canted to one side so as to reduce overall height, the propellor shaft sloping steeply beneath the driver's seat to communicate with a five-speed gearbox of original design, though it seems not to have been made well enough to work as well as it should. All the gears remained constantly in mesh, those on the layshaft being successively locked to it by a selector passing through its axis, controlled by a positive-stop gear-lever linkage giving an action similar to that of a motorcycle transmission.

Chapman had no peer in his ability to eliminate unnecessary weight. The front suspension of the Lotus bore witness to this, the lower wishbones being fabricated from light gauge tubing, the others reduced to single transverse links from the outer ends of which the angled ends of the anti-roll torsion bar contributed some triangulation. At the rear the Chapman strut suspension was used, in which the universally jointed halfshafts were of fixed

145 Lotus 16

146 Lotus 16

147 Lotus 16

length and determined the lateral location of the hub, while longitudinal location was by long radius arms, while a combined spring and damper strut controlled the vertical movement of the hub. Thus the suspension loads were fed into the chassis at points very widely spread (a necessity that too few chassis designers seemed to recognise) and the suspension geometry could be arranged to contribute towards the understeer that Chapman then deemed desirable. Unfortunately he rather overdid it; and in its final full Formula 1 form, with its 2·5 litre Coventry-Climax engine and as much development as time and money would allow, the Lotus 16 was a prey to its own understeer, its rear suspension being too good for its front suspension. It was all very well that its drag should be so low, delightful that its weight should be so slight (the Formula 2 version weighed only 305 kg dry), but lamentable that the excessive directional stability with which it was endowed should so consume power that could better be applied to other purposes. In fact the power consumption of the tyres when the car was driven in a straight line at 100 mph was a mere 10 bhp, but if it was sought to maintain this speed while cornering at 0·68 g the power consumption of the tyres rose to no less than 75 bhp, which in a car that started out with 40 less than most of its rivals could hardly be afforded.

The Lotus 16 will never be remembered as successful, though it lingers in the memory as perhaps the daintiest of all Grand Prix cars. Historically its importance lay in giving Chapman proof, if he needed it, that he was wrong to apply heterodox means to orthodox ends at a time when racing car design had become so stagnant that only the designers who did just the opposite were making any real headway.

The 1958 BRM was well on the way to providing the same proof for its proprietors, and it provided interesting comparison and contrast not only with the Lotus 16 but also with the new Formula 1 version of the rear-engined Cooper. It had been suffering from the same understeer as the Lotus and for the same reasons: Chapman had inspired its rear suspension which gave such superior adhesion that the car became difficult to handle. Accordingly, during the winter of 1957–8 the whole car had drastically to be revised to accommodate changes dictated by the new fuel regulations, a new front suspension restored its handling, while a new space frame assisted the reduction of fuel load in making the car lighter. As for the BRM engine, with its enormous cylinder bores, it had perhaps never been able to work at compression ratios high enough fully to exploit the alcoholic fuels to which it had previously been entitled; but now with petrol as its potion, it was not greatly handicapped, and its 270 bhp were only 18 less than it had given a year earlier, a deficit smaller than was noted by any rival manufacturer other than, for obvious reasons, Ferrari. Thus, with more torque and power than nearly all its competitors and with a frontal area little greater than that of the Cooper, the BRM was a very fast car. Furthermore, thanks to the refinement of its chassis and the elegance of its proportions—its wheelbase was two inches shorter than that of the so-called 'little' Cooper and its track four inches wider—it was also a very roadworthy car. Unfortunately it was rather heavy, weighing 680 kg dry compared with 520 in the case of the Cooper and 320 or so for the final version of the Lotus 16.

From this quick review of the 1958 cars we can see that the time was one in which doubts were spreading about how best to design a racing car, how best to reconcile the promptings of logic with the dictates of experience. It may therefore be instructive to consider how these cars fared against each other in some of the more important and revealing events of the season. At the slowest and twistiest, Monaco, where the fastest lap ever to be recorded had been 101·1 seconds by Lancia and Mercedes-Benz in 1955, the Vanwall proved able to reduce this by 1½ per cent. The next fastest car was the BRM, barely superior to the Coopers, after which the prevalent British racing green of the starting grid was relieved by the first splash of Italian racing red, a Ferrari, managing a place on the third row. The same order applied at the faster but still curvaceous Zandvoort; but at Spa, where the race average might achieve 130 mph, the handling characteristics of the

148 Lotus 16

Ferrari were less inhibiting, and it was to establish the fastest lap, both in practice and in the race. For similar reasons the Lotus fared better too, achieving its best performance to date by finishing fourth—and indeed it wanted but slightly better fortune to have won, for the victorious Vanwall expired at the finishing line, so did the Ferrari which came second, and the third-place Vanwall had sustained a suspension fracture.

Climbing further up the speed scale and down the calendar we come to the French Grand Prix at Reims, a circuit that favours high maximum speed, powerful brakes and good acceleration. In these respects the Dino Ferrari was competitive: in fact it was the fastest car there, followed by the BRM, the Vanwall and the Cooper in that order. The rest of the season confirmed what all this suggested, that while certain cars excelled on fast circuits and certain others on slow, for the majority of give-and-take conditions there was not much to choose between any of them, and races were as likely to be won by attrition as by superior speed. From all this the Vanwall emerged as the most successful, a car which had in the previous year demonstrated that it was consistently the fastest of all, and which had very seldom been surpassed even after being condemned to lose nearly 30 bhp with the adoption of petrol. Only in 1958 did it achieve a high enough standard in handling qualities to allow the best of drivers to use the most advanced of their techniques, and only in that year was the devoted work and superb craftsmanship of those who made and ministered to it rewarded by reasonable reliability. So emerged the champion make, as perhaps befitted its seniority for it was the oldest of the leading contestants. Indeed it was the automotive equivalent of old wine in a new bottle, for despite its space-frame construction, independent front suspension, and scientifically contoured bodywork, the front-engined four-cylinder Vanwall was the apotheosis of the vintage car, rather long, rather narrow, and with the driver sitting high up in the rear to command a distant view of proceedings over a rather tall engine. No car remotely resembling it would ever again win the championship.

At the end of the 1958 season it was announced by the FIA that after 1960 a new formula would apply to Grand Prix racing, under which engine size would be limited to 1·5 litres, superchargers would be banned, 100-octane petrol would be obligatory, and dry weight should be at least 500 kg. Those with an eye to this future realised that the low power but compact dimensions of such a small engine, abetted by the fairly small burden of fuel necessary to race for 300 kilometres or two hours, would favour the rear-engined type of car. Previously the idea had appeared to embody every mechanical and navigational vice to which a racing car might be heir; yet the virtues of the layout were becoming obvious, emphasised as they were by the increasing success of the Cooper. The advantages became most compelling when the engine to be used was one of small cross-sectional area, as was the case with the neat and simple four-cylinder Coventry-Climax FPF for which both Cooper and Lotus were now regular customers. With such an engine in the rear it was no longer necessary for the driver to sit above or to one side of the propellor shaft and other potentially bulkier transmission components, so his seat could be brought as near to the road as was consistent with a reasonable ground clearance. The cross-sectional area of the body was thus determined by the height and width of the engine or of the driver,

150 The revolutionary Cooper: Brabham (1) and Moss lead the world to a new conception of the racing car

according to which was the greater, and if as in this case the driver was the greater, then it could justly be held that the frontal area of the car was being reduced to a naturally irreducible minimum. By this means alone the frontal area could be reduced by at least one square foot, which at the prevailing rate of exchange was worth a good 25 bhp. Further benefits that might accrue from the redistribution of these major masses included a reduction in weight and

197

in polar moment of inertia, though not necessarily any significant change in weight distribution—which was much the same in all Formula 1 cars of 1959 and 1960, regardless of their type.

There were latecomers to the motor racing scene who could not or would not recognise what the future had in store. Aston Martin produced a front-engined six-cylinder machine that was virtually a latter-day Maserati, and that went impressively fast once or twice before being relegated to the ranks of the also-rans. Tec-Mec in Italy sought to revive the Maserati itself in a shortened and lightened form, with even less gratifying results. The rest, either overtly or covertly, set themselves to reconsider all that they had been taught; so that whereas in 1958 the rear-engined car was a rarity on the starting grid of a Formula 1 race, in 1961 the front-engined car could be considered extinct.

During the first part of 1959 the front-engined cars managed occasionally to keep the others at bay, particularly on the faster circuits. The most extreme example of these was the Avus circuit in Germany, where the W196 Mercedes-Benz streamliner had lapped at an average speed of 140 mph in 1954. By 1959, relatively blunt though the new racing cars were, such speeds were put into the shade in the German Grand Prix. The Ferrari V6 could now muster 290 bhp and showed itself conclusively to be the fastest car there, putting up a lap more than 7 per cent faster than the 1954 figure. The value of low frontal area was demonstrated by the Cooper being the second fastest, on an occasion that was

151 BRM changed to the rear-engined configuration in 1960. Their 2¼-litre type 48 was 120 lb lighter than the front-engined type 25; both cars had this single rear brake acting on the transmission

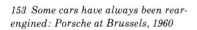

152 *The World Champion in the 1960 Cooper*

153 *Some cars have always been rear-engined: Porsche at Brussels, 1960*

remarkable for being the last proper Grand Prix to be won by a front-engined car. It is true that the Italian GP of 1960 was won by a front-engined Ferrari, but the event lacked propriety in that it was boycotted by practically all other competitors; so it is fair to treat the 1959 German GP at its unusual venue as the last to represent the end of the beginning as far as front-engined cars were concerned. The remaining events of the 2½-litre formula were the beginning of the end.

Before the end of 1959, BRM and Lotus had completed their

initial studies for new rear-engined cars. Indeed the BRM prototype appeared during practice at the Italian GP in September. It was the Lotus that was first to race, however, and to do so very convincingly at its first outing in Buenos Aires for the 1960 Argentine Grand Prix. This was the Lotus 18, a car that followed the lead set by Coopers as far as the general disposition of major masses was concerned, but which adhered to such traditions as Lotus had been able to establish in their brief lifetime. Chapman naturally used a fully triangulated tubular frame that was almost a pure space frame, whereas Cooper equally naturally felt drawn to the use of crude multi-tubular structures, the tubes often bent and made sufficiently massive to compensate for the deficiencies in their design. Chapman also employed techniques developed on his earlier cars which enabled the unsprung mass to be minimised, the suspension loads to be fed in at widely separated points on the frame, and the frontal area to be pruned to the minimum dictated by the half-seated half-supine driver, behind whom was a Coventry-Climax engine of no great power (239 bhp) and no great weight (only 290 lb, 160 less than the Maserati of the same capacity and power as raced in 1956). Behind these was a form of independent rear suspension that was perhaps as important as any other feature of the car: as in the type 16, the universally jointed but non-telescopic halfshafts served as suspension members acting in lieu of other wishbones, while below them were proper tubular fabricated wishbones with their apices almost on the centre line of the car beneath the gearbox, their bases anchored in the bottoms of cast light-alloy hub carriers. By bringing these castings very near to the ground the upper and lower wishbones diverged away from the car's centre line, creating considerable negative camber as they moved upwards towards the full bump position. Thus as the car rolled outwards in cornering the outer wheels

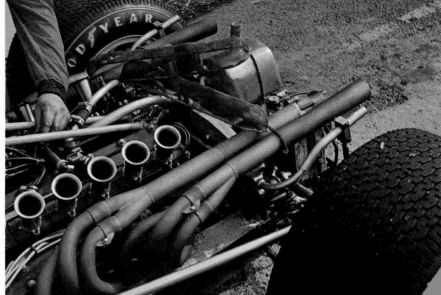

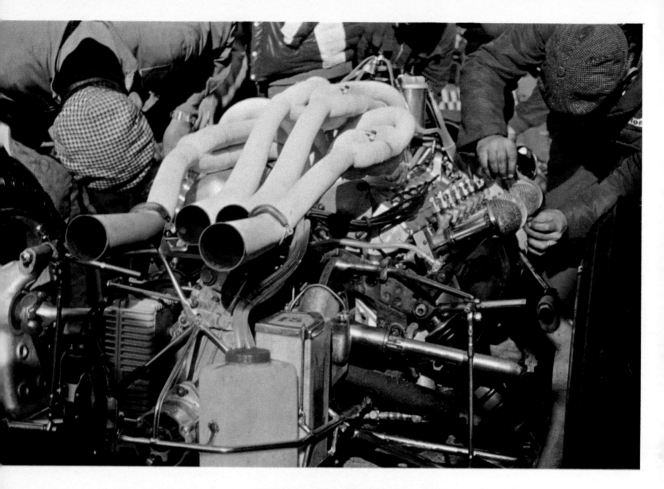

1966-9 V-12 Cars: BRM, Cooper, Ferrari Honda,

IF WISHES WERE HORSES, then beggars would ride, and the H16 BRM would
have been the most powerful and effective engine to be born out of the 3-litre
formula which, in 1966, marked Grand Prix racing's return to power. Instead
it was the most disappointing, leaving a variety of V-12 engines as the most
complex that anyone would thereafter trust. Most of them were also fairly
untrustworthy for one reason or another: the BRM because it had been
intended as a sports-car engine; the Maserati because it was a heavy rehash
of an unsuccessful 2½-litre engine; the Ferrari because something nearly
always went wrong near the end of the race, however often it might start from
pole position; and the Honda because it laboured beneath the impossible
burden of the Honda chassis.

But they were all beautiful, in all their various forms which came and went as
evanescent and ineffective as the first mayfly of a trout's breakfast. They all
sounded marvellous, fitted neatly into established chassis designs, and from
time to time performed satisfactorily. Thus to be damned with faint praise was
all they merited, save the 90-degree V-12 Honda, which was a very clever
engine and deserved a decent car to carry it.

1967-9 V-8 Cars:
Brabham, Lotus, Matra McLaren

THE GREAT EQUALISER of racing was the Ford-sponsored Cosworth V-8 engine; for when everybody had one, all cars (which were already substantially alike in their chassis) would be virtually identical in performance and only the drivers would matter – if anything. Fortunately this state of affairs never quite came to pass; but among those who employed this engine might be seen the moist active pursuit of other means of doing better than the opposition. Wings, for instance, were never tried so thoroughly as by the teams whose custom Cosworth enjoyed: Brabham, McLaren and Lotus were seldom more impressive than during the airfoil era of 1968.

Most significant user of the Cosworth V-8 was, however, Matra. The French V-12, for all its appeal, did not win races. The British V-8 did. But a Matra with a Cosworth engine in it, that was the stuff of which champions were made; and the French firm never lived down the indignity of it.

would remain substantially perpendicular to the road surface and their tyres would be able to accept their full cornering load— and the inner wheels would carry so little load that the angles they assumed would scarcely matter. Furthermore the roll axis of the car was extremely low, the instantaneous roll centre only an inch or so above the ground at front and rear—and at both ends there were anti-roll torsion bars limiting the angular movement of the car around its roll axis to only 4 degrees, a novelty that gave the car superb balance and extremely quick responses. Only a trifle of toe-in variation spoiled a layout that was perfectly suitable to the tyres of the time, but since this variation was dictated by the paired radius rods which provided longitudinal constraint for the rear suspension it was very slight, for they were extremely long.

It is only too easy to underestimate, as have so many commentators, the importance of the Lotus 18 in the history of the Grand Prix car. None would deny Coopers their proper credit for accomplishing the major revolution of justifying the rear-engined cars; but while they showed what could be done, it remained for Chapman to do it. The Lotus 18 was consistently faster (given equal fortune) than the 1960 Cooper, which itself represented a very considerable improvement on the Cooper of 1959; but perhaps more important was that the Lotus was a design that all others were to copy in the years ahead. None of them did so in 1960, being busy enough copying the Cooper of the preceding year; but when 1960 and the $2\frac{1}{2}$-litre formula both came to an end, the Lotus 18 was the world's fastest road racing car, the history of the front-engined Grand Prix machine was finished, and a new volume was about to be opened.

155 The $2\frac{1}{2}$-litre Lotus 18

chapter six

1961 to 1967

O change beyond report, thought, or belief!
Milton

'There is no law, no principle, based on past practice, which may not be overthrown in a moment by the arising of a new condition or the invention of a new material; and the most rational, if not the only, mode of averting the danger of an utter dissolution of all that is systematic and consistent in our practice, or of ancient authority in our judgement, is to cease for a little while our endeavours to deal with the multiplying host of particular abuses, restraints or requirements; and endeavour to determine, as the guide of every effort, some constant, general and irrefragable rules of right.'

These words of Ruskin may be revived to summarise the situation in which motor racing teams found themselves in 1961 when the new formula took effect. Already the old order had been completely overthrown; and the new one was faced with the necessity of finding a new way to do things, a way that had better be the right way because most of the participants now engaged lacked the funds, the support, and the staying power, to remain in racing if they could not become immediately competitive. The days of the great manufacturers going racing with great cars superbly made and with large teams of well-provided and highly-organised men had passed. The racing was now done by little firms making little cars, the simplicity of their design and crudeness of their construction bearing witness to the paucity of their resources. Very few cars were the work of one man or even of a single team of men unified by the loyalties or enthusiasms of a common employer; discrete bands of specialists from various companies within the motor industry now supplied special needs with highly specialised products, so that the design of a racing car might be the joint work of engineers in many different firms, each specialising in certain components—brakes, tyres, gearboxes, engines, ignition systems, fuel injection, dampers and the like—while many other components, ranging from front suspension uprights to gearbox housings, might be adopted unmodified and unquestioned from some humble little family saloon in mass production somewhere. Grand Prix racing, once the arena for tremendous battles between rival manufacturers who were known the world over for their road-going cars, was now the jousting pit for peripheral companies within the motor industry, and these were learning rapidly that in financially underwriting the sport they were buying the right to dictate its terms. The oil companies in particular did so: we have already seen how they virtually put a stop to further engine development by demanding that common pump petrol be the only permitted fuel; and now they went further in contracting with drivers and teams to lend their support (though lend is hardly the word), creating such complexities of allegiance as sometimes seriously hampered the free intercourse of people with knowledge to impart or experience to employ. Before long, other big firms both within the industry and without saw fit to do likewise; and before the decade was out, Grand Prix racing would decline into a brash, self-contained, self-perpetuating closed shop where loud manners, quiet intrigue, ill-concealed avarice, and over-emphasised entertainment value, all combined to make the wares seem almost irrelevant. The new generation of highly paid highly professional drivers, while doing everything possible to further their own interests, genuinely believed in some cases that they were also furthering those of the sport: the condition to which they brought it leaves little doubt as to the order of their priorities.

There may be much in this change to lament or to celebrate, according to taste (or lack of it); but the accompanying change in the design and morphology of the Grand Prix car was so over-whelmingly sudden and complete as to cause not merely pleasure or sadness but shock.

Consider how quickly engineering fashions that had endured for six years, a dozen years, in some cases even forty years, had been swept aside. There had in the past been many phases of great engineering activity and progress in designs, as in the years 1912–14, 1921–4, 1934–9, and 1954–7; but what took place in the first years of the 1960s was something much more revolutionary — and as is so often the case with revolutions, much more dangerous because much more final and irredeemable.

So much that had been received dogma was cast aside, so much accepted theory was confounded, that it is very easy — perhaps too easy — to see in this revolt the source of all the ills to which com-merialised sport may be heir. To be fair, we must not lay the blame for these ills at the doors of the engineers of the revolution: in a sense theirs was a liberating movement, creating a freedom for the expression of new ideas and the evolution of new techniques. They were, no doubt unwittingly, doing just what Ruskin recommended; and if the new laws they propounded have proved to be too con-stant, too general, and altogether too irrefragable, the blame for this probably attaches to those who inherited these new condi-tions, not to those who created them. While there were many so-called designers who were content to be slavish copyists, many who were mere followers, there were a good few who were pre-pared to be pioneers, including Chiti of Ferrari, Broadley of Lola, and Chapman of Lotus, as well as the Coopers father and son; and the greatest of these was Chapman. What these men and others like them did was to consider the many things that had for ages been accepted as necessary evils, and to eliminate those which had become more evil without becoming any more neces-sary.

Let us consider the long list of features that had disappeared by 1961. Most obvious and important, the front engine was no more. Within the engine there were no more four-valve cylinder heads, the last having been the 4CLT/48 San Remo Maserati — though the feature was to reappear in 1964. Fuel injection, that had been used by Mercedes-Benz, Maserati, Vanwall, Connaught, HWM and others for a brief period in the mid-1950s, had temporarily vanished, to reappear within a year or two. Lever tappets had disappeared, as had hairpin valve springs and roller bearings, though the last were to turn up again in the 1965 and subsequent Hondas, and more recently still in the Ferrari 312B. Vertical inlet ports between the banks of opposed valves had enjoyed a brief measure of popularity in engines by Bristol, Mercedes-Benz and Maserati, and were to revive again for a few years in the mid-1960s. Yet engines, which are by definition the work of engineers, were less disposed to change than chassis and suspensions, which can be produced by all manner of men armed with the tools of their respective trades, which may be anything from computers to hacksaws.

Thus we saw the disappearance of the de Dion axle, the final relic of a beam axle tradition that had died slowly and hard, the last Grand Prix to be won by a live-axle car being the Italian GP of 1953 when Fangio took the chequered flag in a Formula 2 Maserati. Leaf springs had gone too, though Cooper had made good use of them in 1959, and it is interesting to see how, throughout the years when the leaf gradually gave way to the helix, there have always been one or two designers who were perspicacious enough to use torsion bars which are light, space-saving and easily admit the use of linkages giving progressive rates, as well as allowing suspension loads to be fed into the centre of the chassis or some other strong point. There was even more interest in independent suspension geometries: all the parallel-action types, such as the trailing link Porsche (except on a few old Formula 2 Porsche cars), the Dubonnet, the Watt linkage (used by Gordini in the $2\frac{1}{2}$-litre era), and various patterns of equal and parallel wishbones, had been abandoned in favour of geometries that gave a useful controlled variation of wheel camber. The wheels themselves were all of cast disc or spoked light alloy construction, only Ferrari doggedly retaining the old wire-spoked wheel for another year or two. Finally the simple ladder-type frame had gone, and in 1961 every chassis was based either on a true space-frame structure or else on a simpler pattern that was multi-tubular if not nicely triangulated.

The regulations governing the new 1961 formula undoubtedly encouraged the development of the rear-engined theme, as has already been explained. They also embodied a number of other apparently minor requirements which in certain ways inhibited originality, though they certainly contributed (as they were meant to do) to safety and practicality. For example, the engine had to be fitted with an automatic starter capable of being operated by the driver when in the car, and the source of energy for this starter (be it electric or otherwise) also had to be carried on the car. This made reasonable the new regulation that an electrical master switch must be fitted as a fire precaution, but it did not explain the universal acceptance of the electric motor as a starting device when other means such as cartridge starters might have been lighter and more reliable. A greater contribution to safety was a new rule that no oil might be added to the car once the race had started. All oil fillers were to be tagged and sealed before the race began, and inspected afterwards. Moreover, catch tanks had to be provided for any oil that might issue from breather pipes, the whole object being to prevent avoidable spillage of oil on the road. Rules such as these had been in force for many years in the United States and provided a welcome encouragement to the development of oil-tight engines.

It was again safety which prompted the requirement that the driver's seat could be emptied or vacated without opening or removing any sort of panel, and that his head and shoulders should be protected from the consequences of capsizing by a tubular hoop behind his seat. A further safety requirement was a dual braking system so arranged that should a pipe fracture or a brake fail there would always be braking available on at least two wheels: the general means of complying with this was to use twin master cylinders, one for the rear brakes and one for the front, connected by a balance beam that could be adjusted to vary the apportion- ment of braking effort between front and rear wheels, a system that had been employed by Mercedes-Benz as long ago as 1934.

The three most important regulations were far more controver- sial. The weight limit, which had originally been declared at 500 kg, was reduced to 450 at the urgent representations of the British manufacturers, and was to be checked with the car's fuel tanks empty, but otherwise with the car in full running order. Nobody seemed to mind that the fuel had to be commercially available petrol, especially since the proscription of superchargers reduced the temptation to use alcohol as the solvent of all thermodynamic problems. What annoyed the British manufacturers, however, was the simple need to produce new engines, for only BRM among their number was capable of it, the rest depending on the continued enthusiasm and support of Coventry-Climax. All sorts of wild protests were made, all sorts of threats of boycotting were made but never carried out, and the clamorous objections of the British fell on deaf ears, while Ferrari and Porsche quietly and methodi- cally got on with the business of designing proper 1½-litre racing engines.

Even these, however, would necessarily produce much less power than even the petrol-burners of the previous formula. With so much less power, some hopes were entertained that what had been lost at the flywheel might be regained in streamlining, so that even if the cars were not particularly ferocious in acceleration and were not made too difficult to drive by an excess of power, they might still be made to go at speeds high enough to impress the paying public. However, the FIA thought otherwise: all wheels had to be exposed, and bodywork was not to cover them in any plane, even when they were at full lock. This may have been inspired by the fear that racing cars were getting too fast and that the 40 per cent reduction in engine displacement might fail as signally as similar reductions had in bygone days to stem the continual increase in lap speeds (with which the CSI committee, like the lay public, equated danger). If this was not the whole reason, the balance was accounted for by a sentimental belief that a proper racing car was a bare-wheeled and shameless thing to which the adornments of the aerodynamicist were as corrupting and improper as the attentions of the fuel chemists had been prior to 1958.

The effect of these regulations was to put even more emphasis on the ratio of power to frontal area than on the ratio of power to weight, and the result was a series of cars lower and slimmer than ever before or since in Grand Prix racing. They were not always as light as they could have been: the early 1961 Cooper-Climax was 67 kg above the regulation minimum, for example, whereas the Lotus was right down to the limit, so that at starting line weights it enjoyed a 10 per cent advantage in power to weight ratio.

However, if this attention to mass and frontal area made the Lotus the best of the British bunch, it still had to make the utmost of its exceptional cornering power if it were to hold its own against competition from abroad. The British manufacturers, in attempting to boycott the new formula and promote their own, perpetuating the $2\frac{1}{2}$-litre engine, were far too dilatory in accepting that the races of 1961 and thereafter would be for $1\frac{1}{2}$-litre cars, despite British objections; and when the 1961 calendar showed that the FIA ruled *de facto* as well *de jure,* only Ferrari was fully prepared—a situation in which Ferrari may almost always be found at the beginning of any new formula, since he is much more proudly self-sufficient than the meaner firms who buy their engines and other components from outside suppliers. Amidst the rash of other names now associated with the sport, several of them new to it, only BRM and Porsche were competent to make their own engines; but neither was ready in the early part of 1961, the former swallowing their pride and using the little four-cylinder

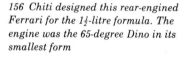

156 Chiti designed this rear-engined Ferrari for the 1¼-litre formula. The engine was the 65-degree Dino in its smallest form

157 *Later the Ferrari V6 angle was widened to 120 degrees . . .*

158 *. . . and fuel injection replaced the carburettors*

Coventry-Climax to tide them over, the latter entering four-cylinder cars that were little more than the previous year's Formula 2 machines.

The first version of the new Formula 1 Ferrari to appear was much more convincing. It was, of course, rear-engined, Ferrari having capitulated to progress with his 1960 Formula 2 car. The 1961 Formula 1 version was new, but essentially similar, its chassis frame a fair imitation of the Cooper's, staunch conservatism showing in the centre-lock wire wheels, and the hand of the designer Chiti showing in the rakish twin-nostril air intake for the radiator in the extreme nose. His engine was the Dino 156, already well known, a 65-degree V6 giving about 180 bhp and running comfortably up to 9,000 rev/min. The Coventry-Climax gave 151 at 7,500, and only by a combination of exceptional driving prowess and advanced chassis design could the Lotus 18 thus powered hope to rival the Ferrari. When at Monaco Ferrari brought along a version of the car with a new V6 engine whose banks of cylinders were set at an included angle of 120 degrees (which led to smoother running, higher revs, and more power, in logical order) the handicap was further stressed; and when Moss in the Lotus 18 outdrove Ginther's new Ferrari at Monaco, it was a triumph of man over machine.

The car to note at Monaco in 1961 was the new Lotus, in which Chapman had sought to do as he had done in the past—to make the car lighter and sleeker than its opponents since it could not hope to have engines more powerful than the others. Superiority in cornering was also sought, the rear suspension now relieving the drive shafts of lateral loads: the hub carriers were extended upwards to connect with short transverse links rising upwards and outwards from pivots on the chassis, while the dangers of binding splines in the conventional telescopic drive shafts were avoided by the use of a large rubber doughnut coupling in place of each conventional inboard joint. The front suspension layout was geometrically unadventurous, but structurally interesting in that the upper wishbone had become a single sheet steel fabrication of streamlined section, cantilevered inboard to operate a helical spring and damper concealed within the car's nose—a development that was hailed as a triumph of drag-abating ingenuity, though it was merely a revival of what Maserati had done in 1948. Chapman's real contribution to drag reduction was in stretching the driver out in a posture even more reclining than had been considered rather extreme in 1960, thus lowering his head and shoulders by at least two inches and the frontal area by nearly a quarter of a square foot. So slender had racing cars become that this alone would decrease the drag by 3 per cent. It availed the new car but little in the streets of Monaco, where the young driver Clark made the third fastest practice lap behind Moss and Ginther; but at Zandvoort he established a new lap record in it and finished third behind Ferrari. It was common knowledge that Coventry-Climax was developing a V8 engine to replace the FPF, and so it became general expectation that when appropriately engined the Lotus would lead the field just as already it had set the trend.

Already it seemed that the new fashions were here to stay; but new doubts, fears and hopes were excited when there appeared in practice for the British Grand Prix at Aintree a car that threatened to turn the whole business topsy-turvy. This was the Ferguson prototype, with its Coventry-Climax FPF engine in front of the driver, the strangeness of which was justified by its four-wheel-drive system. The car was in fact no more than a racing test-bed for this, and drivers were not finding it altogether easy to handle. Even the most proficient, masters such as Moss and G. Hill, had found during testing that they could not check the occasional spin, largely because the later Ferguson feature of a torque-dividing central differential which divided tractive effort unequally between front and rear, the latter receiving the greater portion, was not yet incorporated. Nevertheless the Ferguson proved outstandingly dependable in the very wet conditions of one of the practice sessions, outbraking and out-accelerating the other cars as well as cornering very fast without signs of under- or oversteer. In the dry, it was unconvincing and it started well to the rear of the grid.

Perhaps more important during that rainy practice session was the new D12 rain version of Dunlop's R5 tyre, the nylon carcassed design which had been introduced in the heyday of the Vanwall. The introduction of the Dunlop R5 had been probably the most important tyre development since the very high pressure beaded-edged cover gave way to the high pressure wired-edge type in the 1920s. From that time the continuing trend had been for tyres to increase in section and where possible to diminish in diameter: whereas in 1926 the Type 35 Bugatti wore tyres of 5-inch section on 20-inch wheels front and rear, by 1936 the C-Type Auto Union wore 5·25–17 at the front, 7–19 or 7–22 at the rear, and by 1956 the Maserati Type 250F wore 5·50–16 at the front and 7–16 at the rear. In that year the design of the R5 was begun. The lightness of the nylon which was adopted as the carcass material allowed a reduction of about 2 lb in unsprung weight; its greater flexibility allowed a lower profile (that is, a lower ratio of section height to section width) which brought an increase in contact area of 10–15 per cent with a corresponding improvement in roadholding; and its greater tensile strength made possible the use of a thinner casing, thus providing for cooler running at high speeds and more uniform distribution of heat across the centre section. All these things combined to make possible a lower inflation pressure than before, not only improving the ride but also the adhesion on bumpy surfaces. Compared with the cotton staple of former years, nylon alone improved lap times by about 1 per cent.

The success of the R5 brought all racing car manufacturers to Dunlop's door, even Ferrari eventually breaking free from his onerous contract with Englebert. This meant that for a while all cars competed, literally, on an equal footing; but with the introduction of the D12 rain tyre in 1961 disorder returned, to grow more confounding with each succeeding year. This tyre, employing a synthetic rubber tread having exceptional frictional properties when running on wet roads, brought with it great problems when the weather turned dry, for it could not sustain the high internal temperatures that would then be generated in its tread compound.

Thus a new strategic element appeared in racing tactics. At the Nurburgring for the German GP of 1961, Moss insisted on D12 rain tyres for his modified Lotus 18, despite a directive issued by Dunlop to all competitors that the weather would not be wet enough and that tread temperatures would run too high for it. In fact the roads were damp when the race started, and his tyres gave Moss an advantage which he exploited to the tune of a 15-second lead in five laps. Thereafter there were eight dry laps which tested his nerve and skill as he consistently out-cornered the faster Ferraris, until rain fell for the last three laps and his now severely worn rain tyres kept Moss safely ahead of any challenge until the finish. From that day onwards, the choice of correct tyre for the

159 The British Standard racing car, 1: Coventry Climax V8 with carburettors and two-plane crankshaft (hence the need for crossover exhaust couplings) in a Brabham tubular chassis

occasion has become more and more critical, and errors of judgement have cost many a deserving entrant victory.

That race incidentally saw the first appearance of the new Coventry-Climax V8, which went very well in a Brabham Cooper during practice, although the car went off the road before completing a lap of the race. This was the engine which would in due course power the majority of British Formula 1 cars, but in itself there was nothing remarkable about it: utterly conventional, with twin overhead camshafts to each bank of cylinders, it had a stroke: bore ratio of 0·95, just like the 2½-litre FPF before it. The exhaust pipe system was novel and intriguing, however: pipes from opposing banks were linked in a complicated cross-over pattern that resulted in the total of eight tributaries eventually reaching confluence in two long and shallow megaphone tail pipes. Clumsy and awkward to accommodate though this array was, it was the only way of effectively combining pipes in which the pulsations were dictated by the peculiar firing order of a 90-degree V8 with a two plane crankshaft.

When the Coventry-Climax V8 appeared again at Monza for the Italian GP at the end of this first significant year for the new formula, it met the new BRM V8. This looked altogether more promising: again it was a 90-degree design with a two-plane crankshaft, and with two camshafts above each cylinder head—though they were gear-driven, in contrast to the Climax chain drive. The stroke:bore ratio was much lower at 0·74, so the piston area was 19 per cent higher. The volumetric efficiency promised to be higher too: the exhaust pipes were not combined in the popular pattern (before long they would be separated as short individual tuned lengths pointing skywards), but the breathing restrictions imposed by carburettor chokes had been done away with, fuel being injected by a Lucas mechanism embodying a simple and ingenious distributor and metering system relying on a reciprocating shuttle to feed the injector nozzles. Also new from Lucas was the ignition system, transistorised and free from the treacheries of the old mechanical contact breaker that had been associated with ignition from the earliest days of the petrol engine. Instead, pole pieces on a tiny camshaft-driven flywheel triggered a magnetic pick-up to time the ignition pulses.

Although the new Climax V8 also acquired this transistorised ignition at the same time, most other cars relied on coil ignition. The regulation demanding self-starters implied a substantial electrical storage battery carried on the car, in which case the remaining elements of a coil ignition system would be much lighter and less consumptive of engine power than a magneto. Multiplex circuits were often necessary to satisfy requirements of spark voltage and frequency, especially in engines of six or more cylinders; but high sparking rates held no terrors for this new electronic system. It might not work well at low speeds, but that would come in time. When it did it would find its way, suitably refined, into ordinary touring cars—and whatever objections may be levelled against the formula governing racing after 1960, it did at least foster a number of developments that would eventually serve the common weal. Electronic ignition was one; fuel injection, improved spark plugs, adjustable dampers and a better understanding of suspension geometry were among other boons. Improvements in tyres were more important than any of these, but would have come about anyway, regardless of formulae.

Given a competitive engine—of which by the end of 1961 he had a reasonable expectation—nothing was more vital to the driver of one of these 1½-litre cars than the correct setting of the suspension. It was Cooper who pioneered adjustable suspension in 1958. By 1961 lightness and general chassis refinement had encouraged cornering rates to grow much higher than before, so that despite the fact that the cars had less power than those of earlier years, they were often as fast as their predecessors. This was almost entirely due to improved cornering and braking, so the slightest variation in suspension geometry could have a critical effect. The racing was now very close indeed, the cars being mostly so similar to each other that the drivers were forced to the brink of control in order to remain competitive. The precise handling of these new rear-engined lightweight cars made things easier for the tyro who was not over-ambitious; but the relatively low power of the engine and the great grip of the latest tyres made it very difficult and in some circumstances impossible for the car's

160 (below) *The British Standard, 2: Coventry Climax V8 with petrol injection and crossover exhausts (the single-plane crankshaft did not materialise until late in 1963) in a Lotus 'monocoque' stressed-skin hull*

161 (below right) *The British Standard, 3: BRM V8 with fuel injection, independent banks of exhausts, and tubular BRM chassis*

attitude to be controlled by the use of excess power, so the drivers more or less resentfully suffered the imposition of an equality that was more apparent than real. Racing thus became not only more competitive but also more dangerous: there were several accidents when drivers fought for the best line through a corner, several others when the limits of adhesion were transcended on such a line, whereupon the departure of car and driver from the course was often irretrievably sudden and sometimes irredeemably permanent.

What was beginning to emerge by the end of the 1961 season was that racing was not so much between cars as between drivers, for most of the cars were very much alike. It seemed that all manufacturers were going to build in the image of the Lotus, those who were slowest to copy its chassis being those who had the most powerful engines. Nevertheless the image was not yet fixed: and even at the beginning of the 1962 season it was still developing, when the new Lotus 24 appeared at Pau with the Coventry Climax V installed, mated to a five-speed ZF synchromesh gearbox, and with 187 bhp giving virtual parity in power with the 190-odd now owned by BRM and Ferrari.

A month later the Lotus 24 was out of date. Clark appeared at Zandvoort in a new Lotus, the Type 25, in which Chapman dispensed entirely with the conventional multi-tubular or space frame structure, choosing instead a stressed-skin hull which, whilst not truly a monocoque, came as near to it as an open car reasonably could. The hull was basically a punt formed of aluminium sheet, its sides a foot deep and stiffened by large torsion boxes, while transverse bracing was provided by steel bulkheads and fabricated cross members as well as by the rigidly mounted engine in the tail. The shape of the engine, with its cylinder blocks leaning outwards at 45 degrees, imposed a reduction in the depth of the longitudinal torsion boxes where they embraced it, but additional steel boxes cantilevered from the main structure compensated for this. Similarly the bulkheads and transverse diaphragms before and behind the driver's seat compensated for the deleterious effect of the large hole (necessary for his entry and exit) on a stressed skin structure. We must remember that provision for the entry and exit of the driver and the engine has just as bad an effect on the structural integrity of a space frame. Multi-tubular frames were already outmoded, being excessively heavy; to be light and yet adequately stiff, the tubes must be arranged so as to be free from bending loads, and this demands such complete triangulation that none of the resultant apertures in an ideal structure would be big enough for the passage of driver or engine. Enlarge the hole for these purposes and the structural stiffness suffers. The Type 21 Lotus of 1961 had a torsional stiffness of only 700 lb ft/deg, and although its basic frame weighed only 82 lb, the addition of the brackets, tanks and supports necessary for body, engine, and other essentials, brought the total frame weight up to 130 lb. By comparison, the type 25 had a hull structure weighing only 70 lb, and a torsional stiffness of 1,000 lb ft/deg,

162 The entire field for the 1963 Dutch GP, from the leading Lotus to the trailing Porsche, was shod with the new Dunlop R6 tyre

increased to 2,400 by the installation of the engine. Thus the torsional stiffness was three times greater than that of the 1961 car, while the frame weighed little more than half as much; and to give it further superiority Chapman reduced the frontal area of the type 25 to a mere eight square feet, an 11 per cent improvement on the 1960 Type 18. He achieved this by making the driver lean back further than ever, at an angle of 35 degrees, and giving him a steering wheel only a foot in diameter, packing him and his controls and every possible ancillary well down inside the car, allowing as little as possible to protrude outside.

The die was cast. Thereafter, every successful Grand Prix car would be moulded in the pattern of this Lotus. For years the most adept racing car designers had been searching for those constant, general and irrefragable laws of right. Now the years of bewilderment were ended: the laws had been stated by Chapman. Of course, there would be other designers who would choose to differ: Porsche with a fine chassis and air-cooled flat-eight engine, BRM, Ferrari and Honda with engines of highly individual character. They would all have their brief moments of glory; but over the long term, it was the Lotus 25 and its derivative the type 33 which was consistently and devastatingly successful. This was the theme

163 The flat-eight Porsche of 1962 had a chassis of exceptional merit, but it achieved little

164 Two BRMs sandwich a Cooper in the 1963 German GP. Note the upright attitude of the outer wheels and adverse camber of the less important inner wheels

upon which the passacaglia of subsequent motor racing history was based. This was the car, alone of all post-World War II examples, that deserves to rank with the 1912 Peugeot, the 1923 Fiat, and the 1937 Mercedes-Benz, the rare few to set a fashion for all the world to follow.

Only one thing argues against Chapman being thus honoured with Henry, Cavalli and Wagner: Lotus made racing cars, but they did not make racing engines. These they were content to buy from Coventry-Climax; and until that firm brought its little V8 up to date, the full force of the Lotus lesson could not be felt.

A clue to the next major step in the development of engines might have been observed as early as 1962, when Ferrari made a last effort to get more power from the wide-angle V6: new four-valve cylinder heads enabled this engine to run 5 per cent faster and give over 5 per cent more power, from which it could be inferred that bmep was not significantly altered. At the same time, however, Ferrari was also working on new V8 and flat 12 engines, which, benefiting from greater piston area and the ability to run even faster, naturally produced more power regardless of their ration of valves. By 1964, however, BRM, Coventry-Climax and Honda were all busy with four-valve engines in more or less advanced states of experiment. BRM found themselves in some trouble with combustion, and the final version of their $1\frac{1}{2}$-litre V8 appeared in 1965 with two valves per cylinder again, but with the inlet ports running straight down between them. Honda had already shown in motorcycle racing that there were rich rewards for those who had the courage to break away from current practice, and their tiny multi-cylinder engines ran up to unprecedented rates of revolution, aided by having four valves to each little combustion chamber, and reached specific power outputs that were almost beyond the belief of car engineers.

The first of their opportunities to verify that, if Honda chassis were not up to much, their engines were all that had been claimed, came when the Japanese firm produced an intriguing $1\frac{1}{2}$-litre V12, set transversely across the rear of an otherwise fairly conventional new car. With this multiplicity of cylinders and stroke:bore ratio of 0·81 the engine boasted 49 square inches of piston area and could turn up to 13,000 rev/min. Honda motorcycle practice had been pursued in many respects, including coil ignition and motorcycle Keihin carburettors, needle roller bearings for crankshaft and connecting rods and everything else, and four valves per cylinder. This engine was claimed to deliver 230 bhp. If this claim were true, the V12 Honda was the most powerful of all the engines raced under the $1\frac{1}{2}$-litre formula; but since it was only $7\frac{1}{2}$ per cent higher than the power output claimed for the V8 Ferrari, there is no need to suspect that the Japanese were guilty of any serious deception. The car was run somewhat cautiously in its first races, but when occasionally given head it demonstrated itself to be very fast, eventually winning the last race of 1965 at Mexico City, where it was proved faster along the straight than any of the other cars.

165 *The miserably unsuccessful ATS at Spa in 1963*

166 *Clark in the Lotus 25 at Silverstone, 1963. Inboard front suspension units leave the exterior uncluttered, as in the 1948 Maserati*

Well before this, the final steps necessary for the Coventry-Climax to become fully competitive began to bear fruit. In the 1963 version the stroke:bore ratio had been reduced from 0·95 to 0·76, increasing the piston area from 38 to 44 square inches and permitting the crankshaft rate to go up from 8,500 to 9,500 rev/min. During that year (at the German GP, to be exact), it acquired a single-plane or flat crankshaft, of basically the same shape as that in an in-line four-cylinder engine. This step, which has since been followed by all manufacturers of racing V8 engines, brought with it certain positive advantages, the most apparent being that the complex cross-over exhaust pipe system could be abandoned. Always difficult to accommodate and getting in the mechanics' way at pit stops, the cross-over pipe-work had been essential because of the firing order of a two-plane V8 crankshaft in which the throws are spaced 90 degrees apart. With the flat shaft, the pipes could be grouped more conveniently into two well-separated sets of four, one set to each bank, and led conveniently into tail pipes. There were further advantages in manufacture: when the shaft has its throws spaced at right-angles, the main bearing loads are small but this is only the consequence of balance requirements that make full counterweighting necessary. A single-plane shaft is much easier to make, and it can still be counterbalanced so that the main bearings carry no inertia loads, the primary balance being perfect. There remains one disadvantage of considerable importance: since the crankshaft is similar in shape to the simple in-line four-cylinder engine's, there are secondary out-of-balance forces liberated which act in the planes of the cylinders, and in a 90-degree V8 are resolved into an horizontal force which alternates in direction at twice engine speed. Since these secondary vibrations originate from variations in acceleration of the reciprocating components moving up from bottom dead centre and those moving down from top dead centre, they can only be eradicated by making the connecting rods infinitely long. Coventry-Climax, however, had actually shortened their rods in order to reduce the overall height and weight of the engine. They therefore had to accept and accommodate the vibrations which must be contained by the main bearing webs and the supporting crankcase structure. Presumably Clark was not unduly troubled by the new vibration fed into the fuselage of his Lotus, for it now went faster than ever—as indeed it should, for this revised version with fuel injection developed 195 bhp at 3,200 feet per minute mean piston speed, while the peak bmep had risen a little to 202 lb/in^2 at 7,350 rev/min.

Thus encouraged, Coventry-Climax reduced the stroke:bore ratio of this engine even further in 1964 to the extremely low figure of 0·63. The results were rather interesting, for the piston area was now no less than 50 square inches, more even than the twelve-cylinder Honda and equalled only by later versions of the flat-twelve Ferrari. However, the traditional Coventry-Climax provision of rather small-bore induction tracts, intended deliberately to maintain high air velocities, would not allow this engine to breathe as freely as it needed to if it were to exploit its new dimensions, and despite an increase of 14 per cent in piston area the power rose by only $2\frac{1}{2}$ per cent and the revs by the same proportion, peak-power piston speed dropped by 9 per cent and peak bmep by $6\frac{1}{2}$ per cent.

During 1964 Coventry-Climax sought to profit from the new

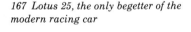
167 Lotus 25, the only begetter of the modern racing car

168 The BRP hull, typical of late 1¼-litre practice, before installation of its BRM engine

169 The Lola-Climax resembled most of the tubular-framed 1½-litre cars of the 1961–5 era, except for its outboard front springs and dampers

dimensions by capping the engine with new cylinder heads embodying pent-roof combustion chambers each containing four valves. Success eluded them, it being thought that the different combustion chamber shape was having a deleterious effect on combustion. Then after weeks of despair, it suddenly occurred late one night to Walter Hassan (erstwhile mechanic to W. O. Bentley and now chief engineer at Coventry-Climax) that the effect of advancing the ignition had not been explored; whereupon leaping from his bed with such zeal as had prompted Beethoven to leap from his bath and run naked through the streets of Vienna shouting Eroica! he returned to the factory, advanced the engine's

170 (above) *In 1963 Ferrari field a new car based more on the British Standard specimen. New V8 and flat-12 engines were planned for it, but as an interim measure the chassis was proven (after some troubles allegedly due to deficient copying!) with a V6 engine installed. Here is Surtees driving it in the British GP*

171 The bodywork of the 1963–4 Ferrari needed only slight alterations to accommodate any of the three available types of engines. The V8 was the most successful, bringing Surtees the 1964 World Championship

ignition, and satisfied himself that he had the answer. The fruits of his labours were 210 bhp at 10,500 rev/min, 195 lb/in^2 at 8,500, and the world championship of 1965. Seldom can a ten-degrees spark advance have achieved so much.

The performance of the Lotus 33 powered by the 32-valve Coventry-Climax was improved even more than these figures might suggest, for it developed useful power over a speed range of 3,500 rev/min, 1,000 more than that of the 16-valve version. Furthermore, the increase in maximum crankshaft rate being greater than the increase in power, it was possible for the car's gear ratios to be lowered, thus multiplying the engine torque so that there was even more surplus tractive effort available at the driving wheels for acceleration.

Thus the 1965 version of the Coventry-Climax FWMD engine completely vindicated the theorists who argued that four small

172 *The early 1960s saw the beginnings of a revolution in tyre construction. Compare the proportions of the Dunlops on this 1962 BRM with those of the 1965 car in Figure 173*

173 *The fastest 1½-litre car of the 1961–5 formula, the 1965 BRM*

valves were better than two large ones. Its value as an example lay in the fact that the rest of the engine remained the same as in the previous year, allowing a true comparison to be reached; and with this evidence before them other manufacturers could not fail to be impressed. Within another four years, four-valve heads were to be the rule rather than the exception in Grand Prix racing.

It might not have taken so long had not the FIA announced in December 1963 the terms of a new Formula 1 that was to take effect from 1 January 1966. The permitted piston displacement under this was increased to 3 litres for unsupercharged engines, while the devotees of forced induction were mocked with the opportunity to use 1½-litre engines and continued restriction to petrol. In most other respects the 1966 formula was much the same as before: the race distance or duration was unchanged, self-starters

174 Its engine altered to take fresh air in betweed the camshafts, and to exhaust between the cylinder banks, the 1965 BRM gave more than 210 bhp

and unfaired wheels remained the rule, but the minimum weight limit was increased to 500 kg.

Thus informed, manufacturers began to plan their new engines before the latest developments in current engines were properly appreciated or even known about. Preoccupation with engines was general: whereas the 2½-litre formula applied through a period of seven years during which designs that were conventional or *avant garde* at the beginning were completely obsolete by the end, the 1½-litre formula was valid for only five years, and the cars racing at its end were little more than advanced versions of those conceived at its beginning. The archetype of the modern Grand Prix car, the Lotus 25, had been seen in action for only one and a half years when the new formula was announced, so it was natural that the cars envisaged for racing in and after 1966 would be essentially similar to it. It was also natural that a new wave of optimism

223

should run almost unchecked through motor racing circles, as the return of power was confidently forecast as restoring to motor racing all the noise, drama, and technical variety that had been somewhat lacking in the first half of the decade. There was talk of engines that would be developing 350 or 400 horsepower within a year of the new regulations taking effect, and reaching perhaps 500 horsepower a couple of years after that. Even though tyres had become broader and more squat upon the introduction of the Dunlop R6 in 1963 and the R7 in 1965, it was thought that such tremendous power would be too much for them, and that four-wheel drive would become essential. It was going to be a brave new world in which the furious intransigence of almighty and brutal power would relieve drivers of the enforced equality they had suffered in the footling $1\frac{1}{2}$-litre cars, and thus sort out the men from the boys.

In 1966, it proved to be more a matter of separating the sheep from the goats. Many of the cars competing that year were of a transitional nature, leftovers from the previous formula and from the Tasman series of winter races conducted in the Antipodean summer under the terms of a peculiar $2\frac{1}{2}$-litre formula, new chassis with old sports-car engines, old-fashioned chassis with new engines based on passenger cars, any and every kind of stop-gap, but nothing that was completely convincing. At slow circuits such as Monaco the type 33 Lotus, with its 32-valve Coventry-Climax engine enlarged to 2 litres, was often the fastest thing in the race,

176 The first 3-litre Ferrari of 1966, winning at Syracuse

though a certain fragility regularly robbed it of success. At very fast circuits such as Spa and Reims a new Ferrari, its chassis an enlarged version of the $1\frac{1}{2}$-litre V8 to carry a 3-litre version of the 3·3-litre V12 that had done well in sportscar races, was clearly the faster but almost as regularly robbed of victory. The new McLaren, built by the former Cooper driver, had a monocoque body of exceptional stiffness, being made of Mallite—an aviation material consisting of two aluminium skins bonded to a sandwich core of end-grain balsa wood—but was handicapped by an engine which

225

177 (top) *A later version of the 1966 V12 Ferrari at Zandvoort*

178 *The Ferrari V12 engine was derived from a sports-car design*

was a de-stroked version of the 4·2-litre Ford Indianapolis engine, insufficiently powerful and excessively heavy.

By far the most successful car of 1966 and the following year was the Repco-Brabham. It defied several conventions, but was a piece of flagrant opportunism rather than a futuristic racing car. It set no fashions except in red faces. Brabham had taken his leave of the Cooper team to produce his own car in 1962, and in its chassis this new one was not significantly different: it had a simple tubular space frame chassis of no great stiffness, basically conventional suspension that displayed a certain refinement in its geometry at the front but was content to wear its springs and dampers out in the open air, and in general its overall dimensions were less than those of the other 3-litre cars. The remarkable thing was its engine, a thing of absurd simplicity and enviable lightness. Its cylinder block was that of a mass-production V8 Oldsmobile onto which had been grafted cylinder heads in which a single overhead camshaft operated a line of parallel valves, two to each cylinder. The crankcase had been stiffened by a steel plate across its bottom,

179 An underpowered overweight
Ford V8 spoilt the otherwise good
showing of the Mallite-bodied 1966
McLaren

the single-plane crankshaft weighed only 45 lb, and the connecting
rods were standard Daimler V8 components chosen because they
happened to be the right size. With a low stroke: bore ratio (0·68:1)
it might have run at very high speeds, but despite its short stroke
the engine developed its maximum power at only 8,000 rev/min
and was neither useful nor safe beyond 8,200, the power inhibited
by the limited breathing ability of the cylinder head, revolutions
checked by mechanical and electrical impediments. On the other
hand, there was an unusual spread of torque over a wide range of
engine speed: there was power at 3,500 rev/min, real useful power
at 4,000, maximum torque (corresponding to 192 lb/in² bmep) at
6,500, and maximum power (285 bhp at the outset, 300 later) at
8,000. The check-in weight of the car was less than that of any
other 3-litre or indeed any 2½-litre car, and the modest fuel consumption made 35 gallons an ample fuel load for the longest race;
so the car's starting line weight was a lot less than that of any car
of comparable or greater power, while the torque and power of the
engine were quite enough to deal summarily with any car of comparable weight. Its handling was inferior to that of the Lotus 33 in

180 1966 Repco-Brabham

slow corners, but in fast bends it was very good; and this may have been because of, rather than in spite of, the torsional weakness of the frame, for its designer Mr Tauranac believed that a little flexibility would ensure better balanced tyre loadings. In this as in most things he was a staunch believer in practical moderation rather than theoretical radicalism; and the Australian team (headed by Mr Irving) responsible for the Repco engine were of the same mind, so that although its 100 bhp per litre was of no great merit it was enough, while the lightness of the engine—which weighed only 340 lb—was of very great value. So was its reliability: in only two of the nine races constituting the World Championship series in 1966 did no Brabham finish, and of the other seven there was only one in which a Brabham did not figure in the first three finishers. Even in 1967, when the Cosworth-Ford-engined Lotus 49 established itself as the fastest concurrent, it was the reliability of the Repco Brabham that saw it through to yet another championship.

By the end of 1968 Mr Rudd of BRM was presenting to the Institution of Mechanical Engineers a paper chronicling the failure of the car—or rather the engine—which should have dominated racing under the 3-litre formula from mid-1966 onwards, perhaps even up to the present day. This was the H16 BRM, for which an ultimate 500 bhp was forecast and in which detailed provision was made for furnishing the four-wheel drive to harness such power, in accordance with all the suppositions and theories that were aired in the days when the return to power was so eagerly anticipated. The concluding words of the paper have a wistful finality about them: 'The engine has so far failed to reach its prime objective, which is to power a car to win the formula 1 constructors championship. The main reasons were that it was too heavy and although now fairly reliable still destructive to transmissions . . . most of the problems arose from excessive caution in the design.' There is here an echo of the old BRM syndrome, which has been evident since the earliest days of the blown $1\frac{1}{2}$-litre V16. Time and time again BRM conceived engines that were adventurous in principle but too cautiously detailed in practice. If the V16 had been given more vigorous cam profiles, vortex throttling, or variable-ratio drive for its superchargers, and more positively sealed cylinder liners . . . or if the $2\frac{1}{2}$-litre engine had been given the four valve heads that Tresillian advocated . . . then perhaps these engines would have been, as they originally promised to be, the ones to beat.

In the early days of 1966, with the 3-litre formula still a matter for speculation, it seemed then, too, that the compact and apparently well-founded BRM newcomer was eventually going to be the engine to beat. So far as we knew or were then allowed to know, it had everything in its favour, for its individual cylinders and most of their adjuncts—valves, springs, cams, pistons, connecting rods and so forth, the things that really count—were the same as in the highly successful V8 $1\frac{1}{2}$-litre engine that had made the 1965 BRM eventually the fastest, though not the most successful, of all the cars built under the expiring formula. When it went to Monza in September 1965 the little V8 had acquired new cylinder heads whose combustion chambers were based on a conjunction of three hemispheres, and in this form it gave all of 220 bhp at 11,750 rev/min. It was expected that the new doubled-up version of the engine would therefore give the best part of 440 bhp at the same revolutions.

But it did not. When, after months of painful disillusion and catastrophic disruption, it was eventually developed to a stage where it was at least worth putting into a car, its best was a short-lived 400 bhp at 10,600 rev/min. Even by the end of the European season in 1966, by which time some major redesign had been effected, output had risen to 420 bhp at 11,000, but things were still going seriously wrong. As for the sopranino realms of 12,000 rev/min, up to which the 1965 engine could sing as clear as a bell—alas, the 3-litre never reached the stage where it could be run at more than 11,000 for long enough to measure much. To make matters worse, it grew most objectionably heavy, more than 140 lb over the original target weight.

As originally conceived, the H16 had much to commend it. Preliminary studies by two independent teams at BRM had indicated that they could build a 48-valve V12 that would weigh 360 lb, be 30 inches long, and would ultimately give 475 bhp; or that they could do the H16, 24 inches long and 380 lb in weight, able eventually to develop 500 bhp. Certainly the H-configuration had much to commend it in making an engine the right shape to fit into a contemporary racing car, an engine which by the nature of its layout could muster the greatest possible piston area, run at the highest possible rates of revolution, be of such satisfying structural stiffness as to lend itself for use as a stress-bearing

229

portion of the chassis in which it would be installed—an engine which would, in short, have almost everything in its favour. There was good precedent. The Napier Sabre, the most powerful piston engine in aviation (it was developed to give 5,500 bhp or 150 per litre, which was fantastic for a big engine) was an H24; and in the early 1940s when the Germans were planning a new generation of aero engines that would range in power from 4,000 to 10,000 bhp, they satisfied themselves that the H layout was the one to adopt.

'Experience was available on H engines including the Napier range,' said Rudd in his paper. Available it may have been, but it does not seem to have been drawn upon in matters of detail. The Sabre, for instance, had an exquisite system of floating gears to balance the loading imparted to the drive train from each of the two crankshafts; but the BRM just had undersized torsion shafts and a crude spur gear connection between the two shafts, and this was developed on the wicked old basis of 'make it stronger if it breaks'. When it stops breaking, something else usually starts; and in fact most of the really serious trouble was the result of torsional vibration problems originating in the shafts. As a temporary measure, heavy steel rings were bolted onto four of the webs on each crankshaft to increase the inertia, and the engine was raced like this through 1966; but eventually a new type of crankshaft with eight crankpins instead of four was made—along with the new crankcase and conrods made necessary by the dimensional changes in the shafts. In effect the difference was that whereas the H16 had originally two cylinders firing simultaneously, it now had the firing order and intervals of a true sixteen-cylinder engine.

At this encouraging new stage, all the new conrods started breaking and a new spate of wrecked engines ensued. BRM had at one stage been using steel cylinder liners but tried cast iron ones because they were much cheaper, and found in the process that the engine gave a little more power when thus fitted. Unfortunately whenever a piston broke or a valve got out of tempo (which was always happening because of the torsional flutter affecting the relationship of crank and camshafts), the iron liner would shatter and the unsupported rod would flail around and smash the engine to pieces. So they had to go back to steel and lose power—though they later tried chrome-plated duralumin and merely lost a bit more oil.

Actually they lost far more oil on occasions through being so hard up for spare parts that they had to salvage bits of old broken engines, with oversize main bearings and worn-out scavenge pumps which left the lower cam boxes swimming in oil. In 1967 smoky exhausts were a frequent sign of hard times.

Also feeling the pinch by then were Cooper, who had started 1966 with a certain amount of optimism and a V12 Maserati engine. Originally they had taken for granted, like Brabham and Lotus, the continuing support of Coventry-Climax; but early in 1965 that company had announced that it would be withdrawing from racing, the cost of which was growing prohibitive. Turning to

Maserati for help, Cooper were offered a 3-litre V12 that had been developed from a sports-car engine, in its turn derived from the 2½-litre V12 that had been so powerful and intractable in Formula 1 racing during 1957. The horde of carburettors had been replaced by fuel injection, the multiplicity of ignition coils by transistorised circuitry; and where the 1957 racing engine had yielded high power output at high speeds and very little at lesser rates, the petrol-burning 3-litre of 1966 gave moderately high power at moderately high speeds (about 315 bhp at 9,500 rev/min, equivalent to a paltry 144 lb/in^2 at 4,150 feet per minute piston speed) but had plenty of torque over a fairly wide speed range. Nevertheless it was a large engine and a heavy one, giving the Cooper a weight distribution that put no less than two-thirds of its total mass on to the rear tyres.

No doubt they had been hoping for more power and less weight. Certainly they had excelled themselves in devising a chassis that for once was ingenious and modern. The hull was a stressed-skin construction, and the suspension more or less conventional, but the front brakes were semi-inboard—that is, the front hub carrier was between the wheel and the brake, the two communicating by means of a live stub axle passing right through the hub. This might increase frontal area slightly, but the brakes could be much better cooled and could be of the greatest possible size without affecting the choice of road wheels that need no longer be large enough in diameter to accommodate them. Thus the Cooper was able to run on 13-inch wheels and enjoy some advantage in unsprung weight and frontal area of tyres compared with what would have been the case with wheels of larger diameter. Furthermore, by bringing the substantial brake calipers and discs further inboard, the moment of the unsprung mass was reduced, permitting lower spring frequencies and a better ride and adhesion.

The grip of the Coopers' front wheels was still not good enough. Despite their weight distribution they suffered extreme understeer in slow corners. Choosing tyre sizes as disparate as the static loads they were called on to bear, Cooper's engineers had perhaps tried too hard to eradicate the oversteer that they felt was likely to spoil the car and had given it an excess of understeer as

231

the result. They also gave it an excess of unreliability, and throughout 1966 the cars were betrayed by an infuriating series of breakages of all sorts of components. Later in 1966, incidentally, the team was joined by the erstwhile Ferrari driver Surtees (world champion driver in 1964 and world champion motorcycle racer on numerous occasions), who encouraged a change from the R7 Dunlop to the new Firestone tyres and virtually eradicated the Cooper's handling deficiencies in a brief spell of development. So successful was this that a Cooper won the last event in 1966, the balance of probabilities being further upset by another win for the same make in the first Grand Prix of 1967. It was, however, a swansong for the Cooper, which was overweight and underpowered; after abortive experiments with new cylinder heads, the Maserati engine was abandoned and Coopers played out their last days in Formula 1 racing with a BRM V12—the engine that had been built as an insurance while work went on with the H16, one that had been conceived as a sports-car engine but was to be developed into one of the most powerful Grànd Prix engines by 1971.

The most significant event in the career of the Cooper was the transformation effected by a change of tyres. The year 1966 stands out as one in which, amid a commercially fomented welter of publicity, the major American tyre manufacturers Firestone and Goodyear set themselves to compete with each other and Dunlop, introducing to Grand Prix racing not only new and remarkable tyres but also what might be called an inflationary spiral of confusion, stupidity, and technological cumber from which there appears to be no prospect of recession.

Ten years earlier, when the 2½-litre formula was getting into its swing, there were likewise a number of tyre manufacturers involved in Grand Prix racing. Pirelli were generally considered supreme, but Mercedes-Benz got good service from Continental, Ferrari fared badly at the hands of Engelbert, and other teams did

1970-1 Tyrrell

THE EMBODIMENT OF ESTABLISHED PRINCIPLES was proved to be sufficient to ensure the satisfactory performance of a new Grand Prix car when Stewart, admittedly the most professional and one of the most proficient drivers of his time, began a very profitable run with the Tyrrell built for him in 1970. His entrant, who had invested in a March for that year, was chary of the fact that the car was an unknown quantity from a new manufacturer; and he therefore took the precaution of commissioning a car of his own from the drawing board of the designer Gardner, whom he had encountered when working on the four-wheel-drive Matra. The conventional Matra of that time was the one in which Stewart had enjoyed an exceptionally successful season, and the Tyrrell was intended to exhibit similar characteristics: a low polar moment of inertia, a very wide track, and craftsmanship of a very high order.

Also implicit in the specification was the Cosworth V-8 engine, in which both entrant and driver had a great deal of confidence. The result was surprising only in the apparent ease with which it proved able to trounce all opposition – which made all the more surprising those occasions when it appeared unable to compete with them. We must accept that this want of consistency was the fault of the car, not of the driver; the latter was always at pains to make this clear.

1969-71 Matra

SOME SUPERB CARS have been produced by the aviation industry,
Hispano-Suiza and Bristol being perhaps the most outstanding. But there have
been some pretty indifferent cars to come from it, too; so it need not be
assumed automatically that the Matra ought to have been good because it
was the work of a leading French aeronautical and missile engineering
company.

The V-12 that appeared in 1968 was a beautiful, thirsty, intractable failure.
The 1969 car was a great success, but with a Cosworth V-8 it could hardly be
seen as a triumph of French engineering. Thereafter Matra prepared a new
V-12 and a new chassis. The latter was superbly engineered, and had
outstanding roadholding; but the former was troubled by oil surge, and
success generally eluded it. For 1971 the engine was further developed, but a
new chassis failed to live up to expectations, and again it was a sad year.
In 1972 yet another chassis appeared, seemingly with all the old virtues in
full strength, and the engine continuing to make the most wonderful noise;
but luck never looked that way. . . .

well enough with tyres by Avon and Dunlop. By 1958, however, the general withdrawal from racing by Pirelli and the introduction of the then remarkable new R5 nylon tyre by Dunlop put the latter firm on a pinnacle whence from late 1958 to early 1966 none could topple them. At the end of that period Dunlop tyres were still looking more or less as they had at the beginning—a bit more squat perhaps, but all the old recognisable characteristics were still there. Already the situation had been complicated a little by the presence of Goodyear, who in 1965 had been content to make (for the use of the Brabham team) tyres according to traditional techniques but perhaps a little lower in profile and a little flatter in the crown. Little attention was paid to this, for Brabhams were not winning races that year. In 1966, however, Firestone came along, pinning their hopes of success on the idea of a tyre of very low profile and virtually flat tread. Thus while the others were content with aspect ratios of 65 or 60 per cent (the figure represents the proportion of section height to section width), Firestone began the year at 55 per cent and ended it below 40 per cent. What became popularly known as the 'tyre war' flared up into an incessant and earnest rivalry between all three tyre manufacturers, the American newcomers demonstrating such overwhelming superiority that by the end of the 1966 season there were scarcely any leading drivers or entrants using Dunlop tyres, and it was not until early in the 1968 season that Dunlop made an effective return to the fray. By that time they had caught up with their rivals in construction techniques; and by that time tyre profiles had dropped in some cases to as low as 30 per cent. Since then the figure has continued to descend, but only by very small decrements, and newly intrusive phenomena (notably vibration, to be discussed later) discouraged further profile abasement in 1971—perhaps scarcely too soon, for extrapolation of early trends suggested that by 1973 some manufacturers might give up conventional tyres and simply wrap a thin rubber tape around the wheel.

Still, if the shape and structure of tyres altered a lot in the two years between mid-1966 and mid-1968, the cars remained the same. They were a little more powerful, and perhaps a little more ugly, but they still had the same sort of shape, the same distribution of major components, the same kind of brakes and suspensions and transmissions. It was somewhat surprising that suspension altered so little: for the variety fashionable then (and indeed still) was originally schemed to exploit the properties of tyres which by 1968 were considered fit for nothing but club racing of obsolescent cars.

In the old days a racing tyre had a visibly convex crown, and suspensions were so adjusted as to display a negative wheel camber when the car was running in a straight line, the ground pressure (between the tread contact patch and the road) varying from a maximum at the inner edge of the tread to practically nothing at the outer edge of the contact patch. With properly arranged suspension geometry, such as was developed during 1961, the effect of roll and weight transfer in a corner would be to press the outer tyres more firmly on the road, increasing the size of the contact patch, changing its shape to a more complete oval and subjecting it to a more uniform ground pressure. In the process the wheel might become a little more perpendicular to the road, but with luck or good judgement it might in extreme conditions still enjoy some negative camber. Too much of this could be a bad thing, as Ferrari discovered in 1961 when the inner edges of their steeply cambered tyres were subjected to gross overheating on high-speed circuits; but in the case of the Dunlop R7 as employed in 1965, maximum cornering force could be realised at 2 degrees negative camber.

This was all very well round corners, but not so good when the car was travelling in a straight line. During acceleration, transmission of power to the ground was hampered by the small contact areas of the rear tyres and the uneven distribution of contact pressure. During braking the effect of forward weight transfer was to force the nose of the car down and in a relative way to force the wheels up, so that both front wheels displayed marked negative camber and thus could not put enough tread on the road to provide the requisite braking effort. Means of modifying the suspension geometry, usually by setting the axes of rotation of the front wishbones out of parallel, had been devised during the early 1960s so as to provide some measure of resistance to braking dive or indeed to acceleration squat; but anti-dive suspension geometry is something to employ with great caution, for when carried to extremes it can be tantamount to a complete locking of the suspension, stopping the front springs from working at all. The consequences of this are imaginable but scarcely enjoyable; and even with a milder anti-dive geometry, complications are entrained during cornering because the castor angle of each front wheel will vary independently with movement of the suspension towards the full bump position.

What was wanted was a tyre that could put more rubber in contact with the road and keep it there with more uniform pressure over the whole of the contact area. At the same time it had to give if possible a higher cornering power and faster responses than existing tyres, and to have as much controllability, predictability and general progressiveness in its behaviour as drivers might require. According to classical tyre-building theory the effects should be sought by reducing the crown angle of the tyre's carcass cords—the angle subtended by the cords through the centre line of the tread. Reduce this angle and the tyre automatically becomes more squat in profile; but, more important, for a given load and inflation pressure it develops a higher cornering power, a smaller slip angle when operating in given cornering conditions, and has a shallower curve of self-aligning torque— which means a less variable pneumatic trail effect and more consistent feel.

It was the pursuit of this theory that led to racing tyres becoming fatter and shallower in section over the years from 1957 to 1965, years which saw the Dunlop R5 make way for the R6 and then the R7. In the process, with the aspect ratio dropping to something

234

like 70 per cent, the contact patch underwent a change in shape as important as the changes in the shape of the tyre itself. It was still oval because of the convex tread; but its major axis was now transverse instead of longitudinal, and this introduced new problems. One was that pneumatic trail (caused by the centre of pressure of the contact patch being behind the geometrical centre of its area) was reduced, and so the degree in variation of castor effect and steering feel became so slight that a driver of less than first-class sensitivity might not detect it until too late. The other and more important was that, since the contact patch was now shorter from front to rear, there was less opportunity in wet weather for getting the road-borne water out of the way so that the tyre tread could come to grips with the road surface. In a racing tyre, as in a road tyre, the foremost third of the contact patch has to shoulder aside the bulk of the water encountered, the next third mops up the remainder, and the final third does the real work of gripping and shoving. Speeds of cars were growing higher and higher, the FIA and its strictures notwithstanding, and this speed alone made it more difficult to get the water out of harm's way. Reducing the length of the contact patch aggravated the problem considerably. In any case there was still no uniformity of ground pressure but, rather, a maximum in the centre of the contact patch and a progressive reduction to zero at the edges of it. This, according to Firestone's thinking, was all wrong: they wanted every bit of rubber to be forced against the road to the same degree as every other bit in the contact patch; and the way to achieve this would be through a rectangular contact patch, in turn demanding that the tread be not convex but flat.

Yet there was no satisfactory way of building a racing tyre of such a shape by conventional constructional methods. Making a flat tread by building up the shoulders would simply accelerate breakdown of the rubber through overheating in the deep layers of tread rubber at the shoulders, where the frictional heat built up with every rotation of the tyre would not be able to dissipate itself with sufficient rapidity. Once again, the old square/cube law was operating, as it had done with inlet and exhaust valves: the ratio of surface area to mass has to be kept high in a racing tyre, as in a racing engine's valves.

It was while puzzling over this that Martin, of the Firestone Racing Division, came across a weird corn-harvester tyre that his firm had made back in 1934, a tyre with huge shoulders and a concave tread whose shape was echoed by its carcass. This was the first-contour-moulded tyre, forced in the vulcanising press to adopt a shape quite different from the simple tubular one that seemed so natural. Thus was born the idea of a contour-moulded racing tyre: and it was an immediate success.

In its uninflated or underinflated state, such a tyre is easily recognised. The tread is concave, and in a new tyre that has never been inflated even the sidewalls are concave too. The carcass cords run right up into the shoulders of the tread and weird things happen to their angles in the course of the vulcanising process,

235

things that result in the tyre having an aspect ratio lower than its cord angles would lead one to expect.

The most weird thing about a contour moulded tyre is the way it flexes. Mount an ordinary tyre on a wheel and inflate it, and the tyre sidewalls will move outwards somewhat while the crown of the tread moves upwards to make it more convex. Roll the tyre on the road and of course the tread becomes more nearly flattened at the point of contact while the sidewalls bulge yet further. Run it at racing speeds and centrifugal force makes the whole tyre expand radially, the crown becoming much more convex and the contact patch becoming smaller in area. The contour-moulded tyre does not follow these rules. On inflation the sidewalls still bulge out a trifle while the originally concave tread becomes flat. It stays flat on the road, the side walls bulging and flexing in accordance with the load being carried. At very high speeds, however, when centrifugal loadings take effect, the sidewalls pull back in towards their original moulded shape and so does the tread, the whole carcass flexing around the shoulders which behave as nodal points. The nodes still move radially outwards, and so may the very centre of the tread in a tyre that is particularly wide, so the overall diameter may still be increased at very high speeds: in certain 1971 tyres an increase of 2 inches in circumference (which is an increase of about 2·6 per cent) has been measured at 160 mph.

It is simply in order to maintain the tyre profile that it remains necessary to increase inflation pressures for circuits that allow very high speeds, even though the tyre might be working sufficiently within its designed load and temperature range for inflation pressure increase to be otherwise unnecessary. One can often see a concavity in the tread in photographs of racing cars travelling at high speed, and this despite the fact that the latest tyres tend to be made with their treads not absolutely flat in the correctly inflated state but very slightly convex. The radius of tread curvature is seldom less than about 30 inches, but car designers feel that this slight convexity gives them a little more latitude in suspension design, for reasons we shall see.

If a tyre appears to be under-inflated, it may be deliberate. Tyre technicians take very careful measurements of tread temperatures and wear rates during practice for a race, and their final recommendations as to pressures and suspension settings have often to effect some sort of compromise between the demands of endurance and the various handling properties required on selected portions of the surface. In general it is surprising how low inflation pressures are: 20 lb/in² is not uncommon, although in the early days of the Dunlop R5 the figure might have been twice as high, while back in the era of the 750-kg cars the huge tyres of Auto Union and Mercedes-Benz were inflated to 50 or 60 lb/in².

The difference is due to the great reserves of load-carrying capacity on the vast tyres upon which the modern lightweight racing car runs. They are made big for traction, braking and handling response; but in the process they are so big that they seldom work anywhere near their peak cornering power, for this tends to increase as the tyre is pressed more firmly against the road and only begins to reduce again as the limits of the tyre's load-carrying capacity are approached. From this comes the curious paradox that it is sometimes necessary to reduce pressure in the front tyres in order to reduce understeer. This went so completely against traditional teaching that tyre technicians for some time had great difficulty in persuading drivers and team managers that reducing tyre pressure would increase the tyres' cornering power. With what opportune aerodynamic cunning the car manufacturers responded in 1968, when they realised all the implications of this situation, will be recounted in the next chapter.

The inflation pressure of the modern racing tyre may be fairly low, but when considered in relation to the volume of the tyre and the weight of the vehicle it supports, the modern racing tyre is still inflated pretty hard—certainly enough to prevent it from deforming much under the load. This is fine for minimising heat build-up and thus improving the tyre's endurance, but it introduces other very serious problems. These modern tyres with cotton-reel proportions, with a tread that is virtually flat and extremely wide, may put plenty of rubber on the road when kept perpendicular to it; but tilt them a trifle as the suspension systems hallowed by the years tend to do, and little more than one edge of the tread may be left in contact with the road. Let the wishbones genuflect just a shade too much in mid-corner, and the driver can find that the grip offered by his tyres has suddenly deteriorated to a tenth of what it was a moment earlier.

You can lose a lot of drivers that way, and designers have lost a lot of sleep in adjusting suspension to minimise camber variation. The most obvious course was to increase the track of the car considerably. In this way the wishbones could remain more nearly parallel while still converging on the same notional point so as to give the car the same instantaneous roll centre as before. At the same time the reduced disparity in angular deflection and length of the upper and lower wishbones ensured a reduction in camber change for a given vertical movement of the wheel, accompanied by a reduction of all the scrubbing and gyroscopic nuisances linked with such changes. In other words, the wider track allowed a given amount of wheel travel between bump and rebound limits to be maintained while the angular displacement of the suspension as a whole was reduced. Thus the increase in the average track dimensions of 1966 cars, compared with those of 1960 and 1961, allowed the same amount of vertical wheel movement to be provided while reducing angular deflection of the suspension by 17 per cent. In this way all problems were minimised. Camber, gyroscopic precession, scrub, roll centre displacement, dive, and squat, all became less problematic. Better still, there was no price to pay. Designers had always fought shy of track increases on the assumption that they automatically increased frontal area and therefore aerodynamic drag; but in

237

fact it was proved that the greater separation of the wheels from the body so reduced aerodynamic interference effects between them that, so far from drag being increased, it was even possible that it might be reduced.

As time went by and tyres became even wider, the drag they themselves presented became a problem; and although it was countered by reducing the overall diameter of the tyre, it began to be realised that there were limits to the value of increasing tyre widths. The more rubber is squashed against the road, the more power is consumed in the process; the wider and shorter the contact patch, the more impossible does high-speed drainage of water become—which is why racing tyres have broad grooves gouged out of their treads for very wet conditions, simply to provide longitudinal drainage paths for the water that would otherwise build up in a wedge ahead of the tyre and lead to aquaplaning—these grooves being first proven in racing by Firestone on the Chaparral which won the 1,000-kilometres sportscar race at the Nurburgring in 1966. Less obvious to everybody except perhaps the driver is the fact that a wide tyre can have an alarming tendency to provoke understeer in slow corners: by 1968 the rear tyres of a Formula 1 car accounted for one-fifth of the car's track width, and yet there could be no differential rate of rotation between the inner and outer edges of the tread. In other words the broad tyre behaves like a solid axle, doing its best to run straight ahead and finally (when it can no longer resist steering forces tending to turn it) losing its grip overall.

This effect is most noticeable at relatively low speeds, despite which team managers continued to specify the widest available tyres for slow twisty circuits simply because of the advantages in

184 By September 1966 new induction and ignition systems were being tried on the Maserati V12. Note the semi-inboard front brakes on Rindt's car, fourth in the Italian GP

traction: a certain twitchiness through corners can be more than compensated by the avoidance of undesirable wheelspin while accelerating out of them. On really fast circuits a narrower tyre may pay for itself in reduced resistance to motion (both in rolling resistance and air resistance) despite being at some disadvantage on bends.

An important factor governing the rolling resistance of a tyre is the composition of the tread compound. To say that the principal constituent elastomers of a modern racing tyre tread are high-styrene butadiene and natural rubber is to attempt a generalisation so broad as to be almost valueless. This is hardly the place, however, in which to embark on a description of the many and varied tread-rubber constituents in use today, to compare the properties of the several natural and many synthetic rubbers and all the various hardeners, softeners, accelerators, activators, oils and carbons that go into tread compounds. It is, however, essential to note that a tread polymer that is right for one circuit may be wrong for another, that a rubber that is superior to all others when running hot may be inferior to all others when running cool, that damp roads and wet roads present quite different problems, and in general that the whole business is most confusing. By 1967 the tyre manufacturers were condescending to identify their different compounds by code numbers or coloured spots on their side walls; but nobody will reveal what the compounds actually are, and Setright knows of cases where a tyre has been falsely marked just to mislead the opposition. Let us just say that by 1968 the racing tyres of all three manufacturers were considerably more up-to-date than any of the cars to which they were fitted.

This was even more true in 1966 when the Cooper last discussed was already obsolescent and the Repco-Brabham clearly could enjoy but a limited future. There were, however, at least two new cars that sought to set new standards: the Eagle, a pseudo-American car of conventional derivation but advanced metallurgy, and the Honda, which was simply too much of a good thing.

Few cars of the time could boast a more attractive pedigree than the Eagle. It was designed by Mr Leonard Terry, erstwhile chief designer of Lotus, his then most recent success being the car that put an end to the tradition that only an American driving an American car could win the Indianapolis 500 miles race. The proprietorship of the Eagle was shared between two American drivers, Gurney and Shelby, with distinguished records in European racing. The principal object was to produce a car that would be effective at Indianapolis, but competent also in European Grands Prix. This meant that the car had to be rather big to accept the larger engine and greater fuel loads appropriate to the American event. Nevertheless it could be made light, and to this end some advanced aluminium alloys were used extensively, and titanium was employed for a lot of suspension and engine components. Nor was there any reason why the frontal area of the Eagle should be particularly great, despite the personal size of

Gurney, and the finished car was certainly of an attractive shape.

For Formula 1 racing the design of a suitable engine was entrusted to the Weslake consultancy, the bulk of the work being done by Weslake himself and by Woods. As the English were still finding out, and as Ferrari had demonstrated from time to time during the past couple of decades, it takes much less time to copy a good chassis than it does to copy a good engine. When there is not a good engine available for copying, then the time required for the power unit grows even longer: so the Eagle first raced with a simple FPF Coventry-Climax engine in its tail, proving to have exemplary roadholding and handling. When eventually the engine materialised it was seen to be a V12 with a stroke:bore ratio of 0·82, four valves per cylinder, the same piston area as the Repco-Brabham, and the ability to run up to 9,500 rev/min, equivalent to 3,740 feet per minute mean piston speed. At this rate 380 bhp were claimed, equivalent to 174 lb/in^2 bmep—the highest peak-power pressure of any 1966 3-litre engine, although the 2-litre Coventry-Climax V8 reached 178 lb/in^2. This may constructively be compared with the figures that have been published for the three-cylinder twelve-valve 500-cm^3 MV Agusta racing motor cycle, which appeared in 1965 and has been fairly consistently unbeatable ever since: this engine likewise developed a bmep of 178 lb/in^2 at the peak of the power curve. On the other hand, one has only to go back to the Vanwall and Coventry-Climax four-cylinder engines in the $2\frac{1}{2}$-litres era to find petrol-burning racing engines with even higher bmep figures. Although figures are difficult to obtain, there seems no reason to suppose that the bmep at the peak torque condition was correspondingly low on the 1966 and subsequent engines. What seems more likely is that, as the science of tuning inlet and exhaust tracts to exploit resonance effects became better understood, so were engines developed to reach artificially high levels of bmep at some chosen speed to the detriment of their breathing at other speeds; and this supposition is

185 Pending readiness of the Weslake V12, Gurney drove his Eagle with a 2·7-litre Coventry-Climax four-cylinder engine

186 *The most powerful engine of 1966 —and for some time after—was the 90-degree V12 Honda. The Honda chassis was much too heavy, and was later replaced by this more suitable Lola design*

lent weight by the evidence of five- and six-speed gearboxes that became standard equipment, the better to keep the engines spinning in the narrowing band of crankshaft rates at which useful power and prompt response might be enjoyed.

If the Gurney Weslake V12 was the 1966 champion of the bmep stakes, the Honda V12 was undoubtedly the top in power: 420 bhp at 10,000 rev/min seemed a perfectly reasonable performance rating when it was announced, and the sight of this big and heavy machine out-accelerating and out-speeding its rivals on the pit straight at Monza was enough to convince any sceptic of the adequacy of the engine's power. It was, after all, an engine of exceptional style and originality. It was very long, because the power take-off was from the middle of the crankshaft between the third and fourth pairs of cylinders, enforcing a longitudinal location of the engine in the chassis, instead of the transverse installation used by Honda in the $1\frac{1}{2}$-litre V12 of the preceding year. The 3-litre machine had its two banks of cylinders set at an included angle of 90 degrees instead of the usual 60 degrees, and its induction pipes plunged between the pairs of camshafts crowning each cylinder head. They were supplied by a fuel injection apparatus of Honda's own scheming, while the exhaust system was as serpentine and tanglesome as any that had yet been seen. Most particularly of all, the Honda engine was distinguished by the use of rolling-element bearings instead of the plain variety now used by all others. Here was successful motorcycle racing practice being applied again; and the same was true of the engine's ration of four valves per cylinder. Knowing what Honda had achieved in motorcycle racing, it would indeed have been a disappointment had this big V12 not delivered such tremendous power.

Unfortunately there was a great deal of car for it to propel. The

241

187 *The 36-valve Ferrari which made its debut at Monza late in 1966*

3-litre Honda actually weighed 40 per cent more than the regulations required, scaling 740 kg empty—nearly as much as the 6-litre C-Type Auto Union of 1937.

A much more practical reconciliation of power and weight was reached by Ferrari in time for the Italian GP in September 1966, when their already established 3-litre V12 appeared in a new guise with cylinder heads containing a total of thirty-six valves. In this case the arrangement of things was that two of three valves in each combustion chamber should control the inlet ports and that one should be enough for the exhaust. Feeding the inlets were pipes which once again dived straight down between the banks of camshafts and valvegear. The profit from all this was an increase in power of about 6 per cent, enough to give Ferrari once more the fastest car, as usual at the end of the season when it was a little too late to be of full use.

There were other companies who organised their affairs somewhat better, as 1967 was to show. The finest commentary on the course of the Grands Prix races accountable in the World Championship of that year may be found in the book of Ecclesiastes, Chapter 9, verse 11. It omits the technical details, which may be summarised by saying that the most outstanding car of the year, the new Lotus type 49, had only won two races by the end of the season, although it had run in and been by far the fastest car present at seven of them.

On the whole 1967 was a year of entrenchment, of development, and of considerable redeployment of forces, with drivers being plugged in and out like light bulbs. From the very beginning of the season it was known that the Lotus team would be joined by Graham Hill in the difficult situation of being joint No. 1 driver with Jim Clark—several years his junior and past world champion twice as often. The reason was no secret—Lotus were soon to have ready their new car, with a brand-new engine for which Ford had paid a mint of money; and if Ford were going to invest like that they wanted to make sure of the best possible results. Accordingly the team contained the best drivers that money could buy. Hill, who had begun his Formula 1 career with Lotus back in the 2½-litre days of the previous decade and had since spent a long, successful and not entirely happy stint with BRM, could be bought.

He soon proved his worth at the third championship event of the year, the Dutch GP where the new type 49 with Cosworth-Ford V8 engine was ready and race-worthy. This was almost the understatement of the year. The car was fastest of all in practice, Hill accomplishing a lap of the sinuous Zandvoort sandpit at a speed 4·2 per cent faster than it had ever been lapped before, a remarkable increment. For the first eleven laps he led the race, but then the Ford's camshaft drives broke. Clark promptly moved forward from fourth place into a lead that he never again lost, prompting yet another reference to Ecclesiastes: *Two are better than one; because they have a good reward for their labour. For if they fall, the one will lift up his fellow: but woe to him who is alone when he falleth for he hath not another to help him up.*

188 The first Lotus 49

The occasion was a triumph for Chapman, vindicated in his pursuit of lightness, traction and controllability, the three things upon which he had for so long pinned his faith. It was a triumph for Cosworth, who did well to gain a bmep in a fairly simple engine such as had not been attained in any unsupercharged Grand Prix car since the days of alcohol and nitromethane. The winning car was interesting but not really astonishing. Its engine justified no wild adulation, for what it gained in bmep it lost in rev/min. It was no lighter than the Gurney-Weslake V12 of the Eagle, was heavier than the Ferrari V12, and did not then appear particularly reliable. It was interesting but not significant that this quite compact V8 should be cantilevered out behind a monocoque hull that ended a little aft of the driver. BRM and Ferrari had done this years before, but Chapman had for a long time adhered to the idea of a stiffened punt formed of two longitudinal torsion boxes to carry his suspension. In general, however, in a class of racing where all the cars were based on principles that derived from earlier Lotus designs, the latest Lotus was just a little more Lotus than the others. Its refinements were many, the detail work fascinating. The deeply dished and ventilated brake discs edged directly into the wind, their calipers steadied by minute tubular

243

triangulations, the suspension uprights dipping crookedly within. The wheels made room for them with fifteen-inch rims, those at the rear no less in width than diameter to carry the latest fiercesomely low-profile Firestone tyres.

These were interesting details, but mere details nevertheless. If the latest Lotus was not fundamentally different from the racing cars of the preceding half dozen years, it was highly improbable that we could expect anything more modern from anyone else; so the whole business would resolve into a dreary competition to see who had the most powerful and most reliable engine. Reliability proved not to be the strong suit of the Cosworth-engined Lotus: it kept on breaking camshafts, suffered a number of other mechanical and electrical boredoms associated with the engine, and suffered a great deal of transmission troubles for which the torque of the engine, the structural weakness of the transmission, and the tremendous grip of those tyres, were all to some extent responsible. While it went, however, the Lotus 49 was always the fastest car, and from its first appearance until the end of the season with the non-championship Spanish GP it always made fastest lap and earned pole position on the starting grid. It really deserved to win many more races than it did, but was betrayed by a variety of engine and transmission troubles, suspension breakages, fuel system malfunctions, and a distressing tendency for wheels to fall off. Evidently when the author of Ecclesiastes penned Chapter 9, verse 11, and commented that the race was not always to the swift, he knew a thing or two.

Never was this more vividly demonstrated than in the Italian GP, certainly the most exciting of the year, one in which the speed of the Lotus was not to be denied but which was won by a Honda by the narrowest of margins from Brabham. At this race there also appeared the latest version of the V12 Ferrari, which had been considerably lightened, cleaned up, and modernised during the year: now it had an engine which was similar in all but its dimensions to the 48-valve V12 designed by engineer Rocchi for Ferrari's latest and quite successful sports-racing cars. This was the Italian approach to the competition to see who had the most powerful and most reliable engine, but its 405 bhp was not enough. As for its reliability, the statistics were to be upset by the announcement that after the end of 1967 the Cosworth-Ford V8 would be made generally available, instead of remaining exclusive to Lotus. There was nothing in this or any other event of the year to show that a motor racing era was coming to an end; but a new era was beginning. . . .

chapter seven

1968 to 1972

forsan et haec olim meminisse iuvabit
Virgil

Since the beginning of 1968 the general availability of the Cosworth-Ford V8 engine has completely changed the character of Grand Prix racing. We had already seen, in the first half of the decade, a number of small manufacturers of racing cars buying proprietary engines, mainly from Coventry-Climax; but they bought them because they could not make their own, and because no better engine was available to them. The fact that some of their competitors who made their own engines had more power simply encouraged these chassis manufacturers to develop better chassis, and this appeared to be all to the good. The case of the Cosworth-Ford was rather different: here was an engine that was demon-

190 The most important feature revealed in this drawing (by Theo Page) is the nearly flat 4-valve combustion chamber of the Cosworth Ford engine

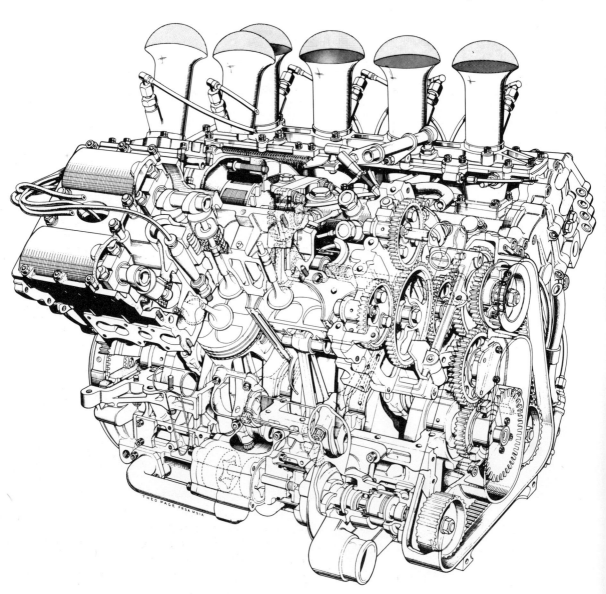

strably as effective as any other, and only the most proud or the most stubborn would think of using something different. Figures tell the story succinctly: in 1956, when Grand Prix racing was at its grandest and perhaps most glorious, there were nine different makes of cars competing, using altogether eleven different types of engine, albeit of just nine makes. By 1968 there were eight makes of cars with seven different engines; and in mid-1972 when this book was written, there were nine cars and six engines.

In these circumstances one might have expected to see remarkable new developments in chassis design. In fact there have been relatively few, the introduction of airfoils being the only one of real importance. For this we may blame the increasing pace of motor racing, which leaves little time for experiment with new designs and little mercy for any new one that is not immediately

191 Poor combustion chamber shape is the shortcoming of the Matra V12 which was announced, shortly after the Cosworth, late in 1967

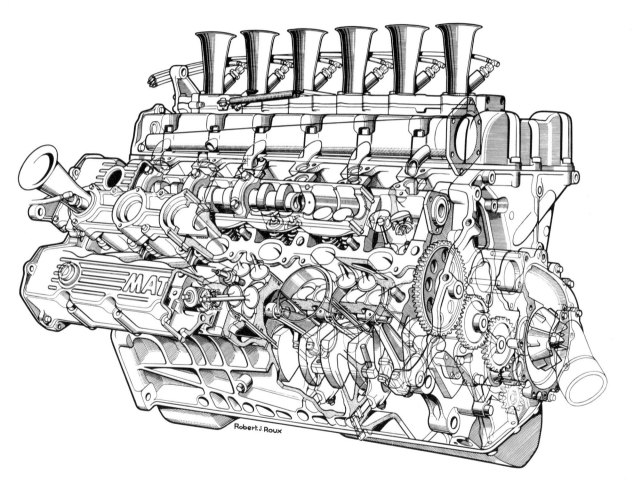

Robert.J.Roux

successful. The years from 1961 to 1967 were, as we have seen, a period in which motor racing became faster, more competitive, more professional, and more money-grubbing than ever before, a period in which the archetypal modern racing car became a stereotype. The emphasis was shifting all the time, from engines to cars and from cars to drivers, so that the mass public now

249

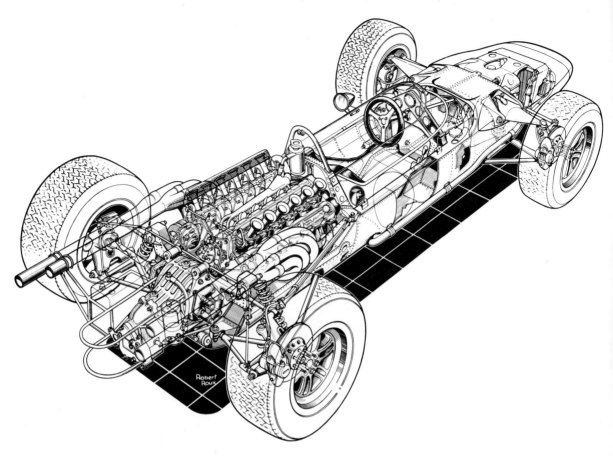

192 The 1968 V12 Matra originally had six exhaust tailpipes, but later in the year was pruned to four

sedulously wooed by race organisers is more aware of the personality of a given driver than of the characteristics of his car. It follows from this that successful drivers and entrants have a vested interest in conservatism: they can attract a better public (more accurately, a larger public, though the adjectives are synonymous in the box office) by regularly fighting close battles in evenly matched cars that are all pretty much the same. Try something new and, if it does not live up to its designer's promise, the car and its driver become objects of scorn and derision. No box-office idol can afford to take the risk.

Compared with the expanse of the sixty-one years preceding it, this last brief spell of four and a half years is too recent for an historical judgement to be passed on it. It may be that motor racing as we used to know it is dying; it may be that the phoenix of motor racing will emerge from her self-imposed immolation before long; but it seems likely that something will be lost in the ashes.

It is equally likely that Setright is being altogether too pessimistic, for the last four and a half years have seen some splendid racing and some beautiful cars. Not for a long time have we seen Formula 1 racing as open, as exciting, as international, and as educational, as it was in 1968, for example. Never had we seen it as fast; and seldom can we have seen it more subjected to the whims of capricious fate.

Not to put too fine a point on it, the results sheet gave a totally false impression of the speed and competence of many of the participants in this most important of all kinds of racing. On a number of occasions in that year the moral victor failed to finish due to some trifling mechanical fault, such as the failure of the fuel pump in Amon's Ferrari in the Spanish GP. Less frequently victory came quite fortuitously to drivers who, however respectable their qualifications in racing, could hardly have been expected to be candidates for top honours. To a large extent the poor weather in Europe that summer made it very much a matter of luck whether the right tyre was chosen before a particular race; and this factor was dominant in giving Matra and Ferrari their victories in the Dutch and French Grands Prix respectively.

Reliability was perhaps the most important factor of all, for the 1968 season saw retirements coming thick and fast. It used to be said that the perfect racing car would be so designed and built, with such mastery of fatigue and other stresses, that it would blow itself to smithereens just after taking the chequered flag. In 1968, after only five cars finished the race at Jarama and again only five at Monte Carlo, it seemed that some makers were in such a hurry to achieve perfection that they could not wait until the end of the race.

A few retirements were caused by drivers trying too hard and running out of road. A few more were the result of chassis failure, notably the suspension breakages that the Lotus suffered early in the season. On the whole, however, chassis and running gear were fairly reliable, which was as it should be seeing that they had not

193 1968 Repco- 4-cam 3-litre V8 on dynamometer test

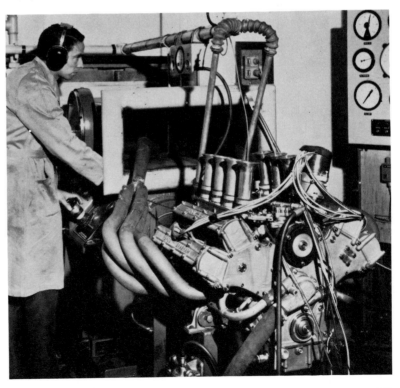

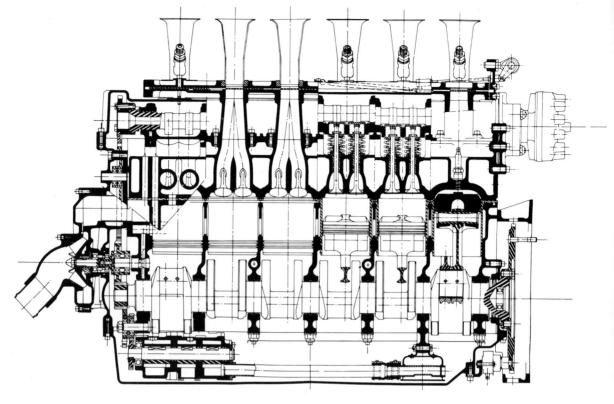

194 *Transverse/longitudinal section of 1968 Matra*

changed in principle for many years and were all basically similar regardless of manufacturer. Naturally there were detailed differences, naturally some performed slightly better than others; but the differences were not great. At the beginning of the year the best-handling cars were undoubtedly the BRMs; but by mid-season the development of airfoils and other aerodynamic aids to road-holding (of which more later) restored the Lotus to its customary supremacy while introducing a new and potentially very dangerous source of unreliability.

Apart from these wings and fins that sprouted in great and experimental variety to adduce evidence of aerodynamic after-thoughts, the least stereotyped feature of the cars was their engines. Superficially they were all either V8s or V12s, but the detail differences were considerable and their reliability varied from the creditable to the appalling. Probably worst was the new four-camshaft Repco V8 employed by Brabham, the most persistent of its troubles being an inability to keep valves in place. By contrast the Cosworth-Ford V8, now in its second year of racing, behaved tolerably well: indeed eleven of the twelve championship events of the year were won by Cosworth-engined cars. Admittedly the engine was used by more than one constructor, the Lotus monopoly of it in 1967 being lifted to allow McLaren and Matra to share it in 1968. Nevertheless, with seven different types of engines being used in eight different makes of cars, this record seems quite outstanding.

If the Cosworth-Ford V8 was well established in 1968, one of the

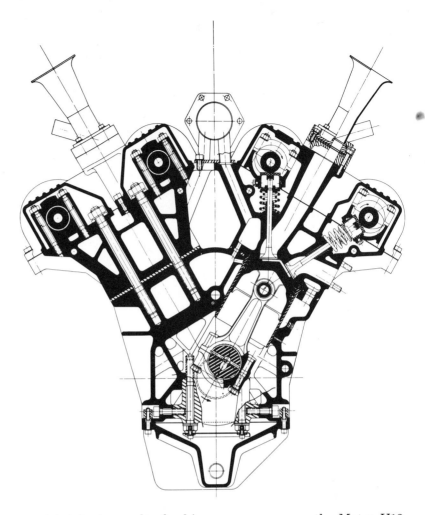

most intriguing and refreshing newcomers was the Matra V12, an engine that not only provided fresh stimulus and more international interest for Grand Prix racing, but also made possible an interesting comparison of what might be considered opposing schools of thought in engine design when compared with the Ford-sponsored V8. For whereas Cosworth in the latter concentrated on good breathing and efficient combustion to achieve power, the Matra firm based their design on the postulate that ample piston area and high rates of crankshaft revolution are the most obvious means to that end.

In fact, of course, these two approaches are complementary and the art of the engine designer is in combining them both. How closely matched were these manufacturers in such skills is evinced by the fact that Cosworth and Matra gave about the same power; but the V8 was the more reliable, and the V12 so much more thirsty that it had to make refuelling stops in the course of a race—something that had been unheard of for years. It was also said that the Matra V12 was more intractable than the Cosworth V8, but this is only a part-truth: in its early form the French engine was graced with a splendid array of exhaust pipes, the two banks of cylinders

being treated as separate six-cylinder engines whose cylinders were coupled by the exhaust pipes so that numbers 1 and 6 fed one tail pipe, 2 and 5 another, and 3 and 4 a third—something that previously only Bristol had had the wit to do with a six-cylinder engine. Thus there were six tail pipes, and a splendid noise, and a respectable 420 metric bhp; but there were also a number of inconvenient hollows and lacunae in the torque curve, and these undoubtedly made the car very difficult to drive. A more conventional four-tailpipe exhaust removed some of these, but removed 30 bhp in the process, so although the engine might now be perhaps more manageable than the Ford V8, whose power came in very suddenly at around 6,500 rev/min, it was no longer as powerful.

There were other engines for which more power was claimed, the highest being that quoted for the Gurney-Weslake V12 of the Eagle which was very rarely seen. At the other extreme the V12 BRM, originally conceived as a sportscar engine anyway, was perhaps the least powerful of them all and very nearly the least reliable. Yet the classical V12 of Ferrari could also trace its ancestry back to a sportscar engine, though there was seldom much question of its reliability and never any of its power. Although the Ferrari was victorious only once in the year, its performance deserves closer examination.

If we consider the five fastest makes practising for each event we find Lotus with a total of sixteen such places, Ferrari with fourteen, McLaren nine, Brabham eight, Matra seven, Honda three, BRM two and Cooper one. Clearly the Lotus and Ferrari were considerably faster than the rest; but the proportions of fourteen to sixteen do not take into account the fact that in one event (the Monaco GP) there were no Ferrari entries, a token of remembrance of Bandini's death there in the previous year, while in the remainder there were never more than two Ferraris entered, whereas Lotus entries numbered two at the first GP of the season, three for the next seven events, and four in each of the last four races. Thus Lotus had thirty-nine opportunities of starting from the first five places on the grid, their sixteen successes being 41 per cent of what was possible; whereas Ferrari had only twenty-two such opportunities, with 64 per cent success represented by fourteen places. Furthermore, a Ferrari was fastest or equal fastest on five occasions, a Lotus on four, a Brabham on two and Matra and Honda once each. On these statistical bases it seems fair to judge the Ferrari the fastest car of the year; yet Ferrari won only one race, Lotus won five, McLaren and Matra three each. Yet there were several drivers of Formula 1 status prepared to admit that had Surtees been with Ferrari, as he was until mid-1966, the year's race results would have looked very different.

Instead he was with Honda, and seemingly did them some good: for the performance of the Japanese V12 improved steadily, particularly after the introduction of a newer and lighter chassis embodying many of the driver's recommendations based on his experience with the Lola. It remained a less wieldy car than its competitors, and the advantages it gained by its unusual engine were somewhat debatable. There have been no more idiosyncratic engines in modern Grands Prix than the Japanese, for the V12 Honda had its cylinder banks spaced 90 degrees apart instead of the 60 degrees common among V12s, and the new V8 that appeared at Rouen for the French GP had its banks at 120 degrees instead of the conventional 90 degrees. The V12 had been changed greatly in detail since its introduction in 1966, appearing halfway through the 1968 season with (inter alia) a new cylinder head design incorporating torsion-bar valve springs and crossflow porting. By far the most interesting engine of all, however, was the air-cooled Honda V8, which was given a tragically premature trial in the French GP. This power unit, with its comprehensive finning and air ducting and its copiously ventilated crankcase forming part of a complex oil-mist cooling system, promised to introduce to motor racing some of the power and mechanical virtuosity for which Honda had established a reputation in motorcycle racing. But it was commercial considerations that encouraged Honda to rush the car into competition before it was ready, to introduce the French driver Schlesser to Formula 1 racing and to the untried V8 for the French GP. If the repercussions served Honda right they were hard luck on the popular Schlesser: for the new engine cut dead in the middle of one of Rouen's streaming wet corners and the car went off the road and burst into flames, killing the driver. Was it coincidence that the deaths of Schlesser, Spence, Scarfiotti, and Clark, which marred the 1968 season, all occurred on the seventh day of the month?

Conditions as foul as those at Rouen, and at Zandvoort for the race preceding it, sorely tried the abilities of the tyre manufacturers to produce tread designs and compounds that would give drivers reasonable control. The most difficult circuit of them all in the rain was the very fast one at Spa, where the drivers bade the organisers of the Belgian GP consider very carefully whether they might do well to shorten or even postpone the race if the weather were wet. It had been wet in practice, when the amount of water thrown up by the new wide tyres made visibility frighteningly bad and overtaking a matter for only the most reckless, especially on the ultra-fast stretches such as the Masta straight. Fortunately the rain held off for the race, which was remarkable for the introduction of wings, for which the tyres were again responsible.

With all three major tyre manufacturers once again active, development continued apace, with racing tyres getting wider and shallower than ever in the quest for grip and response and cornering power; and it was the characteristics of these tyres, and in particular the relationships between their cornering potential and the load they carried, that encouraged the car manufacturers to adopt aerodynamic devices engendering a negative lift (or downward thrust) forcing these tyres down onto the road and thus to develop all the tractive and cornering power of which they were capable. The beginning of this trend was evident very early in the season, when the Lotus appeared with a cuneiform fuselage whose poop deck echoed the repand tail that had been devised by Ferrari (actually by his driver Ginther) for sports-racing and GT cars in 1961. The Ferrari reply to this at Spa in 1968 was an inverted wing or airfoil mounted on struts above the rear of the car. This was quickly copied by Brabham and eventually by all the others. Sixty-five years after the Wright brothers used wings to get a petrol-engined machine up off the ground, wings were turned to the new task of keeping petrol-engined machines forced down on the ground. Theirs are dates that we all remember; but of course both had been preceded by more tentative developments.

Otto Lilienthal, student of birds and pioneer of flight, had made over two thousand gliding flights when, one gusty day in 1896, his home-made wind-rider of linen and palisander went into a fatal side-slip. His last words—*Sacrifices must be paid for*—epitomise the unselfish optimism of the true pioneer. They are also the essence of all engineering compromise; and now that wings have come down to earth as an apparent necessary adjunct of our racing cars, the principle may still be seen to apply.

Sacrifices in ultimate maximum speed on the straights are only worthwhile if balanced by increased speed through the corners. The wing that sets its face against the wind, denying the final build-up of speed along the straight, may literally set its shoulders to the wheels so that the car can go into the subsequent corner faster, go through it and accelerate out of it faster, and thus maintain a higher overall average speed. If it does not do all this, it is not worth having.

That at least might be the technician's appraisal of the situation; but motor racing involves men as well as machinery, so a little psychology may be involved too. Some drivers do not like to feel under-privileged, and I suspect that many of the airfoils we have seen sprouting from Formula 1 cars did nothing except increase the confidence of the man at the wheel.

But this is mere egalitarianism, social security gone haywire. The pioneer's concern was merely scientific. Alas, we tend to forget the pioneers, the great men and fertile brains of the past. As Horace put it, *vixere fortes ante Agamemnona multi*—and there were cars with wings before the Lotus and Ferrari, before the Chaparral even. You can look back to 1924 and see huge stub wings sprouting from the flanks of the rocket-propelled Opel; but that experimental single-seater was so fast and so devastatingly powerful that its designers feared the consequences of it getting slightly airborne over a bump; the wing was simply there to keep the apparatus at ground level.

The true progenitors of our current winged wonders were the Swiss brothers May, who in 1955 mounted a transverse airfoil above the centre section of a Porsche. The airfoil was designed and angled so as to create negative lift, an aerodynamic down-force that would increase with the speed of the car, thrusting it down against the road surface, grinding the tyres into the track so as to increase their grip and cornering power. The car was entered for a race in Italy, but the scrutineers would not or could not understand the principles involved and refused to let the car compete.

So a few years were lost; but history is like that, and we need not

197 In 1968 Matra built a car fitted with the Cosworth V8 for Stewart's entrant Tyrrell

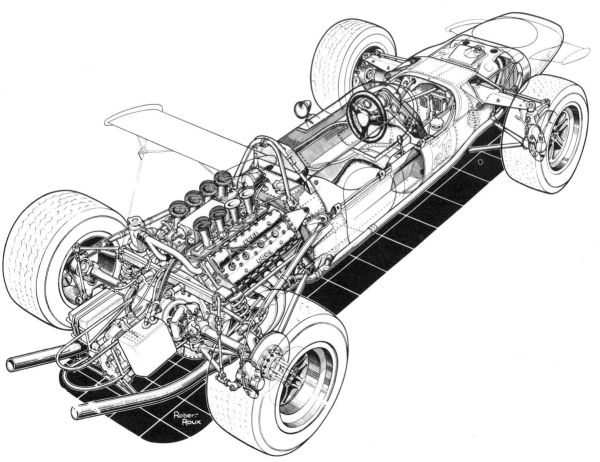

grieve unduly. For the land that fostered the Roman Inquisition also bore Galileo, and if Monza would not have Michel May, Maranello would. He went to work for Ferrari: and it may be no coincidence that Ferrari sports-racing cars were the first to explore the possibilities of those peculiar repand tails that were clearly intended to achieve something aerodynamic, though nobody seemed quite sure what.

More coherent notions began to be formed as the 1950s gave way to the 1960s. Grand Prix cars were limited to $1\frac{1}{2}$-litre engines of not exactly cataclysmic power, but the tremendous potency and all-enveloping bodywork of the sports racers introduced a host of new problems, of hazards lurking unseen in the glips and burbles of the invisible air. The curvaceous bodies were behaving like wings, generating aerodynamic lift at high speeds, hoisting the cars in an aerial hammock that sometimes left the tyres scarcely able to contact the road surface, let alone to transmit the lateral and longitudinal forces that govern stability and agility at racing speeds. So we entered an era of spoilers, diaplanes, cropped tails and similar subterfuges, all intended to check the car's tendency to become airborne and therefore unstable at high speeds.

It was an obvious extension of this process to design bodies that would create a positive down-thrust by aerodynamic means, ensuring that the wheels and tyres were not only burdened with the full weight of the car but possibly with more as well, just to make sure that their full potential was harnessed. It seemed an odd idea, but with tyres now growing to gigantic proportions it was a rational one. If you overload a tyre its cornering power diminishes, and in the days when tyres were fairly slender this stage could all too easily be reached. Now tyres are much fatter, putting far more rubber on the road in the cause of tractive, braking, and cornering stability, predictability and precision. But with big tyres you run against the problem of unloading them, a problem that is just as real. There may be a lot of rubber making contact with the road, but if it is not pressed firmly down on the road it will not grip, but slip and slide. Making the car heavier is a very poor solution to the problem, for obvious reasons: the greater inertia of the greater mass reduces acceleration and increases centrifugal loadings in cornering. The beauty of the aerodynamic down-force on the tyres is that it is simply vertical thrust and no more—there is no addition to the inertia of the vehicle, no penalty save the aerodynamic drag that is inseparable from aerodynamic lift.

A high ratio of lift to drag has been one of the lodestones of aviation technology since the earliest days, even before Lilienthal. An all-enveloping car body may create quite a lot of lift, be it positive or negative, but it will induce a lot of drag in the process, leaving behind it a trail of eddies and vortices and turbulence that is the embodiment of wasted effort. The most efficient tool we have for generating aerodynamic lift with the minimum induced drag is the wing, so it is better to concentrate on getting the body so shaped as to cause minimum drag and minimum lift, either positive or negative, then employ a wing to do the rest. This is why

Lotus resorted to the wing after their brief flirtation with the wedge in the earlier part of the season—though it is not the whole reason, for the possibility of mounting the wings so as to bear directly on the wheels rather than on the chassis introduces other possibilities that are worth exploring.

First, however, what should the wing itself be like? To start with, its airfoil section should be one of the modern generation of laminar-flow types, such as the section chosen for the Lotus; by maintaining attached flow over a greater proportion of the chord of the airfoil, these sections greatly minimise induced drag, enough to make an appreciable difference even at the relatively slow speeds of racing cars compared with those of aircraft. Next, it must have a high aspect ratio—its span must be great in relation to its chord. The higher the ratio, the greater the lift in relation to the drag, until the limit is reached when the wing gets so long and narrow that it is structurally too flimsy. In this respect we can do better than the birds; the aspect ratio of an albatross is not much better than 5:1, whereas a sailplane may approach 20:1. On the 40-inch span of a Lotus airfoil this would give a chord of only 2 inches, which is not enough either for strength or for the necessary wing area, and in fact the Lotus is in the same league as the albatross. At any rate there is a lot to be said for making the wing as large as possible, for the desired lift can then be realised while mounting the wing at a small angle of incidence, which again reduces the drag.

The little end-plates you see on the tips of Ferrari, Cooper, Matra, or McLaren wings are to reduce drag, too, by inhibiting the formation of those power-sucking vortices formed at the tips of all moving wings. Decades ago, however, it was demonstrated that the end-plates have to be so large before they have any appreciable effect that they themselves create too much drag, so they are hardly worth the bother; it is better to shape the wing in plan so as to make it more efficient, the ideal plan-form being an ellipse.

Attention to details such as these will help to minimise drag, but already the lift/drag ratio of established modern airfoil sections is quite low. Estimates of the negative lift developed by car-borne wings vary somewhat, the highest claim yet in Formula 1 being 400 lb lift at 150 mph for the Lotus structure. The induced drag is probably less than 50 lb; indeed, in the case of the Lotus the total induced drag probably does not exceed this, even including the struts upon which the transverse airfoil is mounted, for they are sensibly of streamline section. You would have thought a little precaution like this obvious, but all the others mount their wings on simple crude tubes whose drag can be far higher—another lesson that the aircraft industry learned years ago.

In any case, how much is 50 lb? We hear that the winged Formula 1 cars are losing a bit of speed on the straights, but they don't look exactly crippled, do they? What sort of proportion of the total tractive effort is swallowed up by aerodynamic aids?

None of the manufacturers is likely to give us accurate figures, but reasonable approximations are not hard to calculate. If it were

198 1968 was the year of the wings. This is Hill's Lotus 49 at Brands Hatch

geared for out-and-out maximum speed, a decent clean-limbed Formula 1 car shorn of all its aerodynamic beards and whiskers should be capable of about 200 mph on 400 bhp, and this can be translated into tractive effort at that speed of 750 lb. Suppose you add a wing that would develop a down-thrust of 400 lb at that speed, at the cost of 50 lb induced drag, it would pull the maximum speed down to about 193 mph if the car's overall gear ratio were lowered so as to enable the engine to reach its peak power output at that speed, or perhaps down to the high 180s if the gearing were not altered. Put it another way, at 200 mph such a wing would need about 27 bhp to drive it.

However, the drag of the same wing on the same car at 100 mph will pass virtually unnoticed. Even if the induced drag were the full 50 lb, it would only need 13·5 bhp to push the wing along, which is a mere 4 per cent of the total horsepower available for acceleration at that speed. In practice, of course, since the car is travelling at only 100 mph instead of 200 mph, the wing travelling less quickly through the air will be generating less lift and at the same time inducing less drag, so its effect on the power available will be quite negligible. In fact, it may compensate for the tractive effort it consumes by improving the traction of the tyres and thus actually improving the acceleration.

More important, however, is the effect of the down-thrust on the car's handling, and this depends very much on the manner of mounting the wing. If it be mounted on the chassis or body so that it acts more or less directly through the centre of gravity of the vehicle, as in the case of Michel May's Porsche or the 1968 Formula 1 Ferrari, then it will augment the ground pressure at each tyre contact patch in proportion with the car's static weight distribution. Substitute wings acting at the extreme tail and extreme nose but in each case on the body or chassis of the car, and the effect will be much the same. But in the third case, where the wing at the tail acts not on chassis or body but direct on the wheels through the medium of the hub-carriers, as was the practice of Lotus and Chaparral, a quite different result is obtained. Suppose one of these cars has a static load of 600 lb on its rear wheels, so that when running straight and level each rear tyre is supporting 300 lb burden. Now put the car through a corner so that there is a transfer of weight to the outer wheel, such that it is now loaded to the tune of 400 lb and the inner rear wheel carries only 200; depending on the size of the tyre and its inflation pressure, this may or may not lead to the tail of the car running wide because of this outward weight transference, just as the weight transfer caused by an anti-roll bar at the front of an ordinary car will tend to make the car understeer more than if the bar were not fitted. Now add the aerodynamic downforce of 400 lb total from the wing, remembering that it is independent of chassis dynamics and still added in equal proportions to both rear wheels, and you find that the tyres are now carrying their loads in different proportions: the inner tyre will carry 200 plus 200 equals 400 lb, the outer tyre will carry 400 plus 200 equals 600. Therefore as far as the tyres are concerned, the outward weight transfer is only such as to increase the outer tyre's share of the load by about 50 per cent instead of 100 per cent.

Now we come to the really significant bit. This effect only occurs when cornering at high speeds, when a 150-mph wind in the willows will cause the airfoil to generate maximum negative lift. In the course of a really tight slow corner, something taken at only perhaps 40 mph or 50 mph, the wing will have no discernible effect, and full weight transfer will be apparent to the driver. Thus the wheelborne wing makes it possible for a car to be a convenient oversteerer in slow tight corners and a predictable understeerer on long, fast, sweeping bends. This is what the chassis tuner has long sought, through all the years of frustration when the conventional streamlined body produced quite the opposite effect.

Nevertheless we shall go on to consider the fourth case, where wings at both nose and tail of the vehicle are coupled direct to the hub carriers rather than to body or chassis. In this case the effect of outward weight transfer will be reduced by the aerodynamic downforce applied to each wheel, both at front and rear. This will

261

lead to more consistently balanced handling throughout the whole speed envelope, which might in some cases be more desirable—as, perhaps, in the case of a four-wheel-drive car.

There are other more basically mechanical considerations that must be studied when deciding where to mount the wing. Let it act through the chassis and it will increase the load on the suspension, compressing it more and more as the speed increases and with it the negative lift. If the body of the car is unfortunately one which tends to generate positive lift, this can be a useful antidote and help maintain more or less constant ride height; at other times it is a nuisance, for it limits the amount of suspension travel available at high speeds. At the same time it will inhibit any pitching tendencies created by braking or accelerating.

If, instead, the down-force is applied direct to the hub carriers, then the suspension is less affected—indeed it will have an easier time, for at high speeds the down-force will inhibit wheel-hop, and lighten the burden on springs and dampers because unsprung weight will be counterbalanced when moving in bump. If the body has any tendency to lift, it will be free to do so, and this may have untoward effects on suspension and steering geometry, which can be further complicated by the pitching tendencies that will still be free to develop in acceleration or in braking. Actually the

199 A new Ford-engined Matra for Stewart, the pot-bellied MS80 seen here with wing and grooved rain tyres at the rear

braking condition is rather an interesting one, for although the forward weight transfer may be such as virtually to lift the rear wheels clear of the ground (an extreme case unlikely to be encountered in a Formula 1 car, I admit), the wing will still hold them down and enable them to do useful braking, while all the extra weight on the front wheels will help them to brake with the utmost power. It was rather interesting to watch the fully winged Lotus braking at the entry to a corner, the whole car looking extremely steady and all four wheels digging in hard—despite which the tail of the car had risen quite high on its suspension, the nose was barely clearing the ground, and the whole chassis was tilting forwards through about 3 degrees. It follows from this that the castor angle in the steering geometry was being reduced by 3 degrees, which may not have left much; indeed it is more than some cars have to begin with. This is something that needs to be watched.

There were other things that could be done to make the system more efficient. In particular there was the question of providing a wing of variable incidence instead of the simple fixed structures used initially. At first Chapman was of the opinion that it would hardly be justified on single-seaters, although Hall obviously made the most of it in his Chaparral two-seaters (even when Setright was at school he found Chapman and Hall difficult!), but if variable-incidence airfoils are to be used there are four possible methods of controlling them—by the driver, or automatically according to the car's attitude (nose up, nose down, etc), or according to suspension deflection (as each wheel tends to rise on its suspension it can be pushed down again by what would amount to speed-sensitive progressive aerodynamic springing), or, finally, according to the vehicle's speed (so as to arrange, for instance, constant aerodynamic downthrust over a very wide speed range). All these were perfectly practical possibilities, but only the first and last were actively explored. At the 1968 German GP there was a Matra whose wings were adjustable in flight: electrically operated servo actuators controlled it in aircraft style, its incidence being increased by braking or by downward gearchanges and decreased by upward gearchanges. Then Ferrari introduced speed-sensitive hydraulic jacks with override switch for the driver, Lotus a mechanical system that was left entirely to him, and all the time variations in airfoil size, shape and location proliferated. Chapman argued that his wings were part of the car's suspension, not of its bodywork, and were therefore not subject to the regulation limiting the width of the latter—and produced enormous airfoils 6 feet in span.

Along with all these appendages at the tails of the cars there were a variety of fins and spoilers to be seen sprouting from their noses, either to produce some positive downthrust to aid the adhesion of the front tyres or else to prevent the generation of unwanted aerodynamic lift that could affect the handling. With the exception of the notably wide-span nasal fins of the Lotus, these were less obvious devices tending to be lost amid the unaccustomed welter of advertising decals that became legal wear in 1968, at

200 Wings at nose and tail for
McLaren. The pannier tanks were not
a success and were soon removed

once ruining the appearance of the cars and debasing the once
sporting activity in which they were engaged. It may be that the
withdrawal of some of racing's wealthiest sponsors made it necessary for the competing teams to look to this kind of advertising for
necessary revenue; but if that be the truth it is a deplorable one,
showing that if the highest form of motor racing was in 1968 technically more refined and generally more exciting than had been
the case for some time it was not what it had been in its heyday.

By the beginning of 1969 winged racing cars were getting out of
hand—sometimes too literally. Many cars were now biplanes,
with substantial airfoils above the front suspension as well as the
expected ones above the rear. Too many cars had airfoils that were
insufficiently strong or stiff, either in themselves or in their
mountings; and when a series of high-speed accidents culminated
in a couple of serious ones, everybody began to accept what everybody had known all along—wings were much too dangerous. In
the turbulent air behind another car, at large yaw angles, and
most of all when travelling backwards, a winged car could
become completely unstable and virtually uncontrollable. During
practice for the 1969 Monaco GP the fate of wings was sealed: in
future only a relatively small one, mounted low down and fixed
directly to the sprung mass of the car, would be permitted, along
with nasal fins of similarly restricted size.

It is perhaps a pity that we were unable to assess accurately the
effect of the new wing regulations upon the performance of cars,
for all the leading makes were now enjoying more powerful
engines. In any case it was already recognised that on some circuits
the wing could be more of a liability than an asset: at Monza in
1968 the higher speeds along the straight that could be achieved
without the drag of a wing were worth more than the higher
speeds through the corners that could be achieved with its down-

1969-71 Ferrari

WHEN STANDARDISATION OF DESIGN became so general as to bring the art of racing car design into one of its most depressing periods, the Ferrari was always refreshingly different if not always entirely convincing. In the habit since the 1930s of doing things in his own way, Ferrari could not tolerate the idea that a racing car bearing his name should not also bear on all major components the imprint of his own factory. Other makers' hulls might be monocoques, but his had tubular framework concealed within. Other people might buy their engines, gearboxes, and even their designers, in the market place; but Ferrari's were always home-grown. They were usually very good, but a long run of petty troubles and sheer bad luck robbed the Italian team of much dearly-won prestige in the first four years of the 3-litre formula. The new flat-12 engine, slung beneath the cantilevered beam which was a dorsal projection from the otherwise normal hull shell, was intended to restore the Ferrari reputation.

It had its troubles, but as the embodiment of old Ferrari's spirit, traditionalism, courage, and taste, it was welcome anyway; and when it began to demonstrate itself amply fast and reliable during 1970, and then went on to dominate the races at the end of the season, the welcome was unqualified. Maybe it made its mark a little too late; but while the 59-points winner of the constructors' championship was the Lotus, alias the Gaspers Special, with engine by courtesy of Ford and transmission by Hewland, the make that came second with 52 points was wholly Ferrari. The next two seasons were dogged by labour troubles which affected the whole of the Italian motor industry, including Fiat, who were now Ferrari's patron; but the 213B with either of its chassis was always competitive and frequently on the front row of the starting grids.

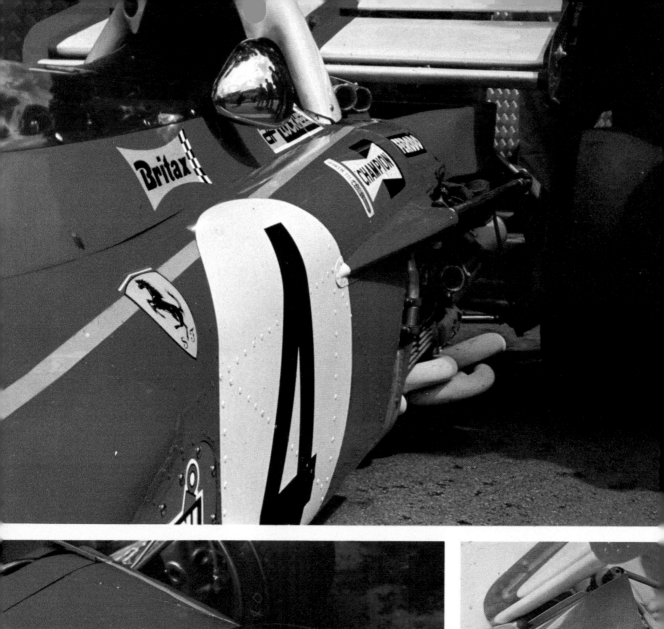

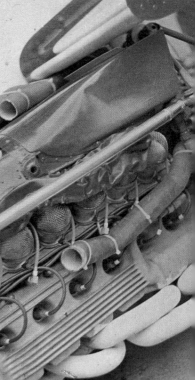

201 *The 3-litre cars were expected to have so much power that four-wheel drive would be necessary. BRM accordingly built this experimental four-wheel-drive car in 1965*

thrust. However, this was a mere side-issue: wings were demonstrably dangerous, and everyone was relieved when finally they were restricted in size, design and effect.

Safety was engaging everybody's minds more and more. New regulations were introduced providing for the cars to carry fire extinguisher systems and leak-proof fuel tanks, and minimum weights were raised to permit these to be carried without enfeebling the structure in any way. Leak-proof tyres would have been welcomed too, for some drivers were growing more and more adventurous in the way they scorned kerbs and put their wheels over the edges of the track, where they would pick up such stones as they did not scatter in their wake. In many ways the new tubeless tyres, which had been surreptitiously introduced in 1966 when their use was still contrary to regulations, were a blessing: it was arguable that they were more susceptible to cuts and punctures, but beyond argument that they were safer in their subsequent behaviour, deflating slowly instead of explosively.

On the whole 1969 can be dismissed as a quiet year, in which drivers attracted more attention than cars. There were three technical developments of note, however.

One was the abject failure of four-wheel-drive, which was tried by Lotus, McLaren and Matra in racing and by Cosworth privately, the last engaging the designer Herd from McLarens to produce a complete car. It was tried briefly but never raced; the other three were raced briefly but never taken seriously. They were obviously very difficult to drive at competitive speeds, and leading drivers (for example, Rindt of Lotus) would have nothing to do with them, refusing to prejudice their careers by having to learn new tricks when they should be getting on with the business of pursuing known goals with known cars.

265

202 *The Lotus Indianapolis gas-turbine car of 1968 set the pattern for future body styles and tempted several designers into four-wheel drive*

The idea of four-wheel drive had been to divide the engine torque among all four wheels so as to reduce the amount of tractive effort applied through any one of them, and thus enable greater utilisation of the engine's torque without fear of wheelspin. It was further argued that by subjecting all tyres to tractive torques (just as they were all subjected to braking torques and cornering forces) the car would be better balanced, there would be less disparity of tyre slip angles front and rear, and handling and cornering would be improved. Further it was suggested that since the rear tyres would no longer have to transmit so much power they would not have to be so wide, and therefore the frontal area of the car could be reduced with beneficial effects on its maximum speed.

Some of these objects might have been attained had not the development of airfoils intervened. With the aid of aerodynamic down-thrust, cars could enjoy as much traction as they needed, and cornering forces could be increased enormously. Indeed there were several transmission failures brought about by the increased grip thus provided, overloading drive shafts in conditions where tyres would have spun and relieved them had airfoils not been in use. Fuel consumption rates rose by as much as a quarter, simply because the extra grip afforded by aerodynamic means enabled full use of available power to be made for so much greater a proportion of the distance travelled. As for the supposedly higher speeds and reduced areas, the truth was that the greater power consumption of four-wheel-drive transmission, and the

203 This four-wheel-drive Lotus 63 ran but poorly in the 1969 British GP at Silverstone

greater weight that it represented, robbed the car of more performance than it might hope to gain. Finally the four-wheel-drive cars were without exception difficult to handle because their steering was very heavy, because the proportions in which torque was divided among the wheels could not be adjusted to correspond with the variations in load transfer during accelerating and cornering manoeuvres, and because in conjunction with airfoils (which had to be retained anyway if the tyres were to be fully exploited) there were too many variables present for it to be practical to get the car set up for a given circuit or even a given set of weather conditions.

The least unexpected of these four-wheel-drive cars was the Lotus. In 1968 this firm had produced an Indianapolis racer powered by a Pratt and Whitney gas turbine, employing four-wheel-drive

204 (top) *The cunieform shape of the four-wheel-drive Lotus is clearly derived from the Indianapolis car, but the engine is the ordinary Cosworth Ford*

205 *The four-wheel-drive McLaren in the 1969 British GP*

and relying on a wedge-shaped body for aerodynamically induced stability. Although it was a failure at Indianapolis, it was only robbed of victory there by cruel luck; and it was confidently predicted that in due course there would be a similar Lotus Grand Prix car. In due course, there was; but it was something that only came about by degrees. The first was the four-wheel-drive car, the Lotus 63, a Cosworth-engined machine which had the same sort of suspension and inboard brakes as the turbine car, although it had perfectly conventional engine location in the rear, with a propellor shaft alongside the driver to carry to the front wheels their share of torque.

In 1969 there appeared another car which was clearly designed to give its driver all the benefits of response and ride that accompany a low polar moment of inertia. This was the Matra MS80, powered by a Cosworth-Ford V8 and managed by Tyrrell. Its radiator was still in the nose, but its flanks were distended with fuel, its wheelbase a trifle shorter than average, its track considerably wider than average (63 inches, compared with 60 or less for all the others). Its broad-bellied shape was produced by a construction that, based on aircraft monocoque practice, was so cross-braced as to allow no possibility of fitting rubber or plastics fuel cells within the tankage space; but on the other hand it gave the car outstanding structural stiffness, and this combined with the central concentration of the heavy masses to produce a car of outstanding capabilities, exploited with outstanding skill by its driver Stewart to win the world championship.

He did not do so without some opposition particularly from Rindt in one of the Lotus 49 cars. In 1970 there came the Lotus 72, and with it the tables were turned. What distinguished it from its contemporaries was the removal of the water radiator from the nose to the middle of the car—there were now two radiators, one on each flank of the body ahead of the rear wheels. Thus the nose of

206 Not quite finished and never raced, the 1969 Cosworth

the car remained a clean sharp wedge, as in the Indianapolis turbine machine, and the polar moment of inertia was reduced by the concentration of weight amidships, while the plumbing should have been somewhat simplified by the short runs involved.

The Lotus 72 was a very fast car, a very stable car, but not a wholly trustworthy car. It took time to discover that the thermal insulating spacers between the inboard brake discs and the universally jointed shafts connecting them to the wheels were not composed of material sufficiently strong for the job, though it had sufficed for Indianapolis. It took time to discover that the brake discs themselves could give trouble due to their inability to shed heat when stationary during pit stops, time to appreciate that the considerable degree of anti-dive and anti-squat built into the suspension geometry made the handling unacceptable to the drivers. Eventually these things were largely overcome, though not until a complete redesign of the suspension. This did not involve any alteration in the basic principles on which it was based, which

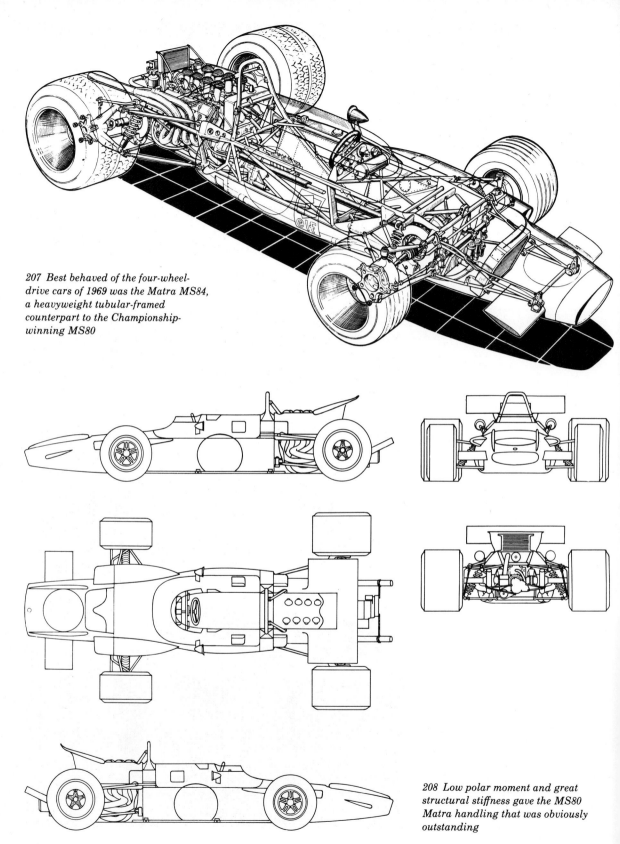

207 *Best behaved of the four-wheel-drive cars of 1969 was the Matra MS84, a heavyweight tubular-framed counterpart to the Championship-winning MS80*

208 *Low polar moment and great structural stiffness gave the MS80 Matra handling that was obviously outstanding*

209 (above) *Lotus 49 in 1969*

210 *Revealing the Indianapolis car as a parent, the Lotus 72 cleaves the rain at Oulton Park*

211 *Amon in the Ferrari during the 1969 British GP*

were in themselves attractive: the front wishbones were so proportioned that they could extend deep within the wide rims of the wheels so as to reduce the amount of offset between the steering pivot axis and the centre of the tyre contact patch on the road. This could only be made possible by the removal of the brake from the conventional position within the wheel, and by the construction of a most unusual looking and compact hub which embraced the outer universal joint of the brake shaft between two unfashionably close-set steering joints. As for the track rods, they had to be fitted in as well as could be, despite the way they encroached on steering lock, and in its earliest form the Lotus 72 had a most peculiar steering linkage, the kinematics of which dictated that the steering wheel should move backwards and forwards as it was turned.

Other aspects of the design were less disturbing. The fuel feed system was much simpler than that which had on occasion betrayed the Lotus 49, and was said to work with as little as one-fifth of a gallon remaining of the forty-eight gallons of petrol with which the car could start a race. Due to the location of the tanks the considerable weight of all this fuel did not affect the car's weight distribution, about 70 per cent of the total mass being carried on the rear wheels. By this time the regulation minimum weight for a Formula 1 car was 530 kg, the supplementary 30 providing for fire extinguisher apparatus, full harness and other safety equipment.

If the Lotus 72 had its troubles in the beginning of the 1970 season, so did most of the others, with the result that the first four championship events were won by four different makes. These were victories won by attrition, rather than by sheer speed. One of the most sorely troubled teams was Ferrari, with a new engine to replace the unsatisfactory machinery of 1969, a new engine which promised to be even more troublesome than the previous one. That had been a very troublesome engine indeed, although in

212 (opposite) *Engineer Mauro Forghieri introduced much of technical merit to Ferrari—for example, the athodyd housing of the oil cooler between the differential-incidence wings of the 1969 car*

213 *BRM designs changed frequently but to little purpose in the years after 1967. This is the P133 of 1969*

214 *The BRM P139 was another 1969 failure in a year when unreliability was crippling*

other respects the 1969 Ferrari had been most attractive. It was one of the lightest cars competing that year, sharing with the Lotus 49B and the BRM P138 the distinction of coming within $1\frac{1}{2}$ kg of the weight limit. Yet despite this lightness the Ferrari did not perform as well as it should. It looked impressive enough: the oil cooler treated by other manufacturers as an afterthought which had to be hung somewhere in the wind was surrounded in the Ferrari by an aerothermodynamic duct of properly divergent–convergent section which reduced the drag induced by the cooler very considerably and improved its performance as a heat exchanger. Flanking it above the engine were little airfoils still permitted by the regulations: the two halves were independently adjustable for incidence and were fitted with end plates. At circuits such as Silverstone where all the principal corners were righthanders, the angle of incidence of the righthand airfoil was set much steeper than that of the left.

Such details do not win a race in the absence of the necessary stamina and power, so 1969 had drawn to an end with Ferrari fortunes and spirits sinking lower and lower—indeed entries were usually limited to one car during the second half of the season. The only bright spot was the new 3-litre flat 12 engine which was intended to be introduced at Monza; but it blew itself up on the test bed and everybody had to start again. Throughout the first half of 1970 this engine continued to be a disappointment. In particular its crankshafts used to break.

Then in the autumn of 1970, when it had acquired a new crankshaft of special American alloy steel, running in four main bearings of which two were of roller type, the flat 12 Ferrari started winning races. Suddenly it was the fastest car in Grand Prix racing and won four of the last five championship events of the year.

Not the least refreshing thing about this was the relief it afforded to the monotony of races being won by Cosworth-engined kit cars. The sheer novelty of a flat 12 after so many years of V-engines was positively therapeutic. Yet it was the chassis which attracted most attention—and it is very seldom that one can say that about a Ferrari. Here the body was substantially a stressed-skin monocoque structure extending over the engine crankcase in the form of a cantilevered beam, from which the engine hung—an adaptation of an idea employed by Honda in their ill-fated V8. Such aerodynamic appendages as were permitted were employed on the Ferrari; but an awareness of the importance of well-controlled airflow was better shown by the careful ducting of divergent nozzles leading air at progressively decreasing velocity and increasing pressure to the twin oil-coolers at the rear of the car.

Undoubtedly the 312B Ferrari would have had to fight harder for its successes at the end of the year had Rindt still been driving for Lotus. Alas, this exceptionally gifted driver was killed at Monza during practice for the Italian GP when one of the front brake shafts snapped while the car was being braked from a very high speed. Nevertheless the abiding impression by the end of 1970 was that the Ferrari was the fastest of all current Grand Prix cars, and therefore the fastest Grand Prix car of all time; and many were the expressions of confidence in it for 1971. No great hopes seemed to be entertained for the new Tyrrell, built around a Ford V8 after the style of the Matra MS80 to keep Stewart competitive after a disastrous start to the year in the new March. As

215 The March 701 was an attempt to secure aerodynamic advantages by simple means, but the airfoil-section pannier tanks were found ineffective

216 The usual modern clutter at the tail of the March 701 ruins airflow over the lower, more important, surface of the wing

for the March, its appearance had been heralded with every sign of glee and approbation from nearly all the established critics, the only expressions of disapproval coming from the pen of Setright — so there was at least one person satisfied with the poor showing of this jejune and lacklustre design! Nor did there appear to be a great future for the new Surtees car, beautifully made but highly derivative in concept.

Matra too had been consistently disappointing throughout 1970. They had redesigned their V12 engine, making the crankcase stiff enough to act as a stressed portion of the total structure, revising the cylinder head completely so as to provide a shallower combustion chamber of better shape, the included angle between the valves being reduced from 56 to $31\frac{1}{2}$ degrees. Inlet valve area was increased, the fuel injection system revised, the inlet ports

277

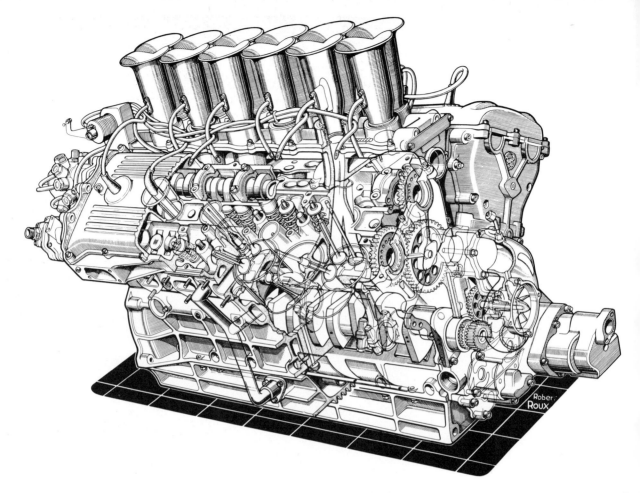

218 Matra's new engine for 1970, the MS12

themselves being placed within the V of the engine rather than within the V of the valves, and all six exhaust pipes from each bank being led into a single tailpipe, to produce the most wonderful high-pitched musical exhaust note yet heard in motor racing. With this glorious sound bearing witness to a claimed 450 bhp, the car should have been impressively fast; but it was betrayed by inadequacies in the transmission and in the chassis. The latter was entirely new, aggressively rectilinear in section, and apparently somewhat lacking in torsional rigidity. Apart from its broad spatular nose, the most distinctive feature was the fuel tank panniers whose upper surfaces were inclined upwards from front to rear so as to constitute aerodynamic downthrust generators, though how effective these could be in the turbulent air behind the front suspension with its outboard springs and dampers was inevitably dubious. Longer in the wheelbase and even wider in the track than the MS80, this MS120 looked the ultimate in lowness and flatness, but it did not handle as well as it looked or go as fast as it sounded.

It was as much changes in regulations as in design philosophy that prompted the new Matra chassis. The MS80 of 1969, it will be recalled, did not have rubber-bag fuel tanks, the curvaceous

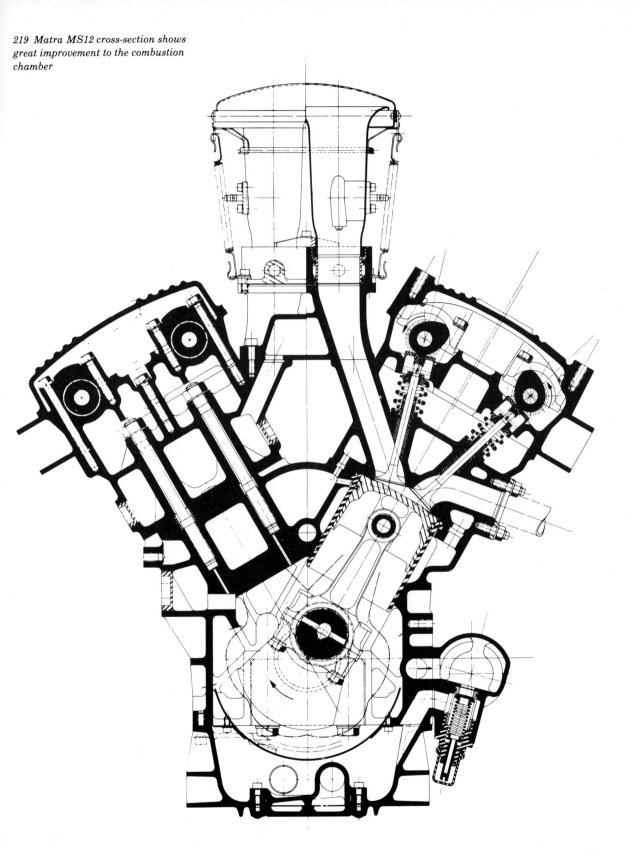

219 Matra MS12 cross-section shows great improvement to the combustion chamber

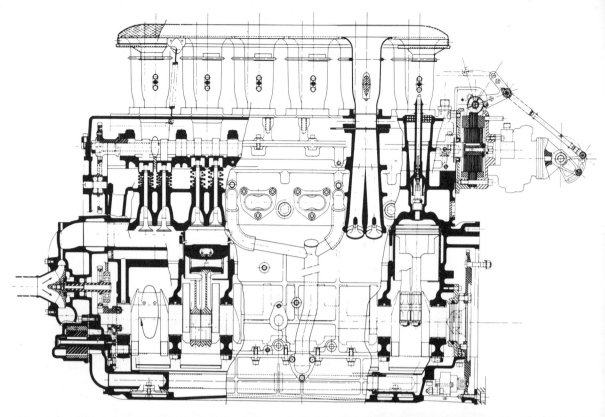

220 (top) Longitudinal section of the
MS12 reveals a very stiff crankshaft,
the result of the low bore: stroke ratio

221 (above) Another attempt to make
a fuel tank into an aerodynamic aid,
the Matra of 1970 proved
disappointingly flexible in torsion. The
number of exhaust tailpipes is now
reduced to two, with no apparent loss
of power

stressed skin boxes on either side being sprayed internally with a
sealant to constitute fuel tanks. Regulations for 1970 made rubber
bags mandatory; and this forced the Brabham designer Tauranac
to abandon his preferred tubular space-frame and adopt monocoque construction in the 1970 BT33 Brabham. This was not the
first monocoque Brabham, that distinction going to the BT25
Indianapolis car; but when the Cooper team abandoned racing
during 1969 some good sheet metal workers were liberated, and
with both Cooper and Brabham factories located in the same dis-
trict it was natural that they should move to Brabham where their
skills would now be in demand. If fuel bags have to be fitted, the

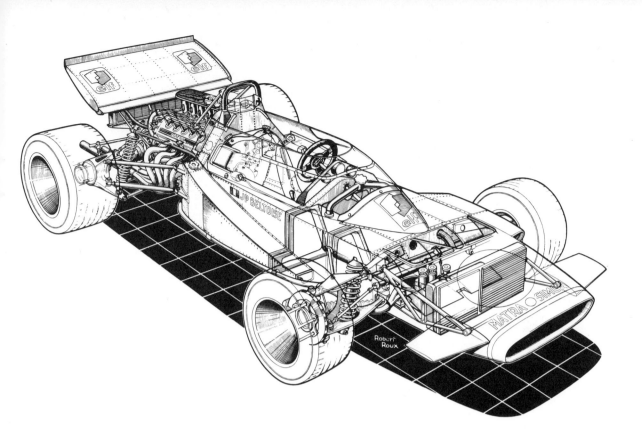

222 *Front wishbones made from sheet pressings are a feature of the Matra MS120, drawn here with four tailpipes*

223 *Probably no GP car has carried as many air-fences as the eight on the 1970 Matra*

224 (left: top) *The Cosworth-engined Brabham BT33 of 1970–71*

225 (left: bottom) *Ickx in the Ferrari 312B, fastest car at the end of the 1970 season*

226 *At the 1971 Monaco GP, Ferrari fielded old . . .*

227 *. . . and new versions of the flat-12 312B*

proper triangulation of a space frame is inhibited, whereas to encase the bags in metal and make them part of the chassis is a natural means to an elegant end.

It was interesting but hardly significant that for 1970, as Matra abandoned the pot-bellied shape of the MS80, McLaren and BRM adopted it, albeit with a different internal structure that permitted regulation fuel tanks to be inserted. More significant was the fact that BRM acquired 48-valve engines, so that now there was not a cylinder head in Formula 1 racing but had four valves to each combustion chamber. The BRM engine was undoubtedly extremely powerful, and there were isolated occasions when the performance of these and the other twelve-cylinder cars suggested that the day of the V8 might be coming to an end.

The form book was completely upset in 1971, however. New chassis from March, Brabham and Matra, modified ones from McLaren and Ferrari, new aerodynamic aids featuring on the Brabham, Matra, and Tyrrell, and new levels of power output in some examples of the Cosworth-Ford V8 engine, all served to

confuse what had previously been a fairly clear cut issue. The Ferrari flat 12 engine was almost certainly the most powerful, its output being in the region of 470 bhp; and according to some claims (others were more pessimistic by 30 bhp) the BRM now enjoyed a good 460. The Ferraris were consistently extremely fast in practice and generally very well placed on the starting grid, but it was a rare occasion when they survived a race, and the same want of reliability plagued the BRM team, which put up some extremely good performances only to fail at a late stage. Each make won an isolated race or two, but throughout the first half of the season it was clearly the Tyrrell which was the dominant car, with the new March constituting a fresh threat to the established order.

The March 711, successor to the 701 of 1970, was much more a credit to the admitted ability of its designer Herd. What distinguished it externally was the shape of its body and aerodynamic aids, the work of none other than that Frank Costin, who had been responsible for the satisfactory shaping of the once-triumphant Vanwall and a number of other uncommonly quick competition cars including early Lotus and Protos, for example. In the March 711 he revived the streamlining techniques that had been perfected in the days when aircraft flew as fast as racing cars now travelled, producing contours calculated to minimise drag while also negating any possibility of lift or instability in yaw by the adoption of the reverse camber line which had previously been the secret of such aerodynamically successful bodies as the Lotus Elite and the Lockheed Constellation.

In perfecting the shape of the March 711, Costin was assisted by Herd's acceptance of the postulate of low polar moment of inertia, so the radiators could be located on the flanks and air to and from them efficiently ducted. This left the nose clear for free

229 The March 711, designed by Herd with aerodynamics assistance from Costin. The car seldom raced with engine cover and lateral radiator ducts in place

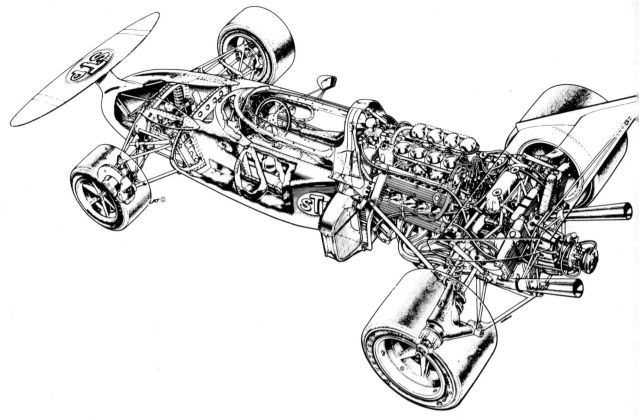

230 It soon became normal practice for the 1971 March to run with bare radiators (and terribly angular plumbing) and engine—the latter in one instance being the Alfa Romeo 48-valve V8 shown here

aerodynamic treatment, the contours reflecting aerodynamic laws—as did the diaplane or transverse wing mounted on it, the first seen in motor racing to embody the elliptical plan form which most efficiently reconciles maximum lift with minimum induced drag.

At the rear of the car Costin was more inhibited by the presence of machinery, which he sought to enclose as neatly and smoothly as possible: but regulations governing the height and width of airfoils enforced the use of a rectangular shallow biplane structure, while difficulties in maintaining equable temperatures in the engine compartment (which could lead to vapour loss in the fuel system, making restarting an impossibility after a pit stop) made it necessary for much of the tail panelling to be removed in early races. Nevertheless the car was impressively fast and clearly handled very well, being driven to a very fine second place in the Monaco GP and remaining strongly competitive thereafter.

If it was not difficult to see in the March 711 the embodiment of principles proven in the Protos which was a Formula 2 car, the windcheating enations around the noses of the 1971 Brabham, Matra and Tyrrell were unquestionably copied from a successful layout pioneered by Tecno in Formula 2 racing in 1970. The principal object of this exercise was to divert air away from the front of the front tyres, and was hampered by regulations which prescribed a maximum width of bodywork not exceeding the track of the car —that is, not extending outwards beyond the centre line of the tyre treads. This, it was realised, would be sufficient to permit a cleverly shaped frontal fairing to relieve the tyre of most of its headwind, and thus not only improve the coefficient of penetration of the car but also, which was considerably more important, to overcome the tendency of these broad rotating tyres to create positive aerodynamic lift.

The fact that tyres could do this had been troubling designers for some time, and had been proved by measurements which made it clear that the tyres were generating sufficient lift at high speeds to reduce by a sensible proportion the vertical loads on them and thus to reduce the grip and cornering power that they could offer. In free air they would, according to the established aerodynamic theories of Magnus, have created a downthrust; but the presence of ground effect (since the tyres were in contact with the road

231 Brabham's 'lobster-claw' car, the BT34

232 The BT34 Brabham proved to have very strong understeer which was not to the driver Hill's taste

surface) reversed this Magnus effect, and in effect the tyre treads were trying to climb up the wall of air against which they were propelled. The frontal fairing diverted the air, and the lift was negated.

287

The neatest embodiment of this idea was on the Brabham, where the radiator was divided into two components, each set in divergent ducts ahead of the outboard front suspension and of as much of the front tyres as the regulations would permit. It was argued that splitting the radiator thus prevented hot air going over the car and driver, and would serve to keep it away from the engine air intakes. Furthermore the vitiated air discharged by the radiators would fill an area which would normally be disturbed and made turbulent by the suspension elements. The radiator cells further acted as natural end-plates for an airfoil mounted between them, increasing its efficiency.

In producing their version of the full-width or hammerhead nose, Matra and Tyrrell did not shift the radiator but relied upon the shaping of the upper surface of a new broad and deep frontal fairing to produce the effects sought with airfoils by other designers. The Tyrrell version was especially successful—as indeed was the whole car, which appeared conventional enough in the light of 1972 standards but was beautified by an unequalled quality of construction and detailed refinement of design. It was commonly alleged that the Tyrrell driver Stewart, by virtue of his reputation, was always assured of enjoying the best service from Cosworth and getting the most powerful engine available; and if there were any truth in the denials that were from time to time issued, at least there was no probability of the Stewart car ever being foisted off with one of the less powerful engines, as sundry others were.

In their efforts to restore parity with the Tyrrell, Ferrari and BRM eventually fitted small fairings ahead of their front tyres, mounted as virtual end plates at the extremities of their usual nasal airfoils. Thus the Formula 1 car of 1972 began to resemble more closely than ever the type 251 Bugatti of 1956, the hammerhead fairings at least finding an echo in other cars of that era including streamlined versions of the Gordini and Maserati.

233 Early in the 1971 season the Tyrrell still closely resembled the prototype design

234 Later in 1971 it grew a so-called 'sports car nose' which was used successfully into the 1972 season. Stewart drives here in the 1972 Argentine GP

The history of aerodynamics as applied to Grand Prix cars does not make encouraging reading: for despite designers' awareness of the induced headwind as the foremost natural enemy of speed, an awareness illustrated as early as 1906 in the very first Grand Prix of all, very little progress has been made. The present state of the art shows a grudging acceptance of the aerodynamicist's importance in a design team, but this has been enforced as a by-product of the almost fissile expansion of tyre technology in the late 1960s, producing tyres that simply had to have aerodynamic aids if they were to realise more than a fraction of their true potential. Yet there had been odd instances of the streamlined racing car being tried perfunctorily at various dates throughout the history of the sport.

The trouble was that in every case the streamlined bodies were designed without reference to the aerodynamic lift they might engender and the extent to which this might degrade the handling of the car. For example, in 1958 during practice for the French GP at Reims, Brabham drove a works Cooper fitted with an experimental fully-enclosed streamlined bodywork intended to allow the car to reach higher speeds along the very fast straights of the Champagne circuit; but the airflow over the nose of the car was accelerated to create a low pressure region which developed so much lift that the nose was raised several inches and the front

tyres were only just maintaining contact with the ground despite the fact that the suspension was at full droop as the car sped down the straight. So the experiment was abandoned during practice and the car ran in its normal form.

In 1957 the Vanwall team had a fully enclosed car at Reims, but the experiment was abandoned. . . . In 1956 Ferrari sent an extensively cowled streamliner to Reims . . . and you can guess the rest. In 1955 Maserati sent a car of similar shape to Monza—and in fact the car did race: it was faster in practice than anything else save two Lancias (doomed not to race because of tyre troubles) and three Mercedes-Benz, two of them streamliners in their own right. During the race the Maserati was hampered by the throttle linkage fouling the bodywork so that the carburettor throats could not be fully opened. In this case, as time after time before and since, efforts to streamline the racing car were half-hearted, ill-prepared, unscientific, and inconclusive.

There were interesting examples earlier. In 1938 Auto Union produced a beautifully streamlined 3-litre V12 for Hasse at Reims in the French GP. But the car did not handle well and the experiment was abandoned during practice. . . . Fifteen years earlier there was the famous little Bugatti tank which had instability problems along the straight at Tours, and there was the wedge-shaped Voisin, which was really a sports car running in the Grand Prix because streamlining had been banned in sportscar racing as giving an unfair advantage! In 1922, as we have seen, Fiat took the sensible step of clothing their remarkable new 2-litre chassis in a smooth two-seater envelope that was perfectly streamlined in plan—though it would be interesting to know to what extent the directional stability of this body might have been impaired by crosswinds. Going back even further there was the long tail

sported by the 1914 Peugeot, and the rakish nose of the 1906 Renault. As mentioned earlier the precocious 1905 Gordon Bennett Renault was even better. Should none but Ezekiel prophesy unto the wind?

In 1954 it seemed that things were going to be quite different. Until that time, all laymen and most devotees of the sport, forgetting the Auto Union pre-war experiment, were convinced that a Grand Prix racing car was a brutish-looking torpedo of a thing whose large and naked wheels, bereft of even the most vestigial wings or mudguards, announced that here was a proper out-and-out racing car. Then at Reims for the French GP the Mercedes-Benz team appeared, their cars clad in fully-enclosing streamlined bodies that covered all four wheels. Daimler-Benz had established by full-scale wind tunnel tests that this body reduced aerodynamic

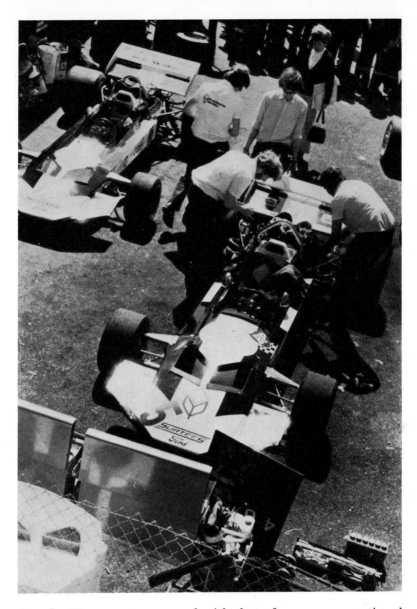

drag by 20 per cent compared with that of a more conventional single-seater. If their engineers had not been so cautious about providing large volumes of cooling air for tyres and brakes, it might have been even better; but they put holes and ducts in various convenient but aerodynamically inopportune places on the body, and these must have appreciably affected the airflow over and around it. Worse still, the bodies looked as though Daimler-Benz stylists had had a say in their design, which was not altogether surprising in view of the company's known policy of treating its racing cars not only as instruments of engineering research but also as tools of the publicity department. Otherwise, such details as the radiator air intakes might have been better, and the cars would have been more efficient still.

Many of a racing car's most important performance factors are intimately related to aerodynamic efficiency. Obviously a low-drag body will allow the car to reach a higher speed with a given power output; by reducing the power consumption at any lower speed, it makes available a greater power surplus that can be used to give better acceleration; by reducing power requirement for a given degree of performance it can improve fuel consumption and thus reduce the amount of fuel that need be carried, in turn reducing the all-up weight of the car and further improving its accelerative ability; while even further reductions in weight can be made in such items as the cooling system, because a properly shaped system of ducts and heat-exchanger matrix allows the cooling system to be more efficient.

Only in the matter of braking does the low-drag body impair performance, by offering less resistance to continued motion. Even this can be offset to some extent in the early stages of a race when the car is travelling with a full load of fuel, for if the low-drag body be exploited to make a smaller fuel load possible so that the car is lighter, then an improvement in braking performance can be enjoyed directly proportional to the reduction in weight. What is much worse is that a streamlined body can have a bad effect on handling characteristics, and it is evident that the generally accepted idea of proper streamline shape for a car in the 1950s was not right. It seems in retrospect that it was aerodynamic side effects that were responsible for Daimler-Benz giving their original streamlined 1954 cars handling characteristics that tended towards extremely strong understeer, a characteristic that made them difficult to drive and that cost them a great deal of power consumption in the form of tyre scrub through corners. It also forced the drivers to adopt drastic methods for provoking oversteer on tight corners, methods so drastic as to make minor navigational aberrations and marker-drum clouting inevitable. The untoward effect of these things upon the car's lap times was sufficiently serious to persuade Daimler-Benz that a simpler, lighter and perhaps uglier body design that left the wheels exposed might be a better proposition in racing; and so it proved.

In addition to such technical considerations, the designers were faced with a human problem. The drivers of the time were convinced that a view of the front wheels was essential to precise high-speed driving on a road circuit, and drivers who were firmly convinced of this found themselves at a marked psychological disadvantage when told off to go and drive a fully streamlined car. It was an irrational, unscientific attitude, the product of ingrained and emotional prejudice, but such foibles cannot be straightway dismissed with the aid of a slide rule and a diagram of forces; it takes time to rid men of such prejudices, time to breed a new generation of drivers who are not subject to them.

In any case, there were other more practical objections to the fully streamlined body in the racing environment. The vulnerability of the bulbous panelling was a constant worry; the extra-territorial forays of the streamlined Mercedes-Benz at Silverstone in 1954, for instance, resulted in quantities of severely crumpled

242 Bell at Silverstone, practising racing starts in his Surtees

243 Redesigned for greater torsional stiffness, the Matra MS120B had a full-width 'hammerhead' fairing ahead of the front wheels, and a high collector to carry air to the engine intake

bodywork, the repair of which could involve difficulties at a racing circuit in some far corner of a foreign field remote from the home factory. Then there was the problem of accessibility: valuable time could be lost in a pit stop while awkward body panels were removed in order that the mechanics might have access to some parts of the engine or chassis. Connaught with their 1955 streamliner took a different approach from that of Daimler-Benz: the car's bodily apertures would not have looked out of place on a high-performance aircraft of the day, while the generous tail fin developing from behind the driver's headrest was evidence that directional stability was a problem capable of a solution in terms of aerodynamics rather than merely in terms of chassis and suspension design. As for accessibility, they sought to simplify matters by making the whole upper portion of the Connaught body detachable in one piece, so that it could in a very few seconds be lifted clear of the car and laid aside while work was in progress. But where on earth do you find room, in the crowded pits of a racing circuit, for a delicate aluminium body shell five feet wide and fifteen feet long?

Problems such as these, presenting themselves at a time when aerodynamics was not yet a sufficiently exact science to enable much profit to be made from its pursuit, doomed the streamlining of racing cars in the 1950s. The inability of the drum brakes of the day adequately to cope with the weight and speed of the cars made a high rate of heat dissipation from their drums essential if performance was to be maintained, and this could only be achieved by abducting the heat in a constant and generous flow of cool air. Such draughts were automatically excluded by the all-enveloping streamlined body, and if holes and ducts were cut and fitted to guide air through to the brakes, then the aerodynamic losses they caused would degrade the efficiency of the body design as a whole. The same applied to tyres, which in the case of some cars of the period (notably the Ferrari team which was under contract to Englebert) were teetering on the brink of disaster: temperatures could easily climb to the danger limit if ample cooling air were not ducted to these tortured amalgams of rubber and cotton fabric—so bang went several more per cent of drag.

244 Matra devised a new shape for the side tanks of the MS120B

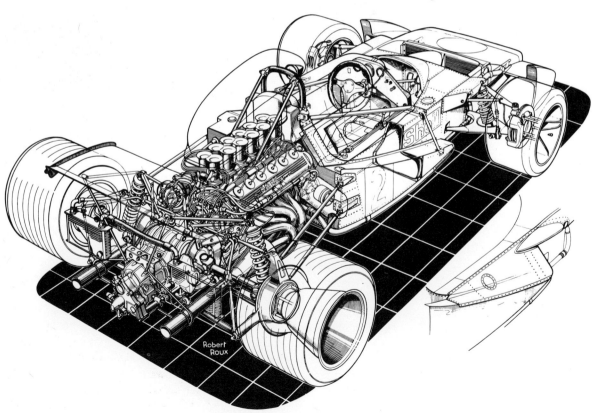

1969-72 Lotus

THEY STILL HAVE FOUR WHEELS (this could have been the title of this book)
but otherwise the latest racing cars have very little in common with those
which set Grand Prix racing on its way so many years ago. Yet the Lotus 72
is on its way to becoming a classic, for even in its fourth year of competition it
has been good enough to defeat all competition in race after race; so that at
the end of 1972 Lotus were once again the champion constructors. The work
of designing a Lotus Grand Prix car may no longer be entirely the province of
Chapman, but those to whom he delegates the duty are clearly imbued with his
attitude to design. This Lotus, like all those preceding it in this class of
racing since the beautiful slim little Lotus 16 – and indeed the Vanwall which
earlier still owed its chassis to Chapman – is the work of an engineer more
imaginative, more creative, and more critical of established practice, than
any of his contemporaries.

On the evidence of three cars in that elite family – the 18, the 25, and the 72 –
Chapman is entitled to be considered one of history's band of great and
creative racing-car design engineers. Their number, despite the advocacy of
retrospective romanticism, is very small: it includes Henry, Fornaca, Bugatti,
Wagner, Porsche, Uhlenhaut, Jano, and Colombo, making an average of about
one great man every eight years. It is interesting to speculate, not who will be
next, but what novelty or resurrection of principle will justify his inclusion;
for history supports the prediction that the pendulum will swing again.

It is possible that all these objections could have been overcome—but for another practical objection, probably the greatest of all: the time necessary for the perfection of an effective streamlined shape. Time is a commodity sadly lacking in the frantically crowded racing calendar, which seldom allows more than a week or two in which to rebuild the car, after the disasters and extremities of the last race, before the next comes along. A great deal of painstaking experimentation is necessary to evolve a proper body shape for a given car with a given performance; slight modifications to the weight distribution, power characteristics or gearing of the car can have a disproportionate effect on its performance and controllability. For these, designers, engineers, test drivers and financial comptrollers could afford neither time nor money.

So it was that fully-streamlined Grand Prix cars disappeared from the world's racing circuits, after a none too promising beginning. The Mercedes-Benz streamliner, so greatly ballyhooed as the Silver Arrow when first it appeared, was convincing enough on the simple Reims circuit but proved a catastrophic mistake at Silverstone, and was thereafter never fielded as a first-string car except at Monza. It was also at Silverstone that the fully clad Connaught made a most unpropitious start, thereafter campaigning with the wind blowing quite undiverted about its naked wheels.

An altogether more practical and more elementary approach to the problem was shown by Lancia, whose D50 enlivened the end of the 1954 season. To all intents and purposes this was a conventional exposed-wheel single-seater, but the turbulent area behind the front wheels was filled in by a deep and narrow outrigger or sponson that occupied all the space between front and rear wheels and should thus reduce the losses due to turbulence. It was an old trick, but one worth copying, since it promised to give worthwhile results in return for scarcely any handicap. The only aerodynamic shortcoming of the arrangement was the fact that the sponsons were not separated from the flanks of the fuselage by a distance great enough to avoid interference effects between the two bodies, so that airflow between them was far from smooth. When Ferrari took over the running of the Lancias in 1956, one of the many modifications embodied in the cars was a filling in of the gaps between body and sponsons, so that over the entire length of the car behind the front wheels and ahead of the rear wheels the body was of full-width construction. In this way the frontal area was increased, but the aerodynamic drag was not increased in like measure, for a seething mass of turbulent high-speed air trapped between two closely spaced walls can be as costly in drag as the slight increase in frontal area consequent upon filling the space with metal. Alas, Ferrari would never be happy until he had stopped the Lancias looking like Lancias and made them look like Ferraris, and in 1957 the outriggers disappeared altogether. In the meantime the potential virtues of the between-wheel infill had not been lost on Maserati, who fielded a car similarly shaped at Monza, with additional nose and tail fairings intended to reduce the coefficient of penetration without involving any increase in frontal area.

This has always been the essential balance to be struck in the design of a low-drag car. All other things being equal, a reduction in projected frontal area will give the same benefits as a similar reduction in the drag coefficient; but it is in the nature of the four-wheeled single-seater car that a low drag coefficient can only be achieved by the use of fairings that considerably increase the frontal area. Careful arrangement of the essential mechanical components of the car will make it possible to produce a very slim hull of remarkably low frontal area, but from this hull the wheels, brakes and suspension elements necessarily protrude; and although these are invariably of aerodynamically clumsy shape,

246 As usual in modern 'scientific' racing cars, half the machinery is bare and unfaired. The clutter round the engine of the MS120B Matra cannot disguise the beautiful detail design and workmanship, however

enclosing them in streamlined cowl and fairings can involve a crippling increase in frontal area.

For a long time people did not bother because it seemed that most of a racing car's drag was caused by its tyres—in which case why bother too much about the shape of the body? The excrescent wheels and suspension media of the 1936 Auto Union accounted for 95 per cent of the car's total wind resistance, those of the 1939 Mercedes-Benz 90 per cent. But things have improved, and the 1966 Cooper-Maserati owed only 40 per cent of its total drag to its wheels and suspension, despite the fact that these items account for a slightly greater proportion of the total frontal area than was the case with the Mercedes-Benz or the Auto Union. The explanation is to be found again in the matter of interference. The latest GP cars have tremendously wide tracks in an effort to minimise camber variations (during suspension movement) such as would impair the performance of the latest ultra-wide tyres. So the air flowing past the body flanks was made less severely turbulent by the wheels of the Cooper despite their impressive width, than was the case with the Auto Union.

Now this is important. At last we have reached the point where the tyres' share in the total aerodynamic resistance of the car is very nearly equal to their share of total frontal area, a parity that has not been known for decades. Whereas in the case of the Auto Union any improvement in the shape of its hull would have little effect on the total drag, since the entire hull represented only one twentieth of the total aerodynamic burden, we now find in the latest manifestations of the Grand Prix car that the hull accounts for 60 per cent of the total drag: therefore a 20 per cent improvement in its aerodynamic efficiency would be worth as much as a reduction of $1\frac{1}{2}$ square feet in frontal area. Now let us see how this can be exploited.

We have seen that by tucking all possible suspension components inside the car's fuselage, and by setting the wheels as far apart as possible, the aerodynamic interference effects between the wheels and body can be minimised. This trend became marked in 1966, with the track of Formula 1 cars increasing from an average 54 inches to 59 or 60, and it goes on. Although there are certain mechanical disadvantages in following this trend to extremes, from the drag point of view a further increase in the track from 60 inches to 66 would increase the overall width of the car from, say, 72 to 78 inches; and although this 8 per cent increase might suggest an increase in superficial frontal area of one square foot, in fact the widening of track could be achieved at a cost of no more than a few inches of wishbone and driveshaft, which

247 The 48-valve BRM P160 drawn up on the front row of the grid for the 1971 British GP, next to a Tyrrell (revealed by its nose fairing) and a Ferrari. This BRM was more troubled by tyre vibration than any earlier version

would involve a frontal area penalty of less than $1\frac{1}{2}$ per cent.

So wide a car would promptly present tremendous frontal area if fitted with fully enclosing bodywork, and its performance would almost certainly suffer as the result. In any case the present hamstringing regulations would not allow a Formula 1 car to be so bodied—but paradoxically the current cars have become so set about with excrescences in the form of radiators, engine air intakes, lateral fuel tanks, and cumbersome exhaust systems, as once again to present a substantial frontal area and almost completely to fill the space between fuselage and wheels. Thus the frontal area of the typical 1972 Grand Prix car is no less than $14\frac{1}{2}$ square feet, so that it enjoys rather less than 32 bhp per square foot of frontal area. This may be compared with about 36·5 for the H16 3-litre BRM of 1966, 42 for the 1939 Auto Union, 52·5 for the 1953 V16 BRM, 51 for the 1937 Mercedes-Benz W125, or 20·8 for the 1958 Vanwall. All these cars were geared to reach approximately similar maximum speeds on the straights of the fastest circuits, and the current cars are no exception to the rule that it is usually advisable to gear down for acceleration and accept that maximum speeds are of merely academic interest. In other words the whole force of current aerodynamic thinking is applied to the negation of upward lift and the generation of downward thrust, while the reduction of drag is relegated to secondary importance, receiving no more priority than the provision of suitable ducting for heat exchangers, combustion air intakes, cockpit cooling and the like.

Where the current cars score over their forebears (in straight-line performance, ignoring their obvious superiority in cornering) is in acceleration and braking ability. When running light—that is, with the sort of fuel load that might remain at the end of a race or be carried during practice when the ultimate potential of the car is generally displayed—the most powerful of the 1972 cars will deploy about 750 bhp per ton, and this is considerably more than was enjoyed either by the best cars of 1951 or even the monstrously powerful cars of 1937. Moreover, the 1972 car can make better use of its propulsive effort, suffering less from wheelspin and loss of tyre traction during acceleration than did these earlier cars. This was so even before the advent of airfoils to increase downthrust upon the tyres; with their aid the latest Formula 1 cars can sustain 1·2 g acceleration up to about 100 mph. There have been similar advances in cornering and braking rates, which have increased by fits and starts from about 0·6 g in 1954 to about 0·9 in 1959, 1·2 in 1966 and as much as 1·7 now. Indeed, braking figures are sometimes even higher than this, and there is no reason to suppose that Formula 1 cars cannot match the deceleration in excess of 2 g that has been measured by Porsche in their sports-racing cars.

In all these accomplishments the most important part is played by the tread polymer of the tyres which makes possible the realisation of coefficients of friction between tyre and road surface in excess of unity. In fact it is not too difficult to show that all technical novelties introduced to Grand Prix racing since 1966

248 *The 1972–3 Tyrrell, bodily revised in order more closely to resemble the fashionable wedge shape*

(excluding the four-valve cylinder head, which is in any case no novelty) have been brought in either to succour or else to exploit the latest tyres. The most mysterious thing is that no serious efforts seem to have been made to evolve a form of suspension more suited to these tyres—though Lotus are known to have experimented with de Dion axles in a 1967 prototype. Such a system could be made to work extremely well, needing only a very wide track to relieve it of problems of gyroscopic precession that might impair the stability of a narrower-track beam axle suspension. With front tyre diameters down to 20 inches and track widths up to 63 inches in 1971, it is hard to see why a beam axle should not afford the best control of all currently available systems.

If the modern pneumatic tyre is the fount of so many competitive virtues, it is also the source of a vice or two. One of these had been especially troublesome in 1971, following the adoption of even lower tyre profiles, but it has been evident to some degree since early 1969. This is tyre vibration, so violent as to damage cars and even to impair their drivers' faculties. The gravity of this situation at the time of writing is beyond exaggeration; suspension components and even basic structural elements are being fractured by vibrations which occur during cornering, when drivers experience difficulties in breathing and sometimes suffer total blackout of vision.

The vibration is of quite low frequency and large amplitude, so that it can sometimes be seen with the naked eye. It is the rear tyres which suffer it, the resulting distortion being as much as an inch at the tread centre line, reducing towards its edges. The frequency is commonly about 20 to 25 Hz, though Ickx has reported shakes as slow as 3 Hz in the Ferrari—possibly a heterodyning vibration. This car seemed to suffer more than most of its rivals; similarly Firestone tyres as employed by Ferrari seem to be more afflicted than others. There is evidence to suggest that Firestone found ways of identifying and so perhaps overcoming this crippling disability; but in the meantime they were forced as a palliative to make tyres of 1970 dimensions (which were higher in profile) and in 1971 polymers so as to give Ferrari and other affected teams a reasonable chance of surviving a race intact.

Already the significant factors are forming a recognisable pattern. The violence of the vibration increases proportionally to the tractive torque transmitted to the tyre, to the stiffness of its tread, and to the slip angle at which it operates, and inversely according to the aspect ratio of the tyre—the more squat its profile, the worse the vibration. From all this it follows that a power-oversteer condition aggravates the vibration, which is why Ferrari reset their cars' suspensions before the British GP so as to keep them understeering at all costs. To such an extent was this done that their cars were having to be brought into the pits with front tyre troubles halfway through the race. Moreover, because the multiplication of tractive effort amplified the vibration, the Ferrari drivers once under way eschewed use of their lower gears and (at Silverstone at least) confined themselves to fourth and fifth only, even though it might mean some loss of acceleration at certain points on the circuit.

There are also other factors at work. The vibration appears to be worse in a round-shouldered tyre than in one with square shoulders, a rather unexpected state of affairs that may be related to the surprising distortions that only lately have been detected in the contact patches of the latest breed of racing tyres. Furthermore—and in this lies the most likely clue to what is happening and how to cure it—the type of differential employed in the final drive can have the most critical effect of all.

The problem persisted, despite the zeal with which this clue was pursued, throughout 1972. This was scarcely surprising, for the cars of that year were not distinguished by any novelty from those of earlier seasons. On several occasions, tyres of higher profile were restored to in order to alleviate the vibrations; experiments with two or three different kinds of differential mechanisms were pursued; and certain components that suffered particularly from the shakes were moved to locations where they would be less perturbed.

The fact that the four-years-old Lotus 72 dominated the 1972 season is perhaps sufficient evidence of the stagnation within Grand Prix racing. True, there were one or two new cars, and not all of them were (like the short-lived Connew) kit-cars composed of the inevitable Cosworth engine and Hewland gearbox plus a British Standard chassis. The Tecno appeared on a few unconvincing occasions, powered by a flat-12 engine of obviously derivative design, though the credit for it was attributed to the brothers Pederzani. More disappointing, March began the year with a car that was intended to pursue the ideal of a low polar moment of inertia as far as possible, by location of the gearbox between the engine and the final drive. This enforced the use of an unsatisfactory Alfa Romeo gearbox which was of sports-car origin and could not offer the quickness of change necessary if valuable seconds were not to be lost: the car was simply too slow for its handling qualities to be of significant value. The March designer, Herd, was forced to forgo the development of a design in which his considerable gifts had been deployed, in order to provide the team with something immediately competitive: and he did so by shoehorning the standard Cosworth-Hewland aggregate into a March formula 2 chassis, to produce a little machine of repellent aspect but fair agility and reasonable reliability.

One of the factors affecting the general suspension of progress in 1972 was the formulation of new safety regulations which were scheduled to be operative with effect from the date of the 1973 Spanish Grand Prix. These rules, calling for wider bodies with built-in provisions for the better protection of the drivers in a crash, inevitably imposed handicaps in weight and frontal area (the maximum allowable width was to be increased to admit the necessary deformable structures on the body flanks) that most teams would be reluctant to carry until they were compelled so to do. An exception was Surtees, who took his new TS14 model in 1973 regulation trim to Monza for the Italian Grand Prix in September 1972. The race was won by a Lotus, as had been most of the preceding Championship series during the year; but as it happened the Lotus was to win no more until the following year, the Tyrrell suddenly finding a second wind that bore it to success in the Canadian and United States events which concluded the series.

In terms of results, the 1972 season was not in the least surprising. Of the twelve major events, Lotus won five, Tyrrell four, BRM one, Ferrari one, and McLaren one. Second place went three times each to Ferrari, March and Tyrrell; third place was taken by McLaren cars no less than seven times, and was the highest position ever occupied by March or Matra, despite the fact that the latter demonstrated on more than one occasion that it was the fastest and perhaps the most stable car present. Alas, its driver Amon continued to be the unluckiest.

In this account of sixty-six years' engineering advance in motor racing, personal fortunes and foibles among the drivers have not been our concern; and there seems no reason why this attitude should be relaxed in our examination of the last full season. Perhaps Amon was unlucky, but that is not uncommon; and why should it disguise the possibility that in some ways Matra were unwise, or Ferrari incompetent, or BRM chaotic? By this time the kit-cars ruled a situation for which they were created, and that is no surprise at all. It was even possible to forecast, as did some astute commentators, that before long Ferrari would bite the bullet and create his chassis in the British Standard idiom; and in due course, it became known that Ferrari was even going to the lengths of having his next chassis tubs (the word *monocoque* is too freely applied to these things) made in England. In chassis terms, everything has become a great deal too predictable.

And yet there is always the hope that some free-thinking

designer, fretful at the constraints of custom and resenting the all-pervading equality enforced by sporting fashion upon a band of contestants who are in truth unequal, may one day advance some new concept of structure or suspension, and with it escape from the base contagion of mindless mimicry. It is but a faint hope: the last time such a thing happened was when the fertile mind of Mr Hall, creator of the sports-racing Chaparral, produced a perfect response to the banning of the airfoils that he had done so much to make effective. His last car, before he abandoned the business of innovator in justified disgust, had suction fans to evacuate the air beneath the hull, which was skirted down to ground level: the difference in pressure above and below the car gave it unmatched adherence to the road, by a means which was independent of the car's speed or attitude, which was unaffected by the proximity of other traffic ahead or elsewhere, and which was inherently much safer than the airfoil. After a few brief appearances the car was outlawed by a peremptory bending of the rules. What a pity that the Greeks ever propounded democracy: for the mob was ever loth to tolerate a nonconformist. The banning of Hall's ground-effect car was just as predictable as all the other events of motor racing in the beginnings of the present decade. The way is set for tighter control of design by legislation, and chassis design is probably doomed to be entirely foreseeable—a sad way for the author to wriggle out of the judgement of Friedrich von Schlegel who wrote that 'an historian is a prophet in reverse'.

249 The blister fairing on the right flank of the Tyrrell windscreen is supposed to give the driver's right hand enough room to change gear

250 Herd put the final drive of the March 721 behind the gearbox, in an effort to reduce the polar moment; but he was forced to use an Alfa Romeo gearbox that was unsuitable, and the car was never fast enough

Would that the future course of engine development might be forecast with any sort of accuracy. Year in, year out, decade in, decade out, the engineers pitch and toss between one extreme and the other of a gamut that they are careful to keep narrow for fear of finding themselves in uncharted wastes. Two valves or four valves per cylinder? Roller bearings or plain? Split big-ends or built-up crankshafts? Castings or forgings? Large-diameter pistons or lots of them? The pendulum swings erratically but always within known limits—and since 1924 the only novelties have been multi-stage supercharging, ram and resonance type unsupercharging, and fuel injection. Certain things have grown progressively better rather than happening suddenly, far and away the most important of these being developments in metallurgy and tribology, for both of which we can thank the aviation industry, the arms race, and kindred activities.

There can be little doubt but that the governors of the sport, the FIA, are responsible for the fact that today's engines, transmissions, and so forth, are in essentials no different from what they have always been. It is highly probable that they will take this as a compliment rather than as a criticism; and it is certainly possible that they may be right. It is nevertheless a pity that so little has been done to foster and so much actively to discourage the use of other interesting modern power units such as the Wankel engine or the gas turbine, though Lotus deserve immense credit for fielding a Formula 1 version of their Indianapolis gas turbine car in selected events during 1971, despite the fact that the regulations as at present framed condemn it to the status of an also-ran. It is tempting, however, to consider that if someone had the courage to stage a mid-winter Grand Prix rather than pursuing the sun, the Lotus Pratt and Whitney might fare rather better.

Of course the real answer would be a thermal efficiency formula based on the issue to each car of a quantity of fuel of given calorific

*251 (opposite) By the time of the 1972
252 French GP, March had hurriedly assembled a new GP car, based on an existing and very successful Formula 2 model, but powered by the usual Cosworth Ford V8. On the right sort of circuit its agility was valuable*

253 (opposite) *The Lotus 72 appeared in new colours for 1972, substantially unaltered except in details, such as the refined air-collector box above the engine intakes. In this car the driver E. Fittipaldi could seldom be beaten*

254 It would at least make a change if the Pratt & Whitney gas turbine powering this Lotus were to be a prelude to greater turbine participation in motor racing

content: this was discussed at the beginning of this book, and at the end of it there seems no greater hope of the idea receiving any official endorsement. It is certainly not too early for a new fashion to be launched.

Index

Index

Figures in italics refer to illustrations in black and white

Michelin, 25
Milan GP, 91–2
Miller, 11, 73, 80–1, 82, 85, 100, 128, 131, 158
Miller, Harry, 81, 100
Minerva, 31, 44
Minoia (racing driver), 56
Miramas, 91
Modena GP, 187, 188
Moglia (engineer), 91
Monaco GP, 97, 170, 171, 191, 192, 195, 209, 210, 225, *225*, 254, 264, *283*, 286
Monroe, 50
Monte Carlo, 251
Monza car, 97, *97*, 98–9
Monza circuit, 71, 77–80, *78*, 92, *93*, 100, *103*, *105*, 113, *136*, 148, *153*, 168–9, *184*, 187, *192*, 212, 229, 241, *242*, 258, 264–5, 275, 291, 298, 304
Moroccan GP, 187
Mors, 22
Moss (racing driver), 169, 183–5, *184*, 187, *191*, *197*, 210, 211
Motor, The, 75
Musso (racing driver), 185
Mussolini, Benito, 109
MV Agusta, 240

N

Napier, 37, *38*, 230
Nazzaro, Biagio (racing driver), 71
Nazzaro, Felice (racing driver), 26, 27, *27*, *28*, *29*, 30, 38, 71, 78, *82*
Niebel, Dr Hans, 113, 115
Norton, 178
Nurburgring, 97, 111, 113, *121*, 166, 167, *179*, 211
Nuvolari (racing driver), 97, *103*, 111, 126, 139, 142, *142*

O

Ochelhauser, 92
Oldsmobile, 226
OM, 91
Opel, 257
Orsi (constructor), 147
Oulton Park, *271*

P

Packard, 119
Page, Theo (artist), *248*
Panhard, 20, 21, 24, *31*, 52, 126
Parry Thomas, J. G. (engineer), 91
Pau GP, 79, 134, *135*, *159*, 214
Pederzani brothers, 303
Pescara, *134*, 187
Peterson (racing driver), *290*
Petit, Emil (designer), 98, 117
Peugeot, 11, 34, *43*, 43–4, *44*, 45–50, 51, 53–4, *55*, 56, 57, 58, 59–60, 67, 68, 81, 94, 127, 162, 217, 292
Piccard Pictet, 53
Pirelli, *190*, 232, 233
Plancton (designer), 76–7, 145
Pomeroy, L. H. (designer), 34, 42, 45, 48, 60, 65–7, 80
Porsche, 118–9, 120, 125, 138, 141, 144, 155, 180, *199*, *200*, 206, 207, 208, 215, *215*, *216*, 257, 261, 301
Porsche, Dr Ferdinand (designer), 113, 122, 130, 131
Porthos, 35
Posthumus, Cyril (author), 110
Pratt and Whitney, 267, *309*

R

Racing colours, 29–30
Railton, Reed (consultant), 143
Reims, 144, 164, 165, 196, 225, 289, 291, 292, 298
Renault, 11, *23*, 24, *24*, 25–6, *25*, 28, 30, 292
Repco, *251*
Repco–Brabham, 226–8, *227*, 239, 240, 252
Resta (racing driver), *81*
Ricardo, Sir Harry, 48
Richard Brasier, 24, 26
Rigal (racing driver), 46, *55*
Riley, 144
Rindt (racing driver), *238*, 265, 269, 275
Rocchi (engineer), 245
Rolland–Pilain, 64, *65*, 67–8, 72, 76, 80
Rolls–Royce, 127, 151, 152, 176, 178
Rome GP, 163
Roots, 77, 91, 122, 127, 129, 131, 139–40, 144, 156, 163
Rosemeyer, Bernd (racing driver), 121, *121*, 123, *123*, 126, 130, 131, 139